THE BEAUTY OF DEER

THE BEAUTY OF DEER

Photographs and Field Notes by
Robin Henderson-King
Published by Robin's Nature

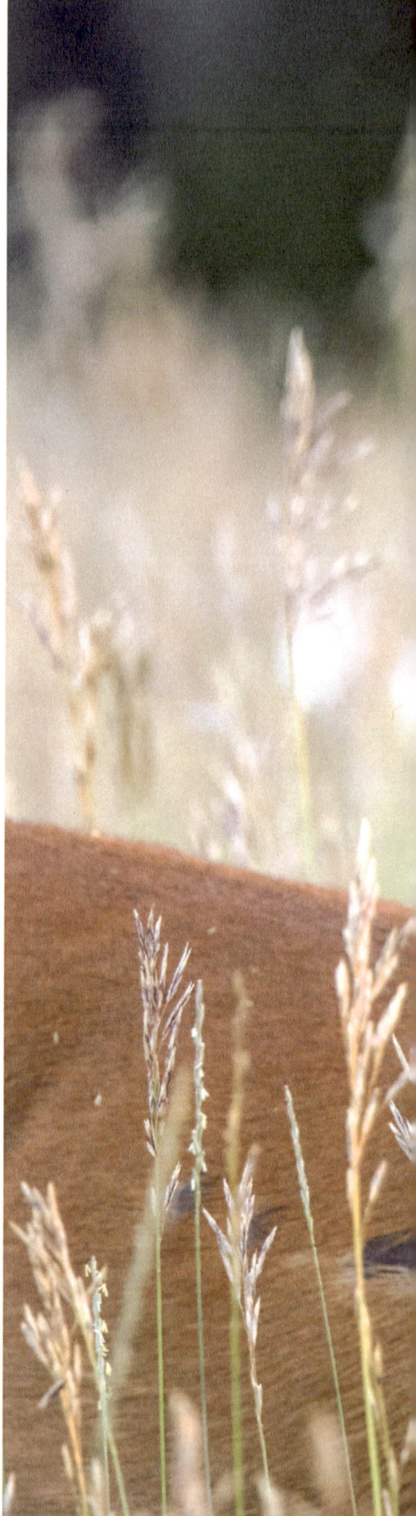

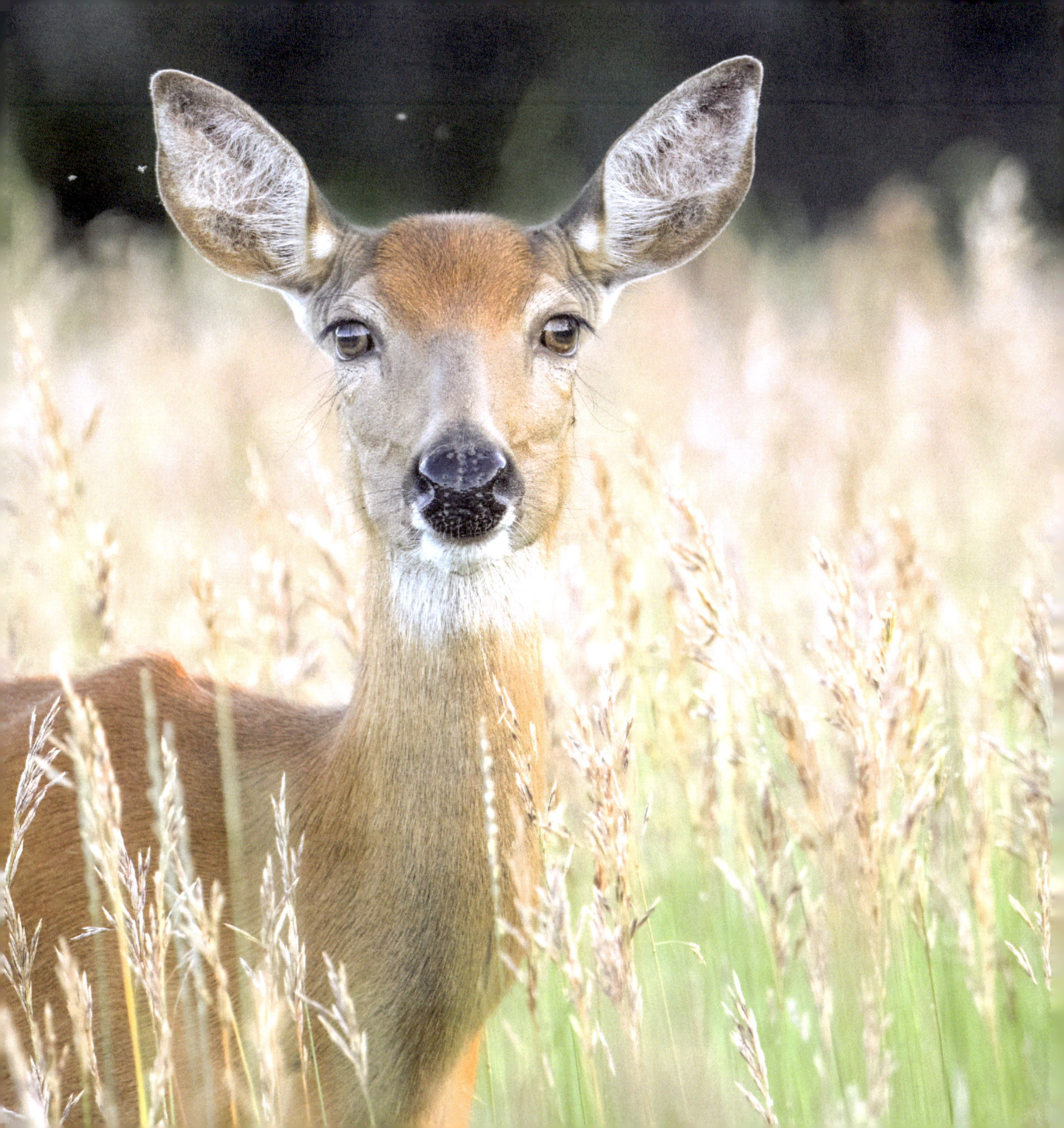

ISBN 978-1-957077-82-6

Robin's Nature
P.O. Box 107
Greenwood Village, CO 80112
robinsnature.com

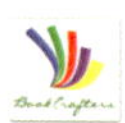

Publishing assistance by BookCrafters, Parker, Colorado.
www.bookcrafters.net

Dedication

This book is dedicated to my father for sharing his love of wildlife with me.
To my mother for her support and encouragement.
To my husband for providing me the opportunity to spend time on the trails
and to my son, who started this deer journey with me.

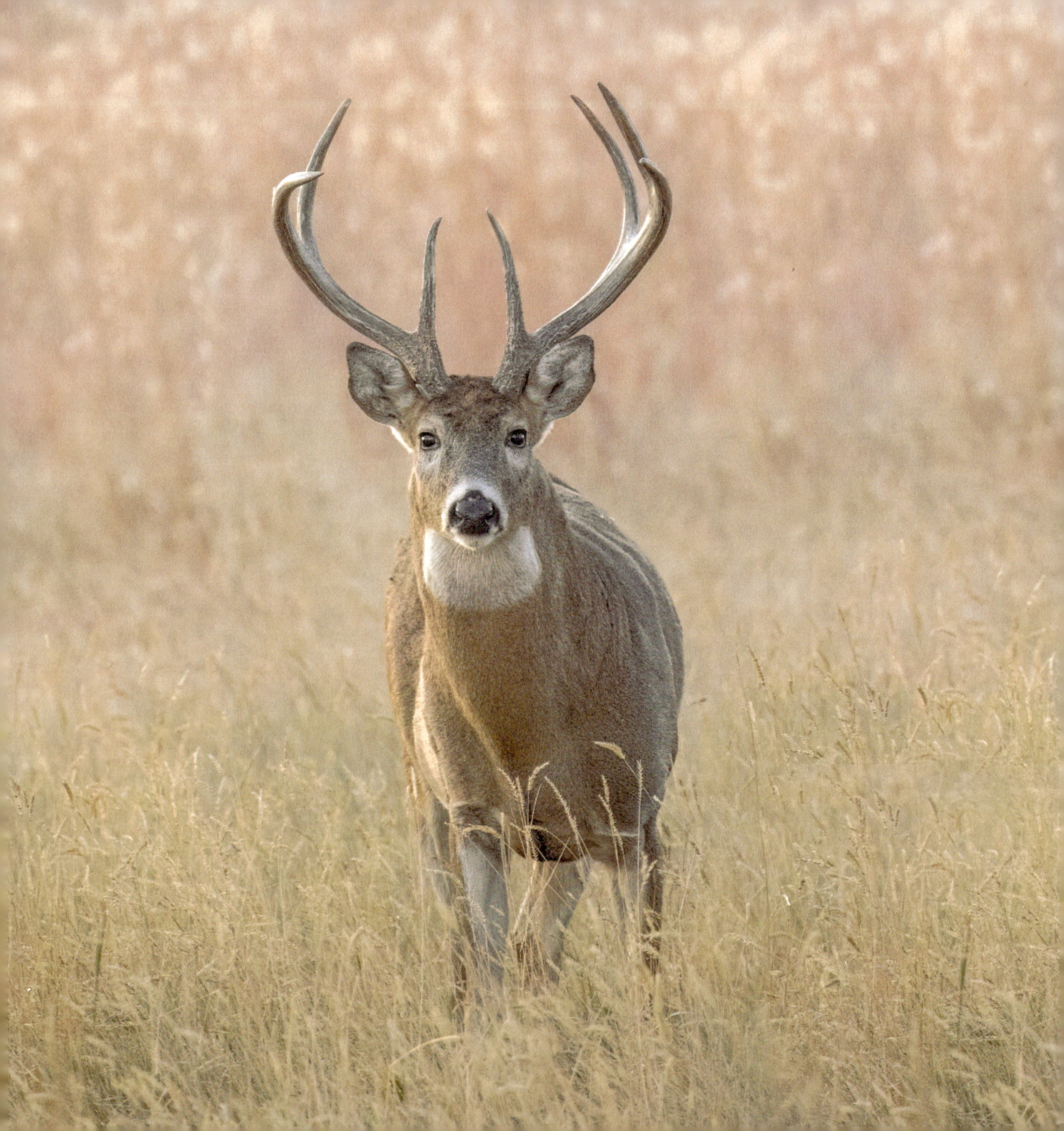

Table of Contents

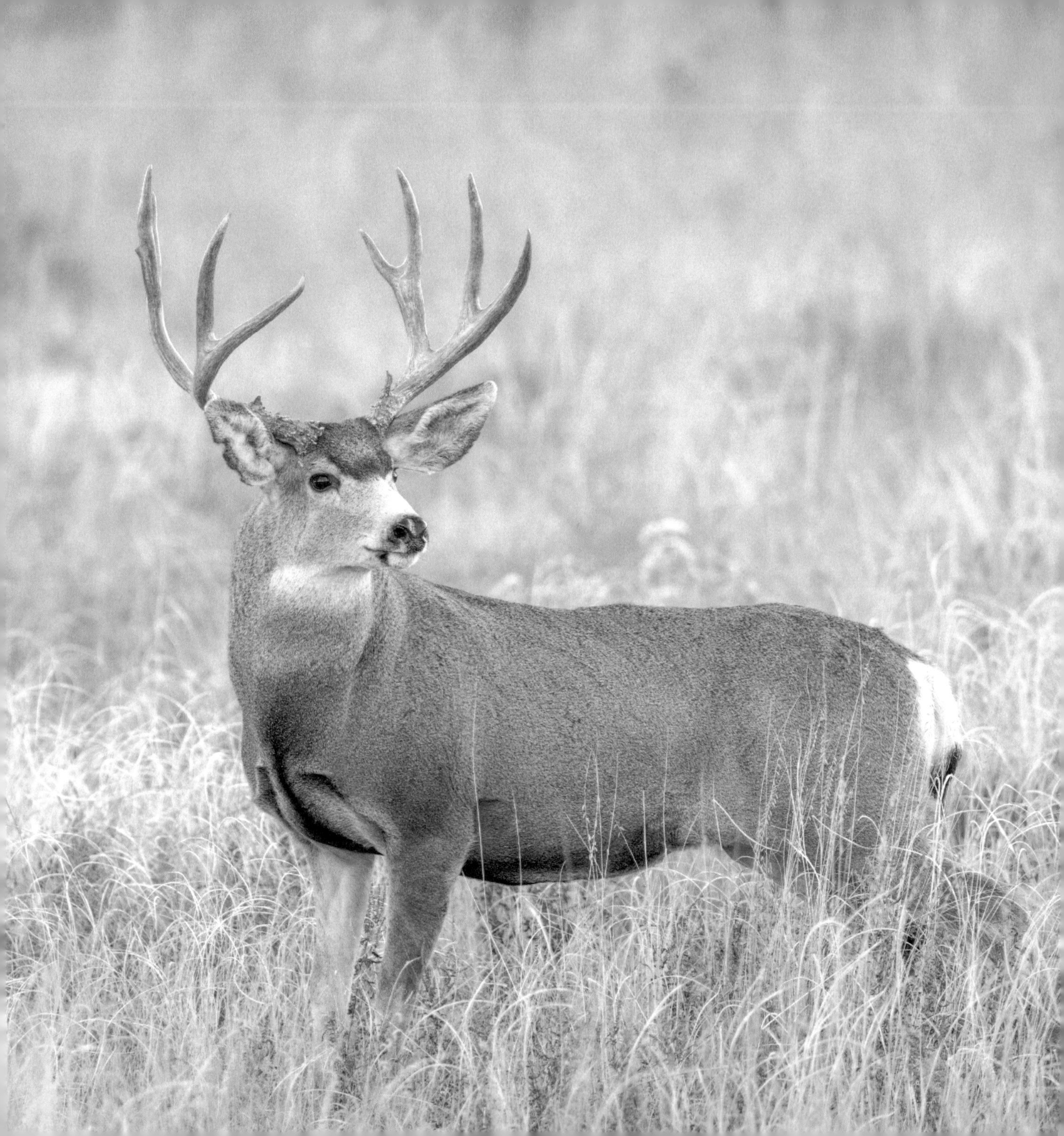

Introduction

Many people ask me, "Why deer?"

As long as I can remember, deer have fascinated me.

They are such beautiful and interesting animals.

All the photographs in this book were taken in my home state of Colorado. And both Mule Deer and White-tailed Deer are featured throughout the pages. Although Mule Deer make up most of the deer population in Colorado, White-tailed Deer can be found in the Eastern part of the state.

Through my photographic journey, I have observed their routines, social structures, and their unwavering will to survive.

I have witnessed new beginnings of newborn fawns and heartbreak watching the last hours of life of an older or injured deer.

Each day, deer must focus on survival and each breeding season they must do everything in their power to ensure their existence.

The challenges for them to survive and thrive continue to be more difficult with the loss of habitat, extensive growth, alteration of migration routes, and the availability of natural resources.

I hope you enjoy this book and can see into the lives of deer, their unique personalities and behaviors, and just how beautiful they really are.

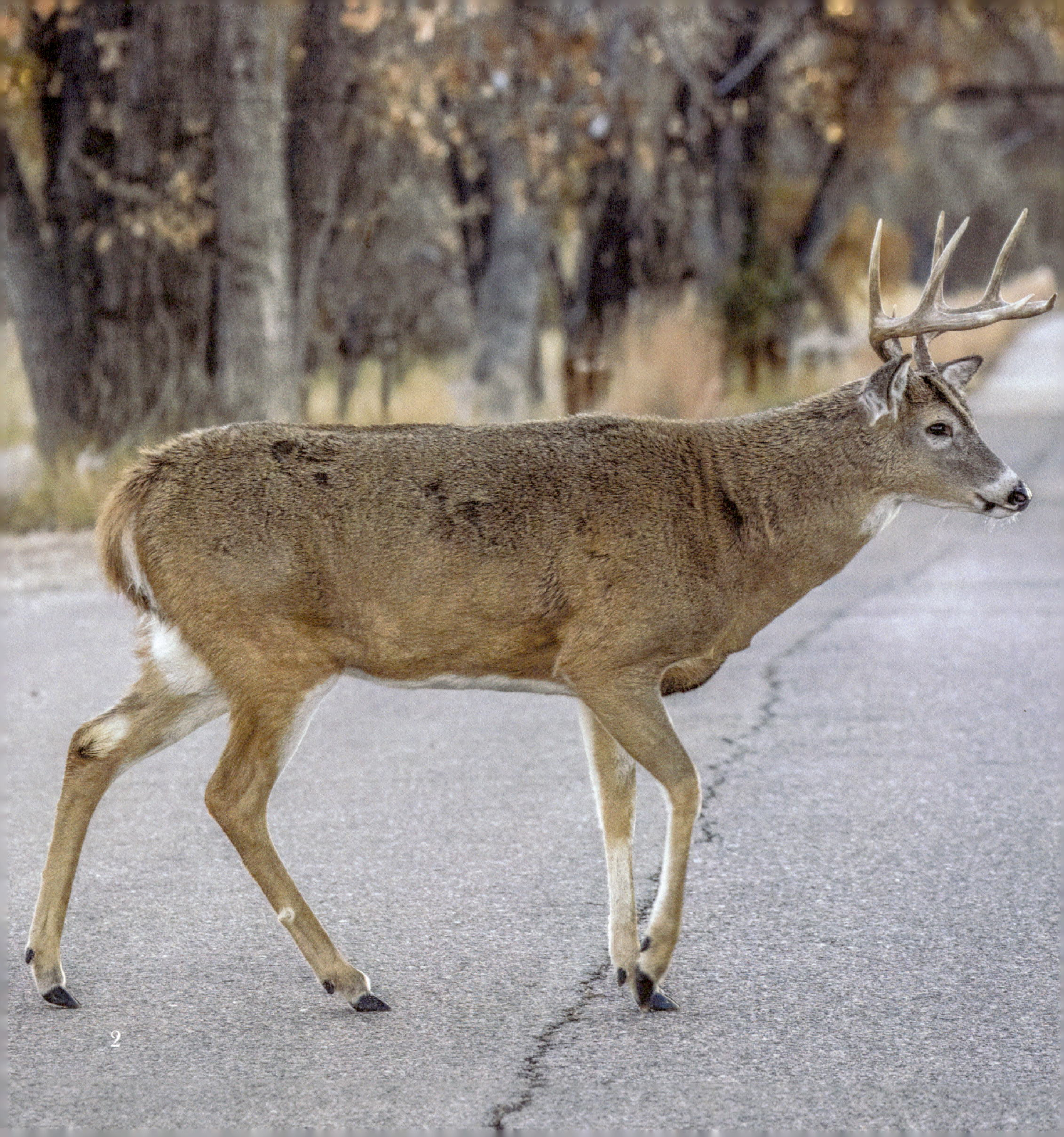

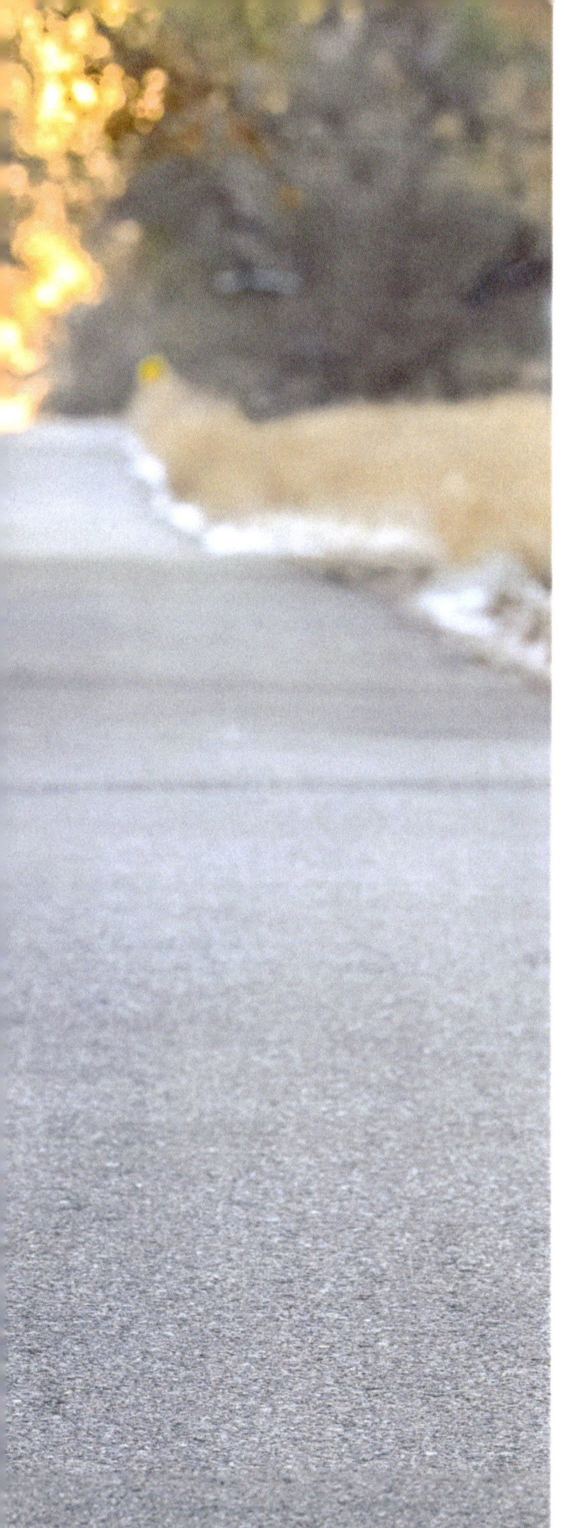

"You can't go
back and change
the beginning
but
you can start
where you are
and change the ending."

—C.S. Lewis

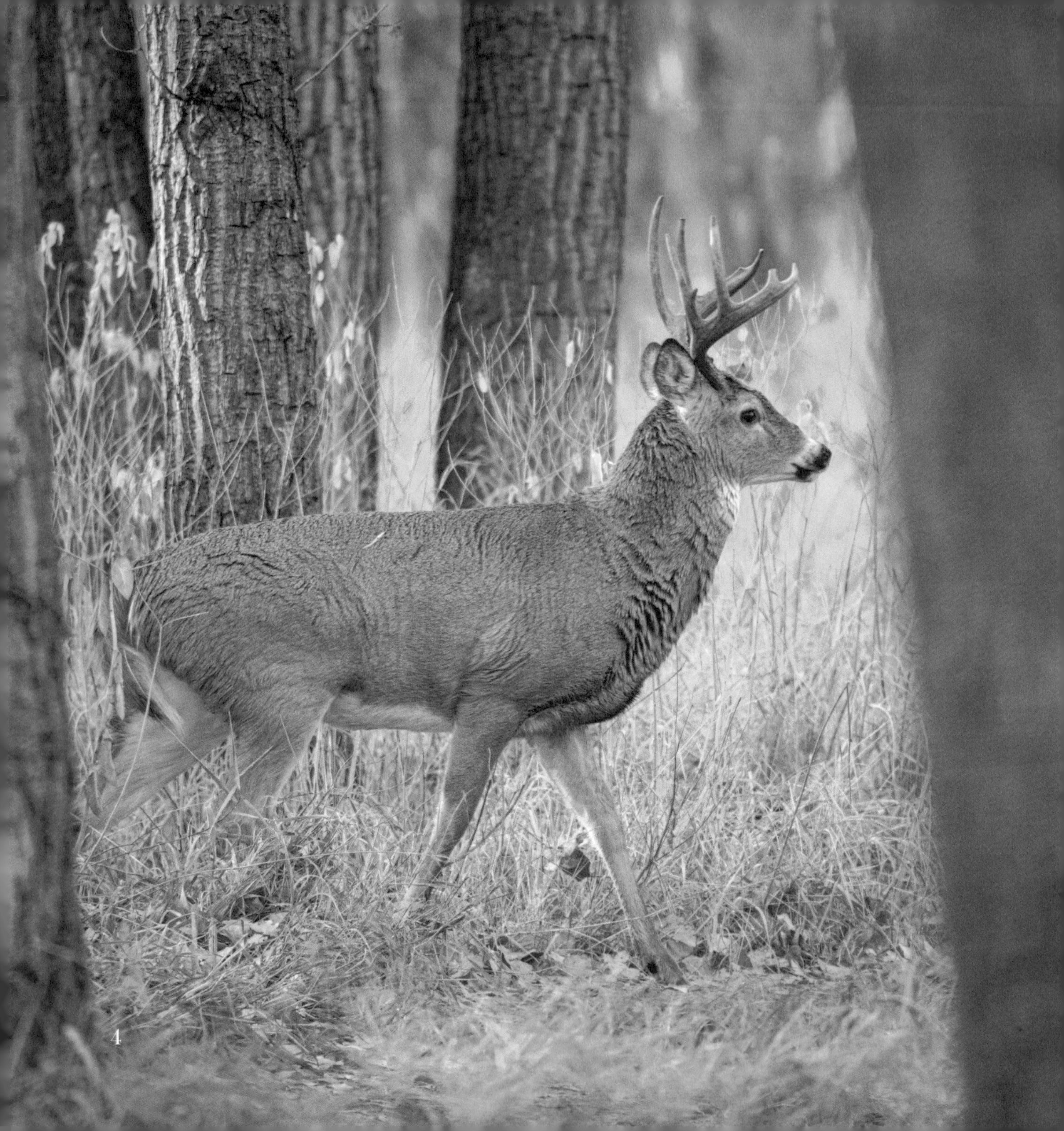

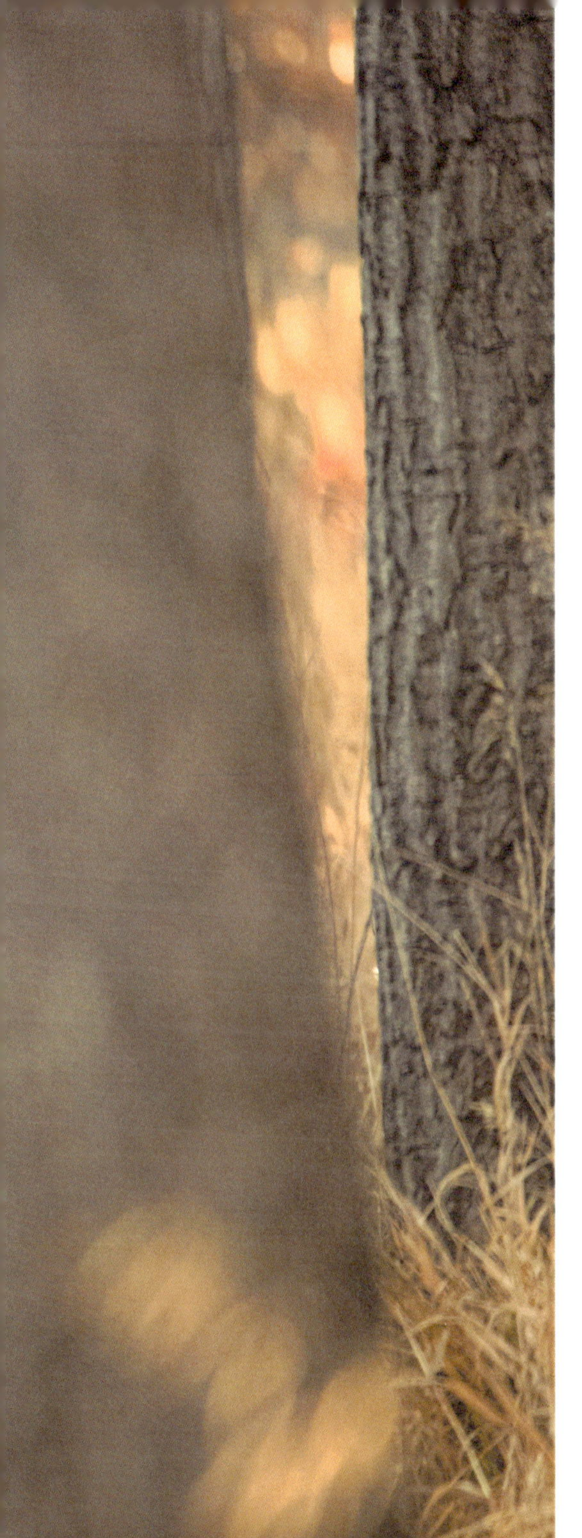

The Deer Woods

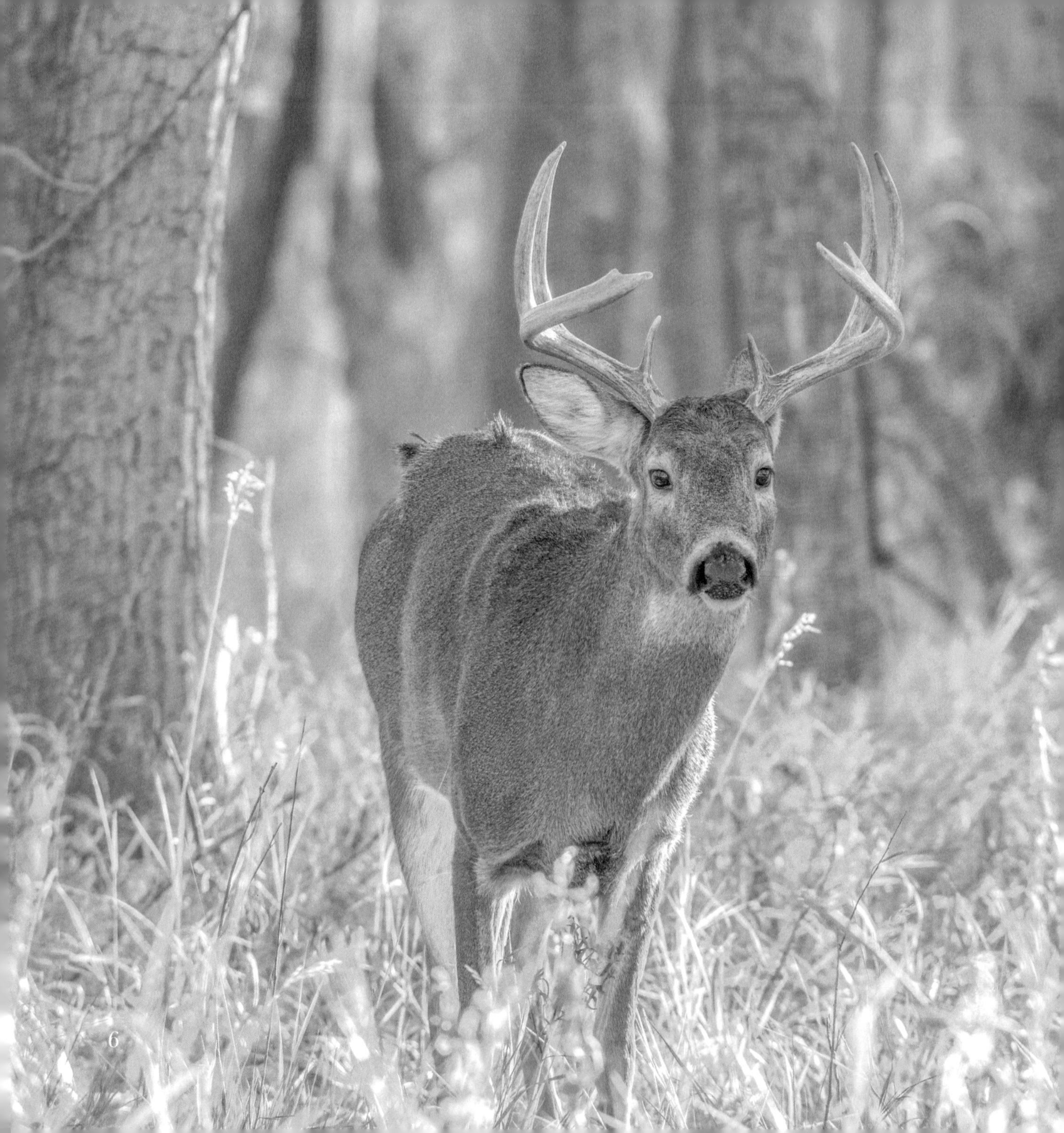

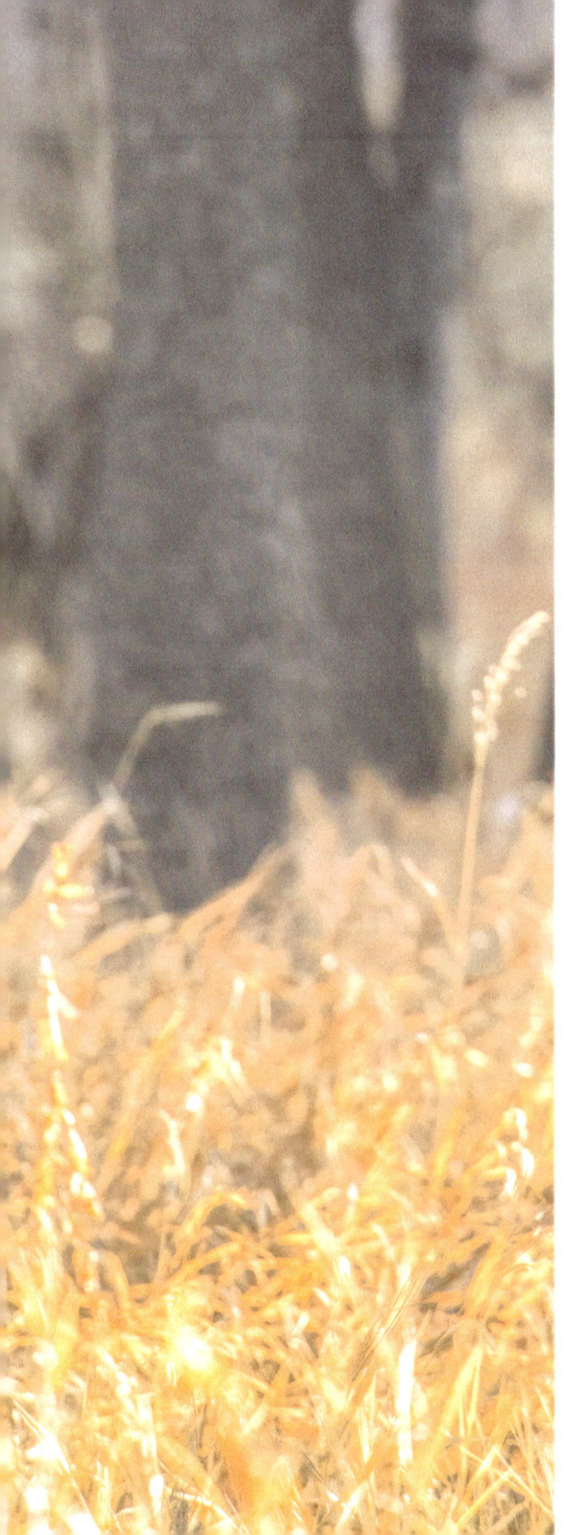

I took a walk
in the woods
and came out
taller than
the trees.

—Henry David Thoreau

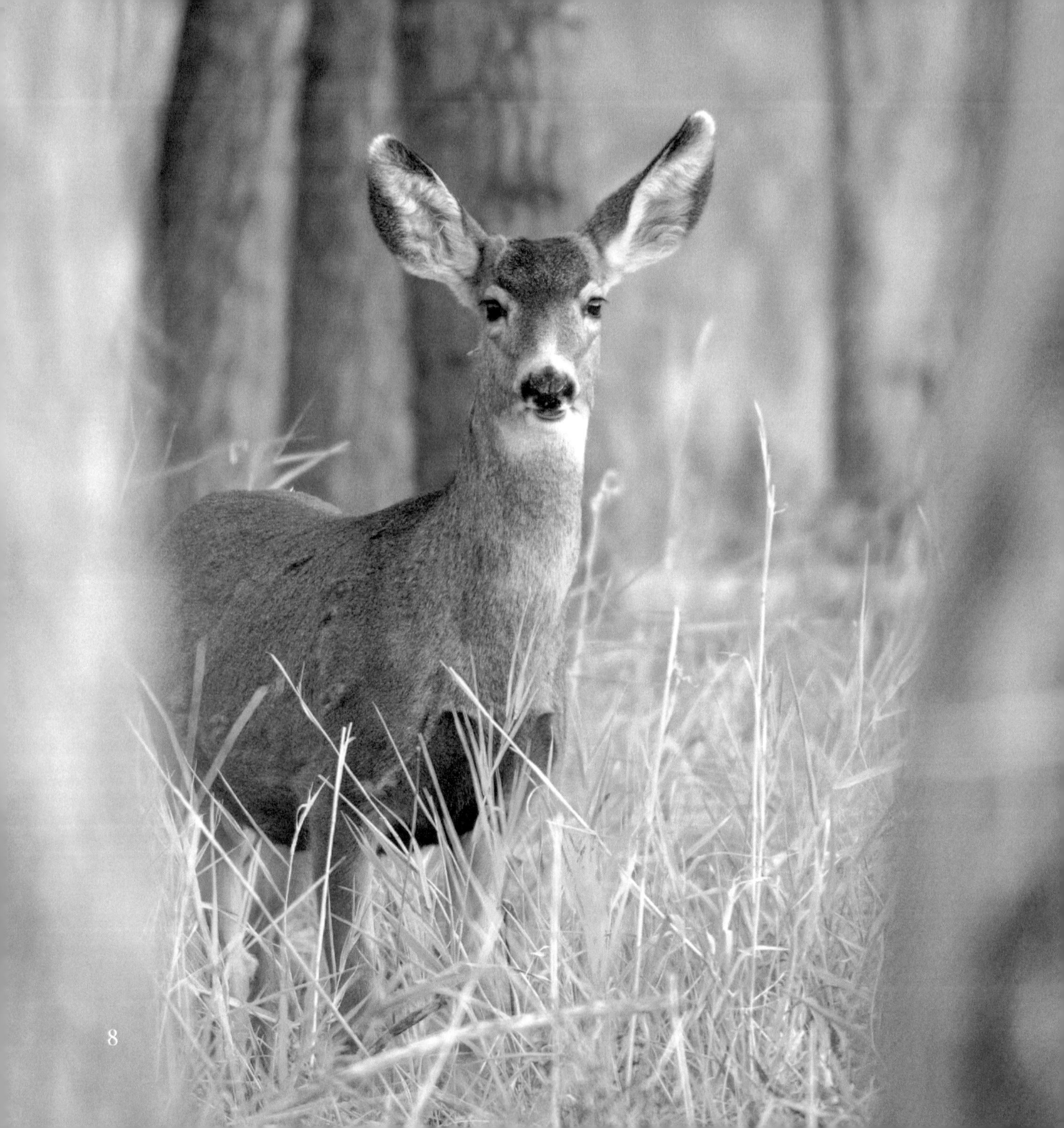

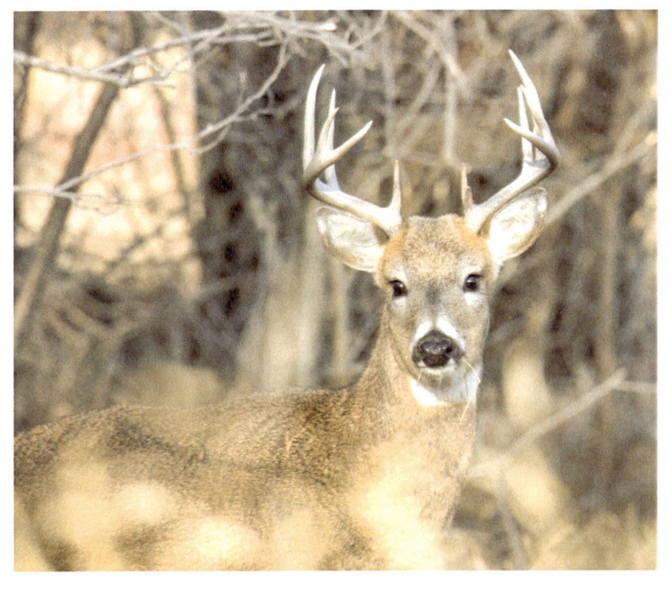

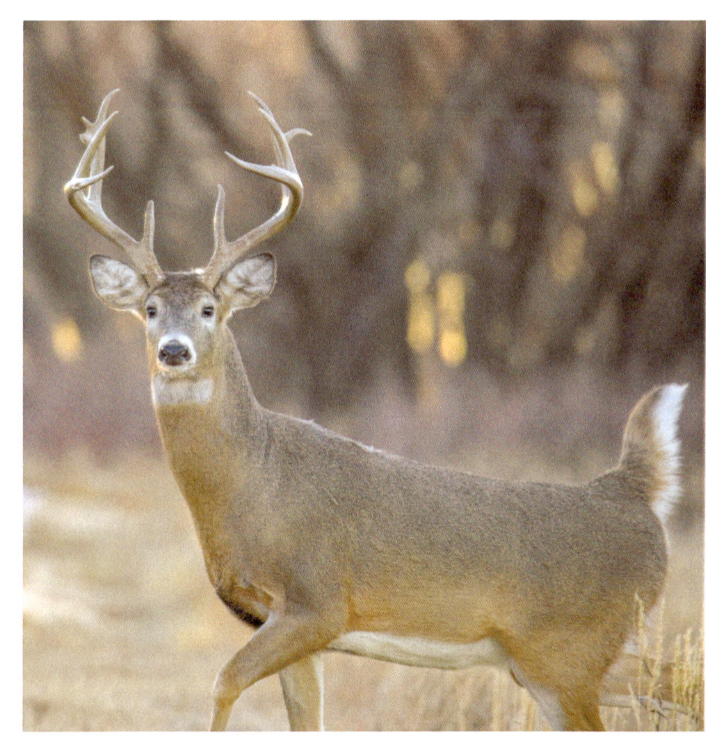

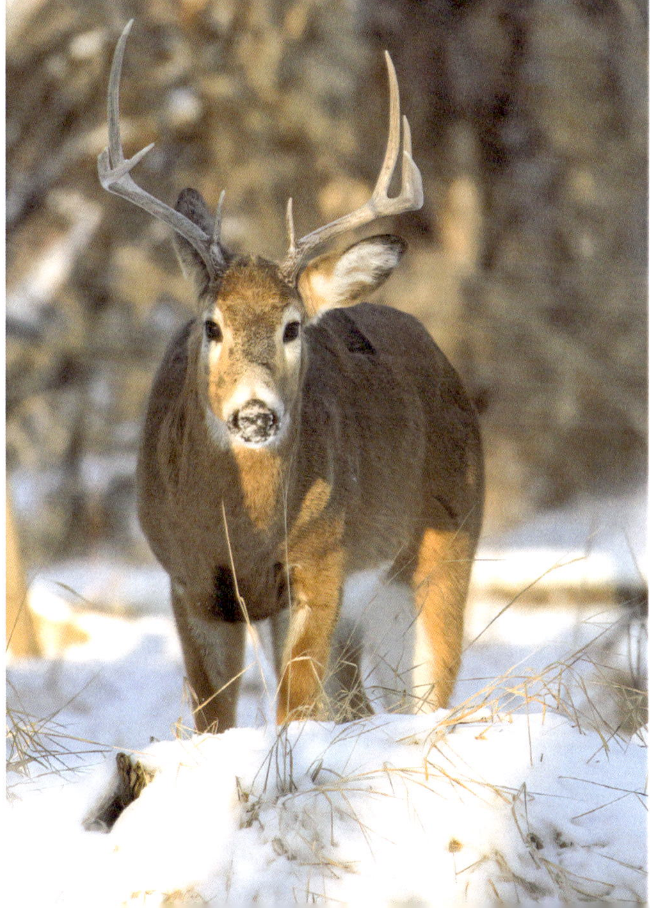

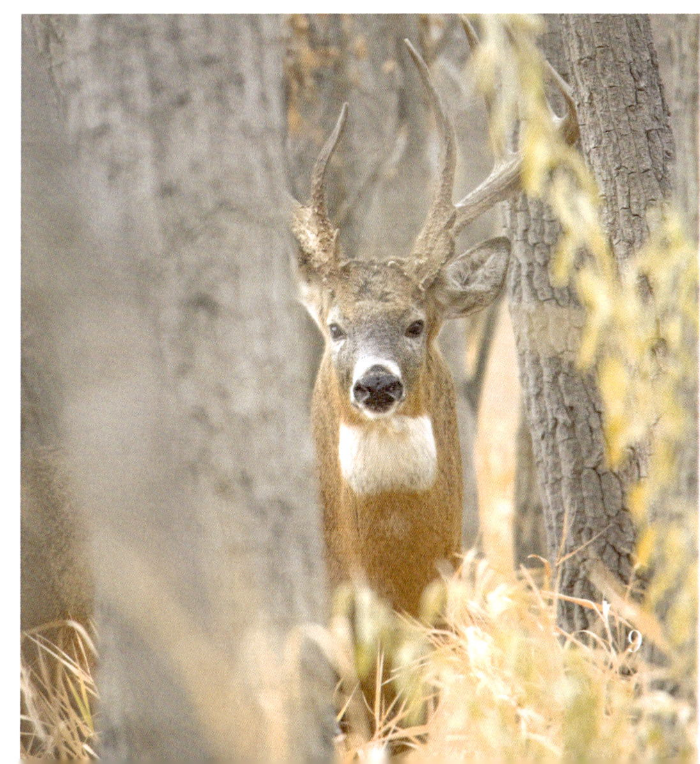

The deer woods are one of the most special places on earth.

The beauty and peacefulness are good for the soul. The concerns of the day seem so far away.

I have seen such beautiful interactions between the deer. At times, it can make me feel a little melancholy wishing my father was still here so he could see them too.

While in the woods, I pray and thank God for the beauty he has created. To be alone with your thoughts and with the deer is an experience like no other.

Many times, I have sat down on a log or rock, my camera on my lap and just observed the fascinating behaviors and habits of the deer.

Taking pictures of these beautiful animals is truly a blessing. But being there in their world, is the true blessing.

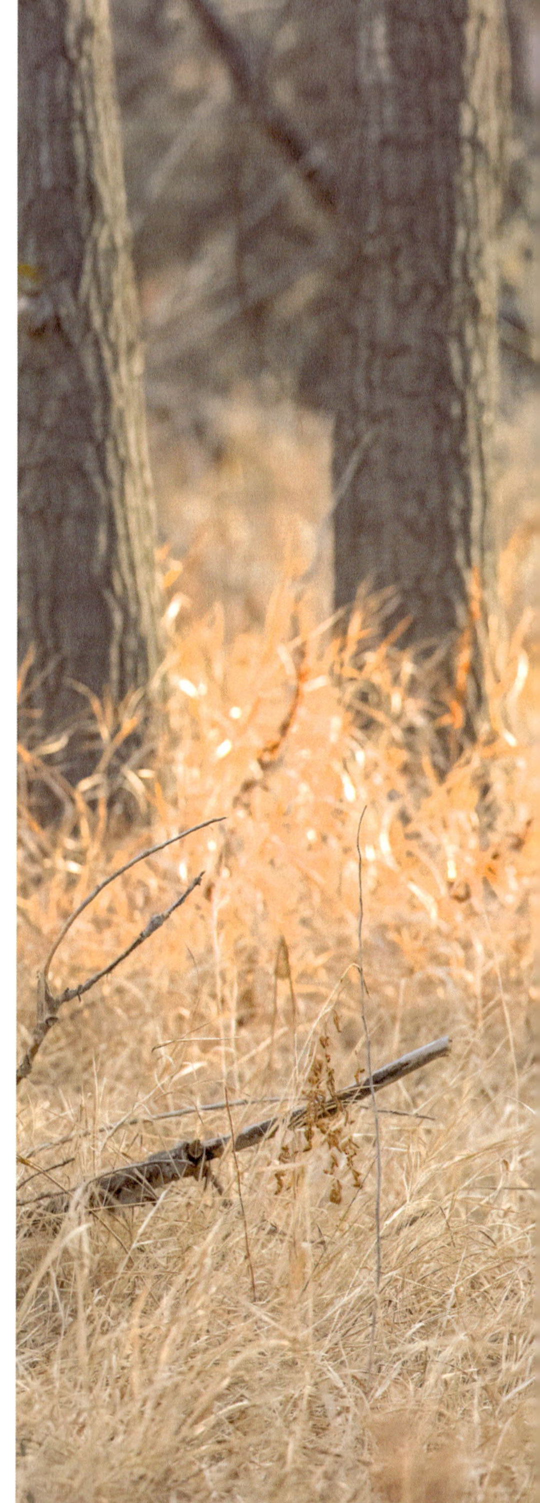

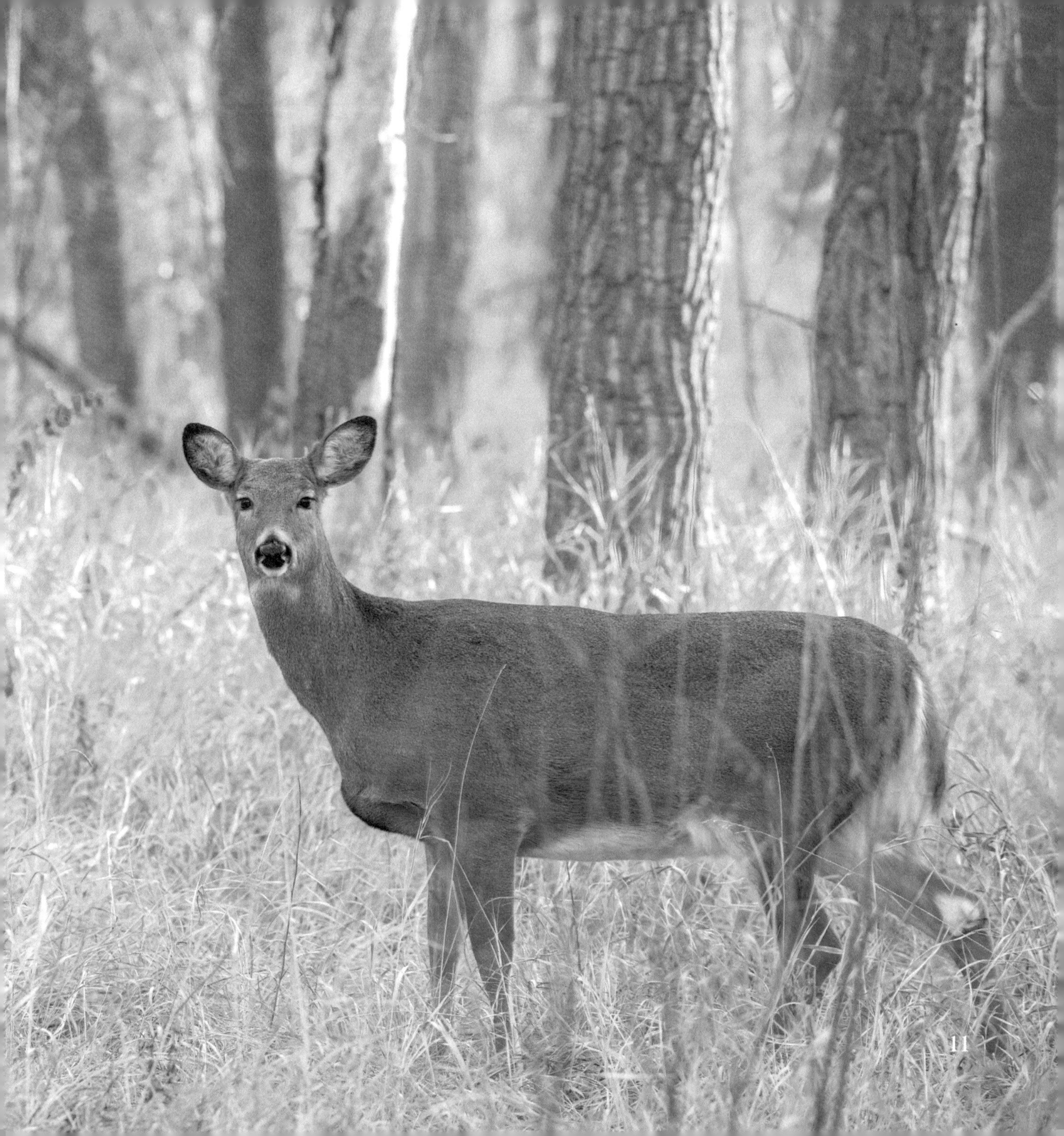

The deer woods
come alive with
the vibrant colors
of fall.

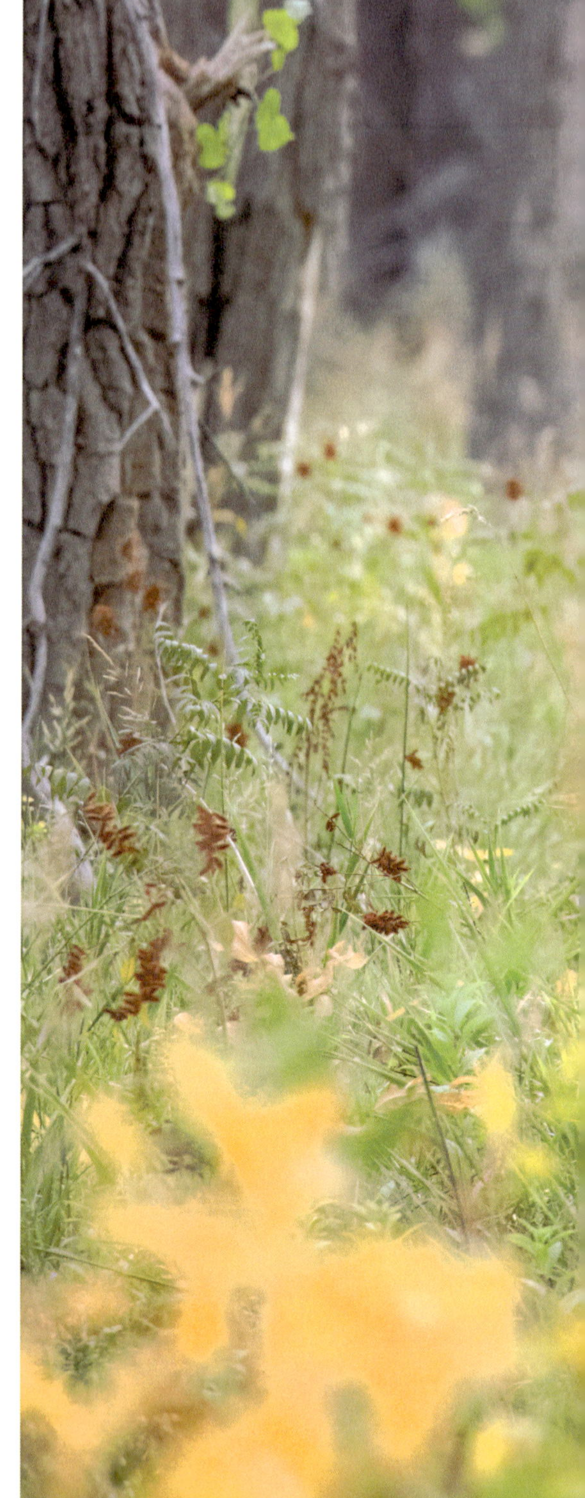

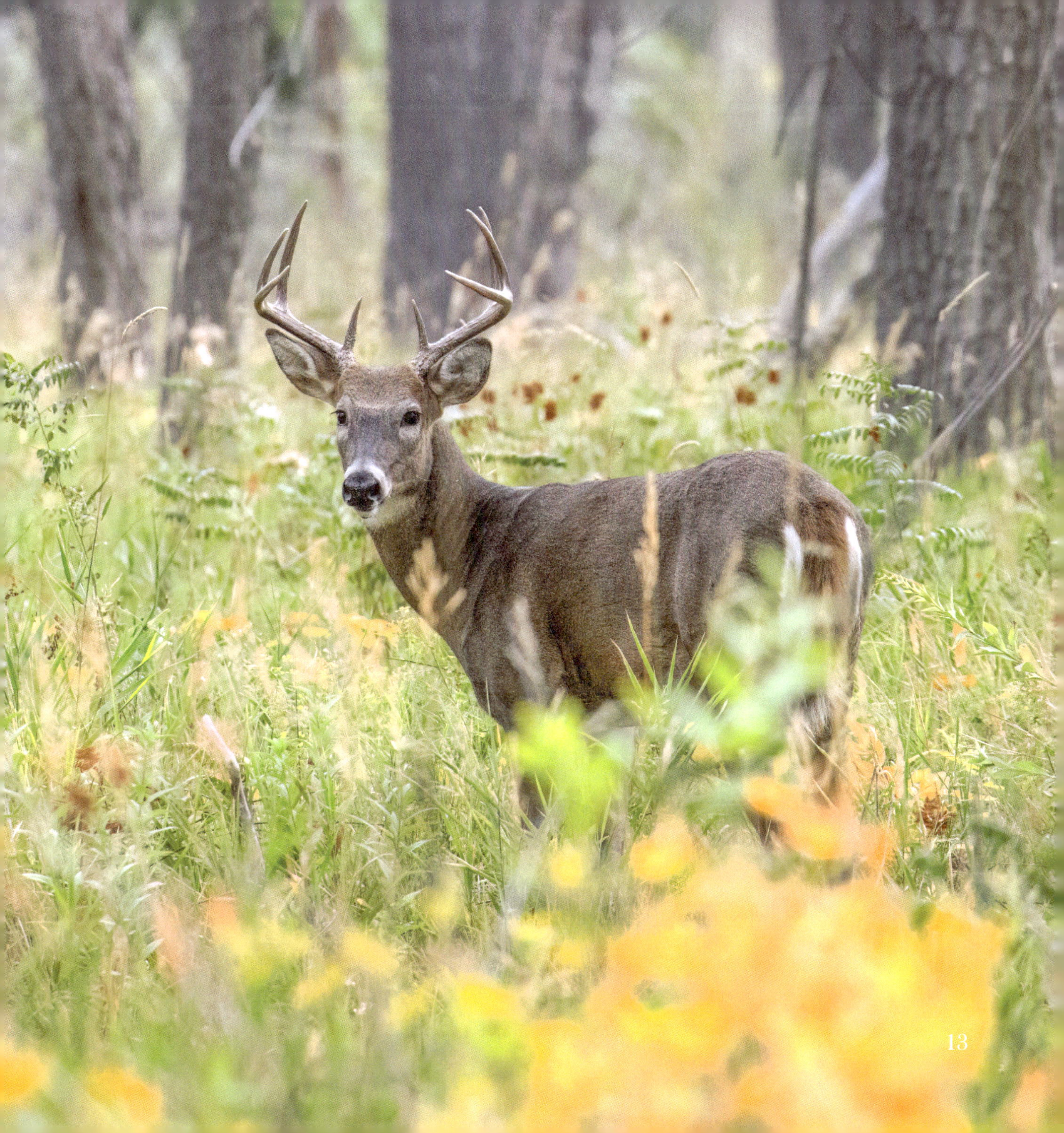

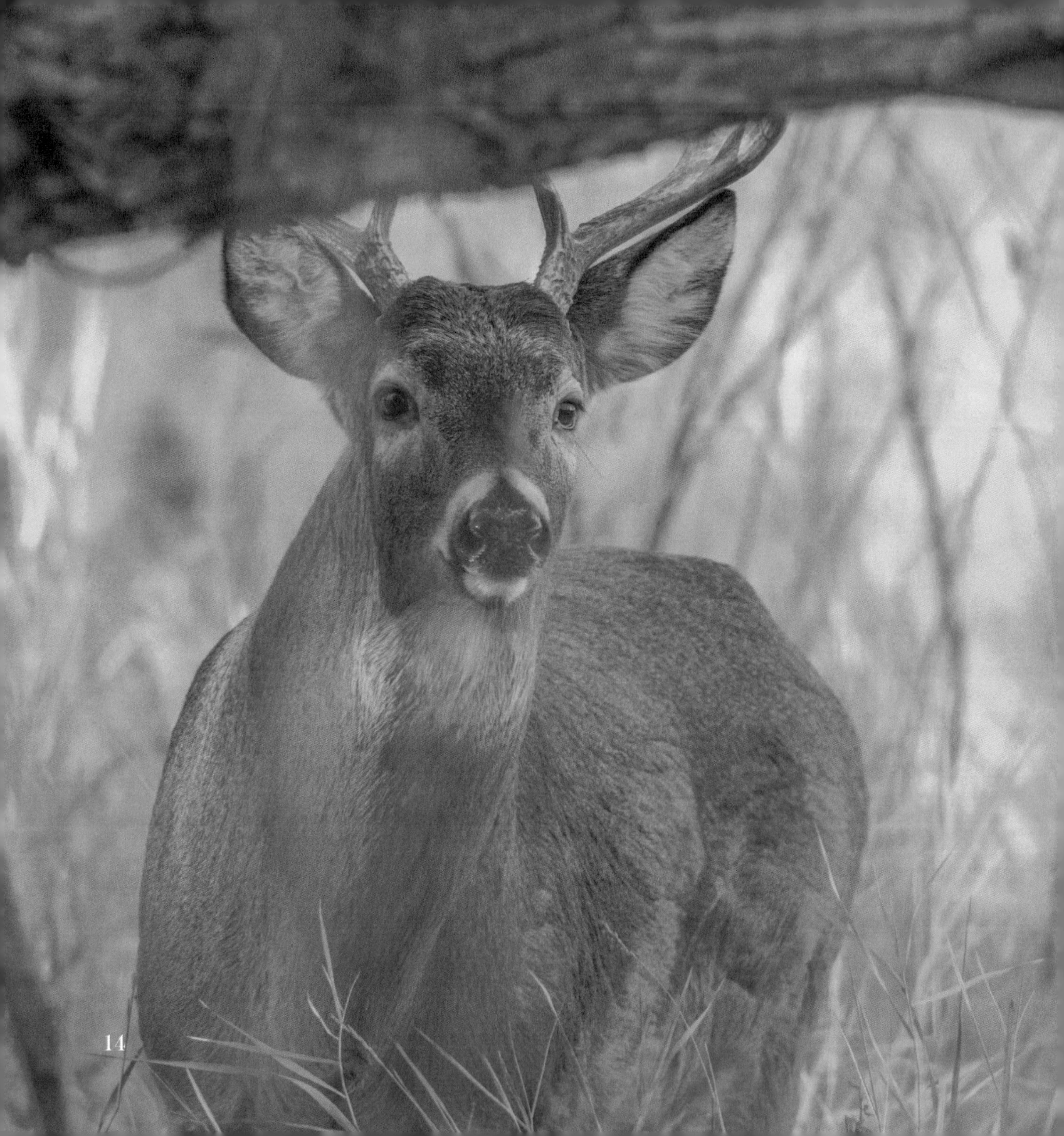

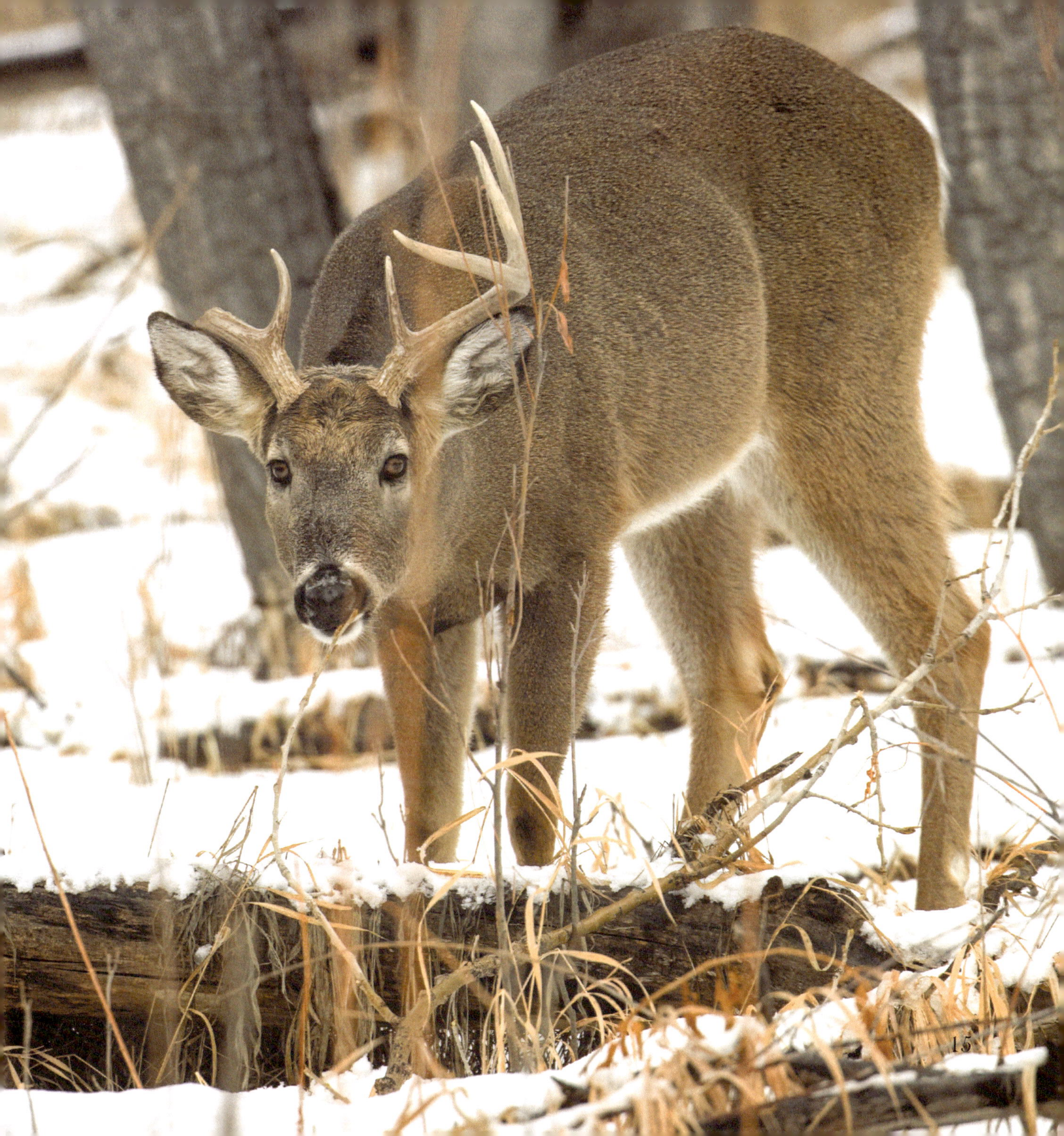

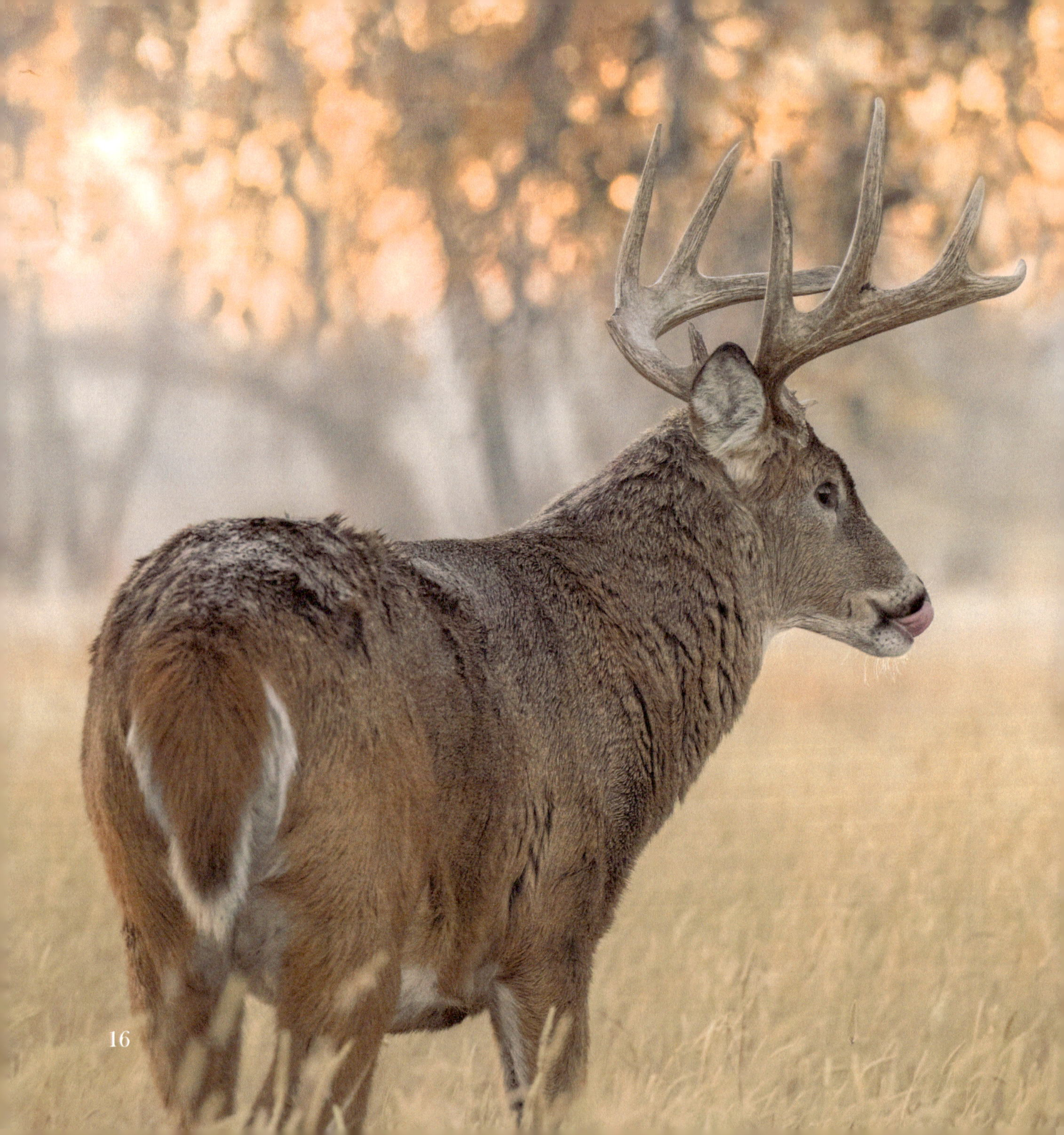

Beautiful Light

Early Morning Splendor

I love photographing deer in
the morning.

The colors, how they move, and
the way the light is captured in the
grasses and trees.

So much happens in the deer world
while the rest of the world sleeps.

Although getting up out of bed
before sunrise and driving in the
dark to look for deer may not be for
everyone, it's for me.

There have been mornings that
I turned off my alarm, and those
are the mornings that I regret.

Regret does not happen when
I spend the morning looking for
these beautiful creatures.

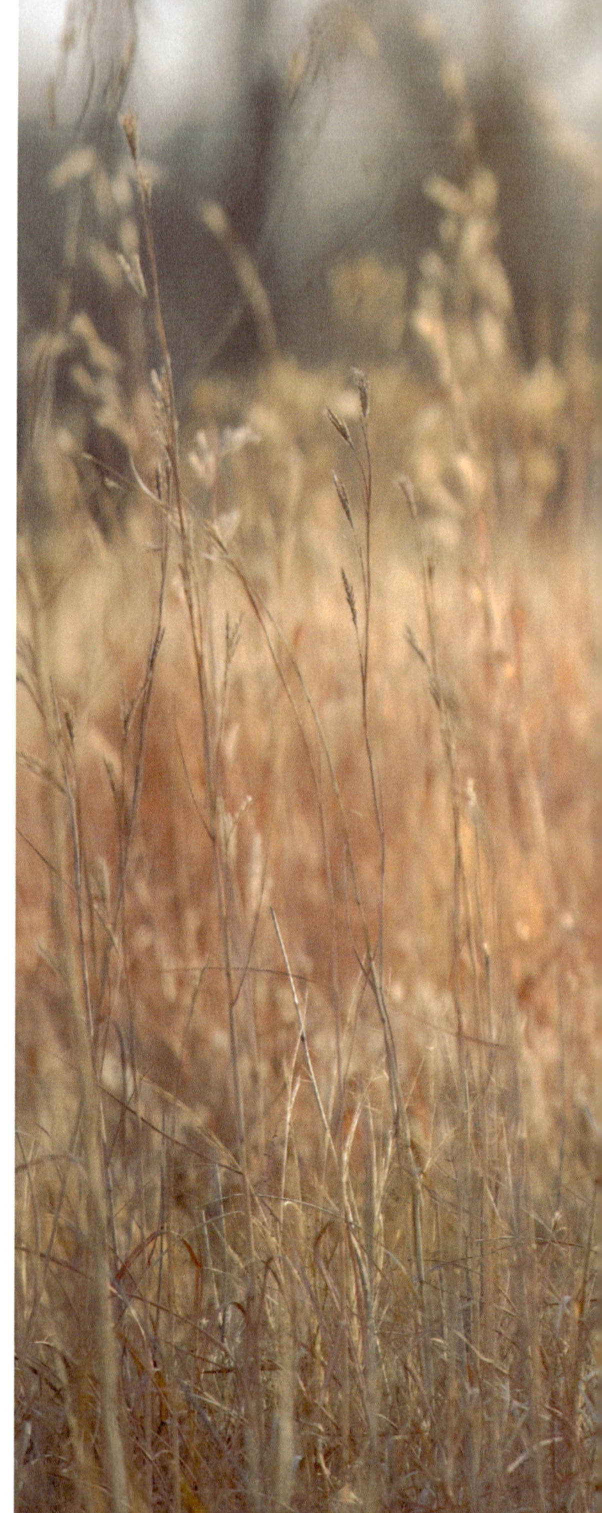

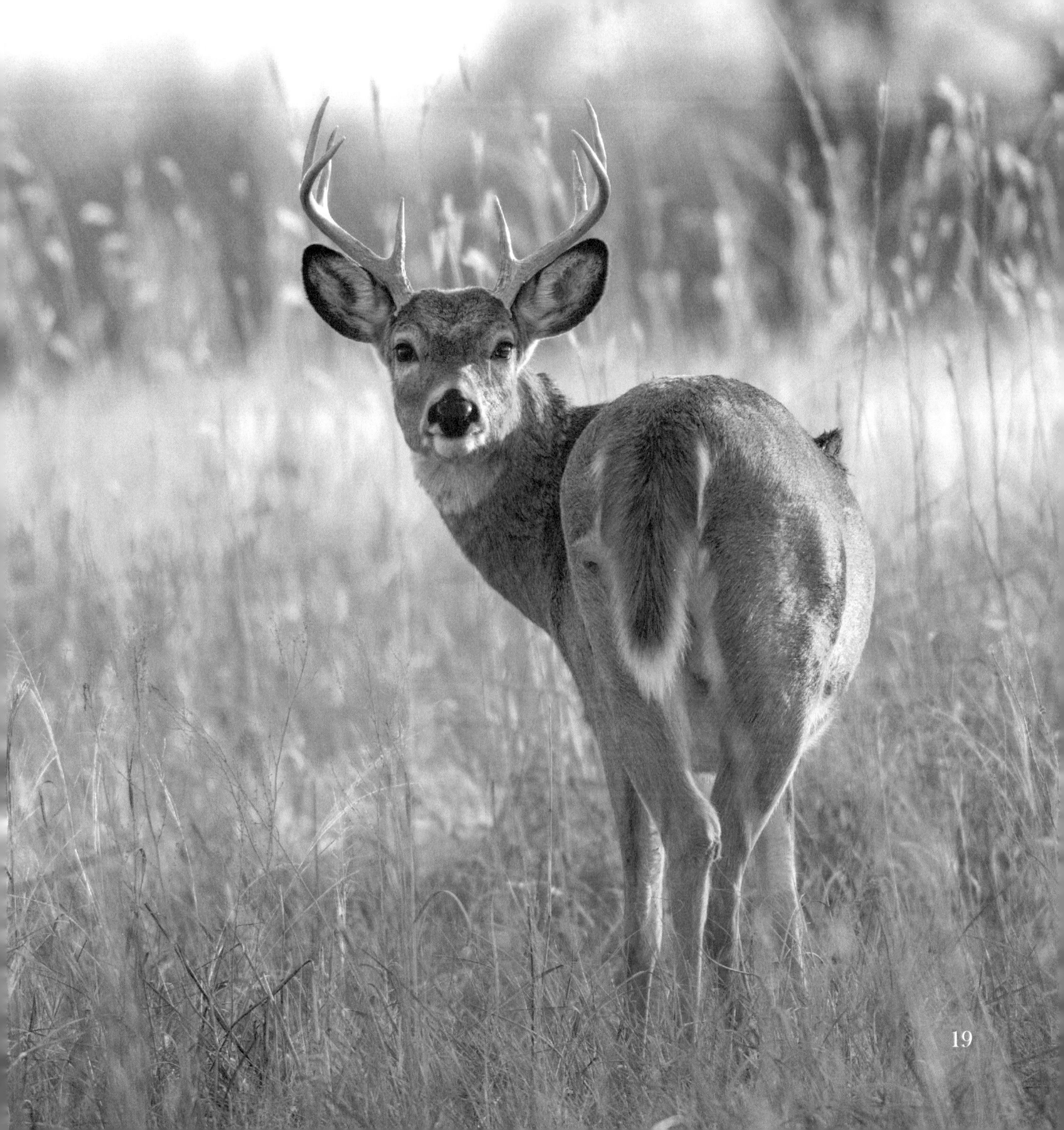

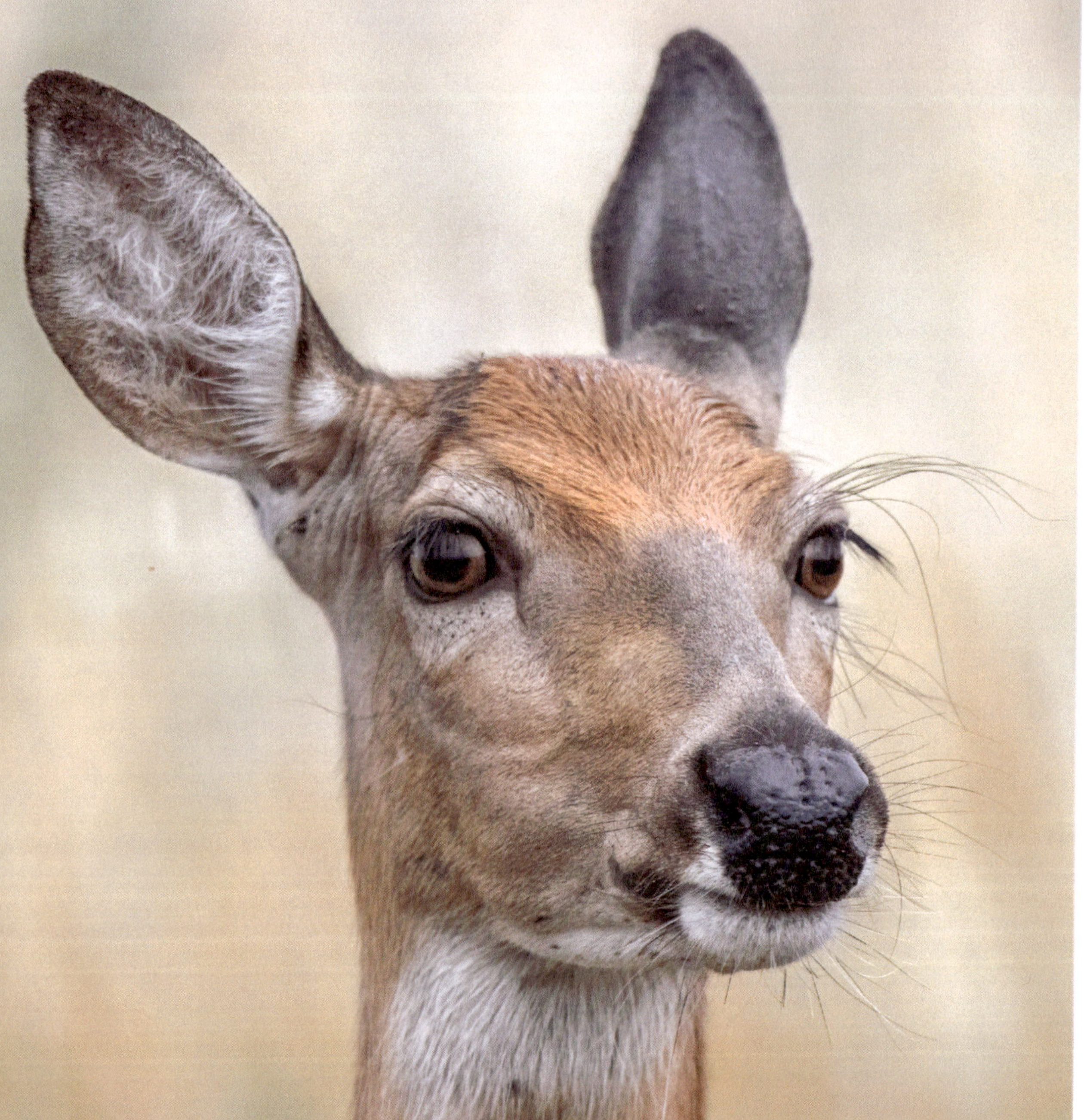

The lighting, and the camera angle, made this photograph of a doe look more like a painting.

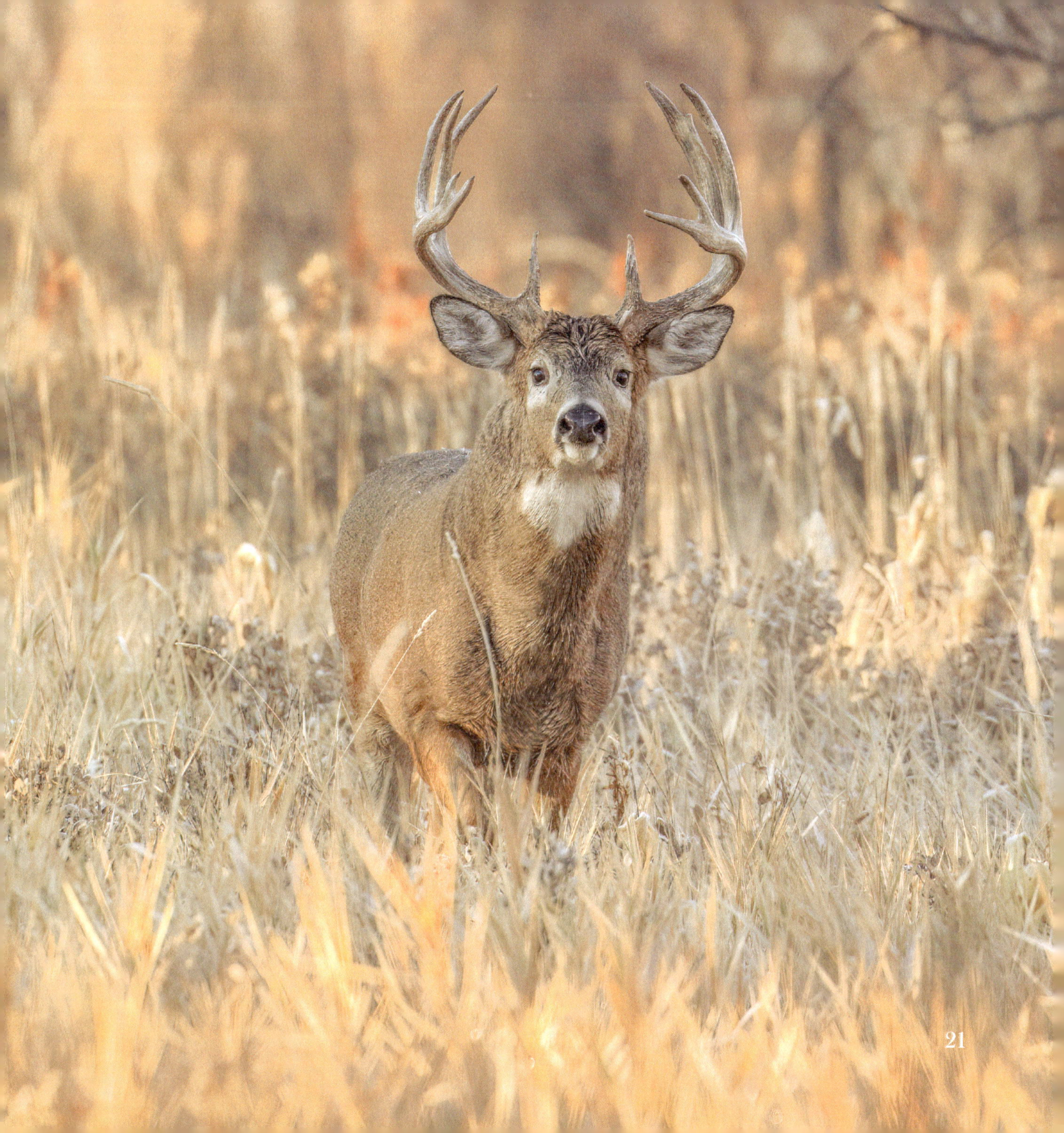

Just before the sun set, I was walking
in a meadow that was filled with
golden sunlight.

Out of the corner of my eye,
I noticed a deer in the distance.

Slowly, I walked closer and closer.
The deer in the distance turned out
to be a large Mule Deer buck
who was very focused on eating.

The light was amazing, the deer
was big and beautiful, and I took
as many photos as I could.

He never looked at me once.

Then when he was done eating,
he glanced over for a moment and
then continued on his way. I stood
very still as he passed nearby.

As I left the meadow, I could not stop
smiling. What an amazing experience.
Whenever I look at this photograph, I
can almost feel the sun on my back.

Some days, the beauty is almost too
much to take in all at once.

Those are good days.

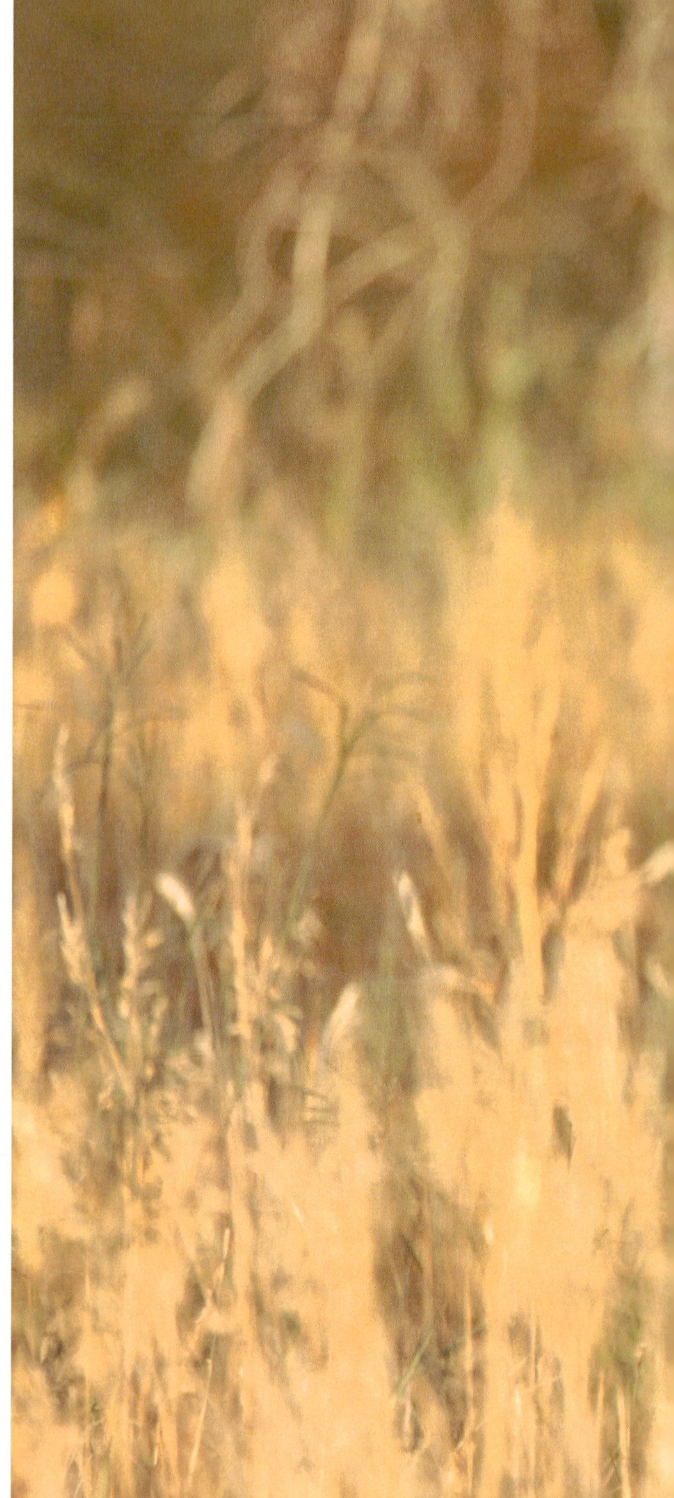

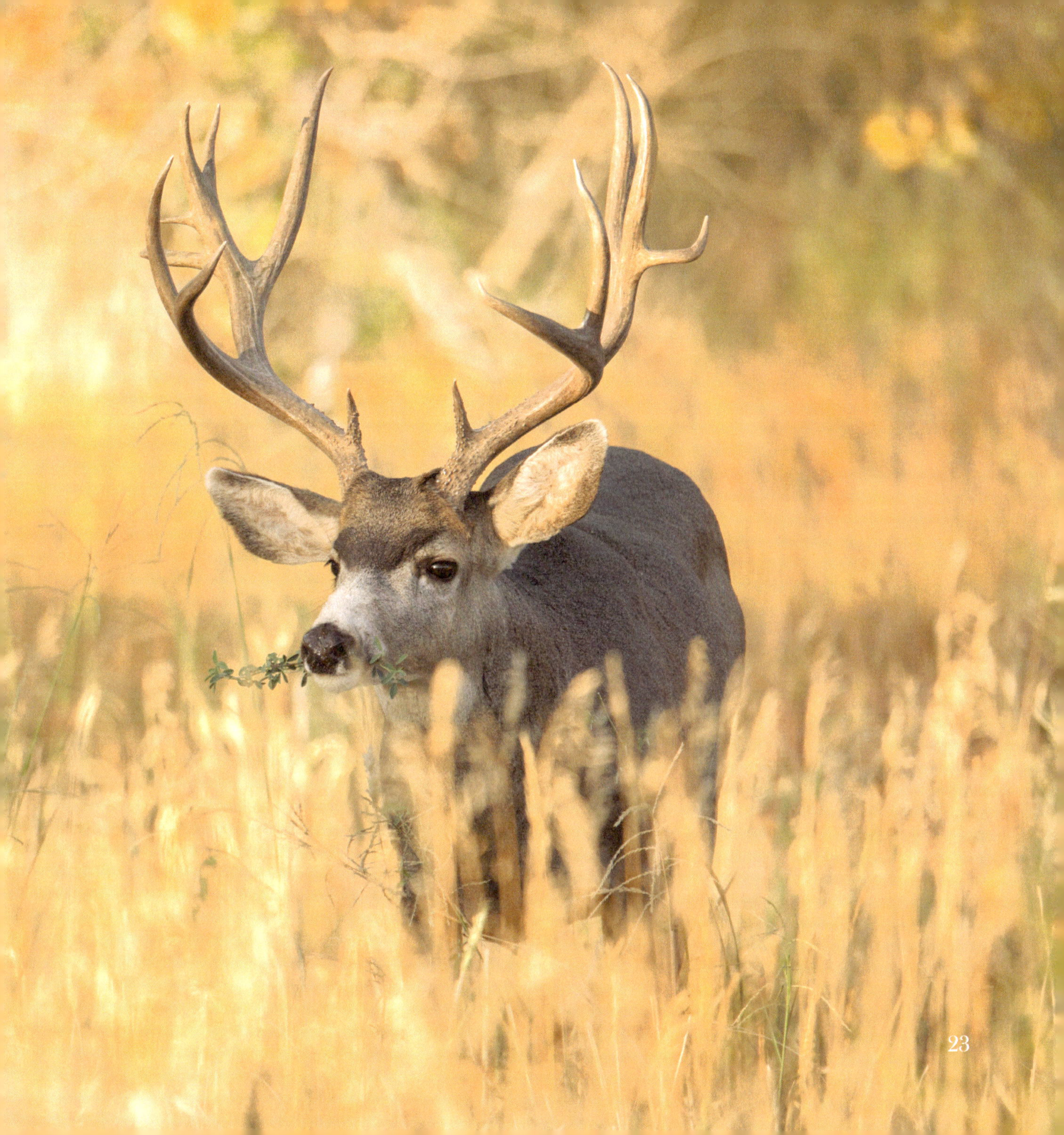

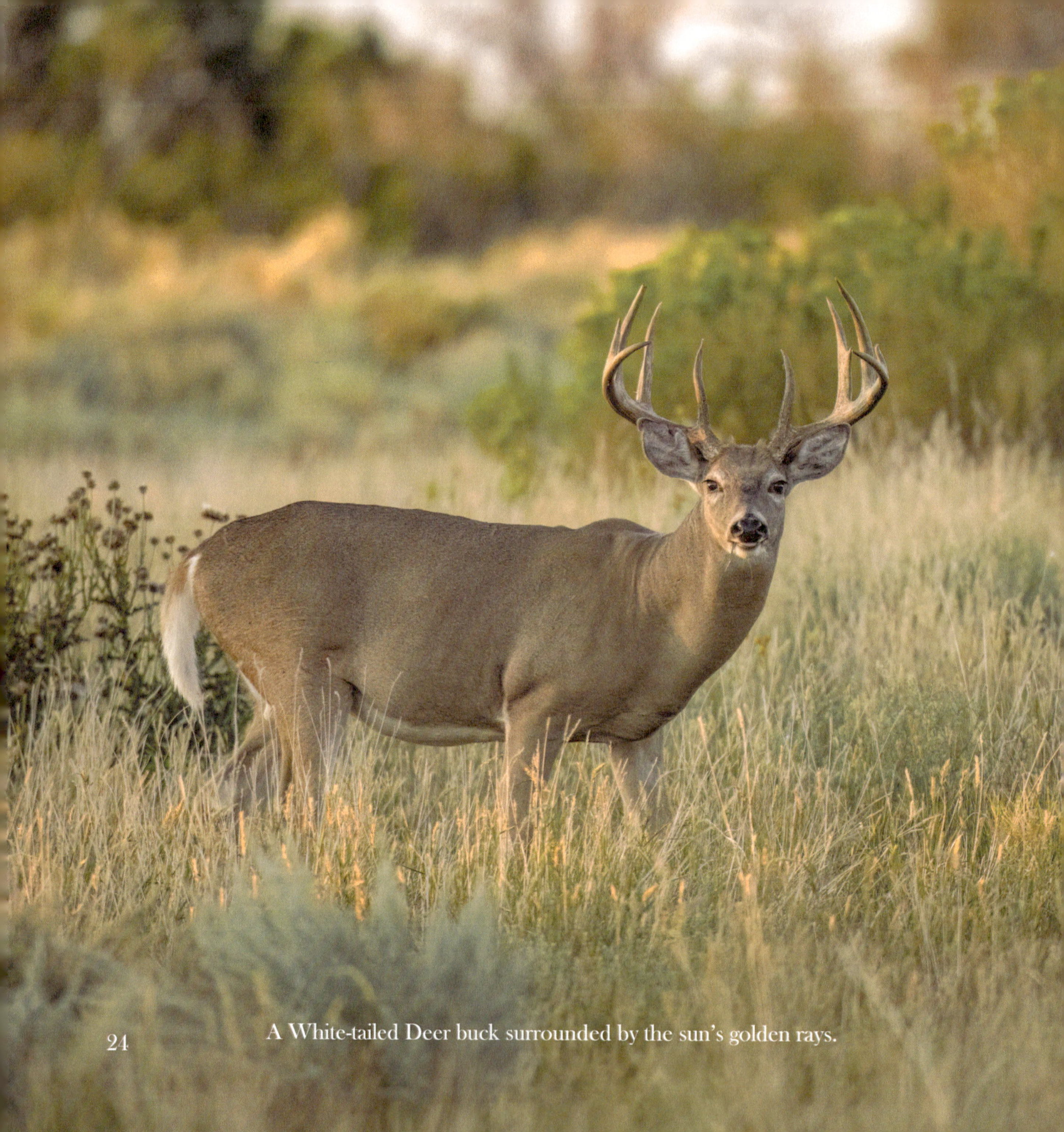

A White-tailed Deer buck surrounded by the sun's golden rays.

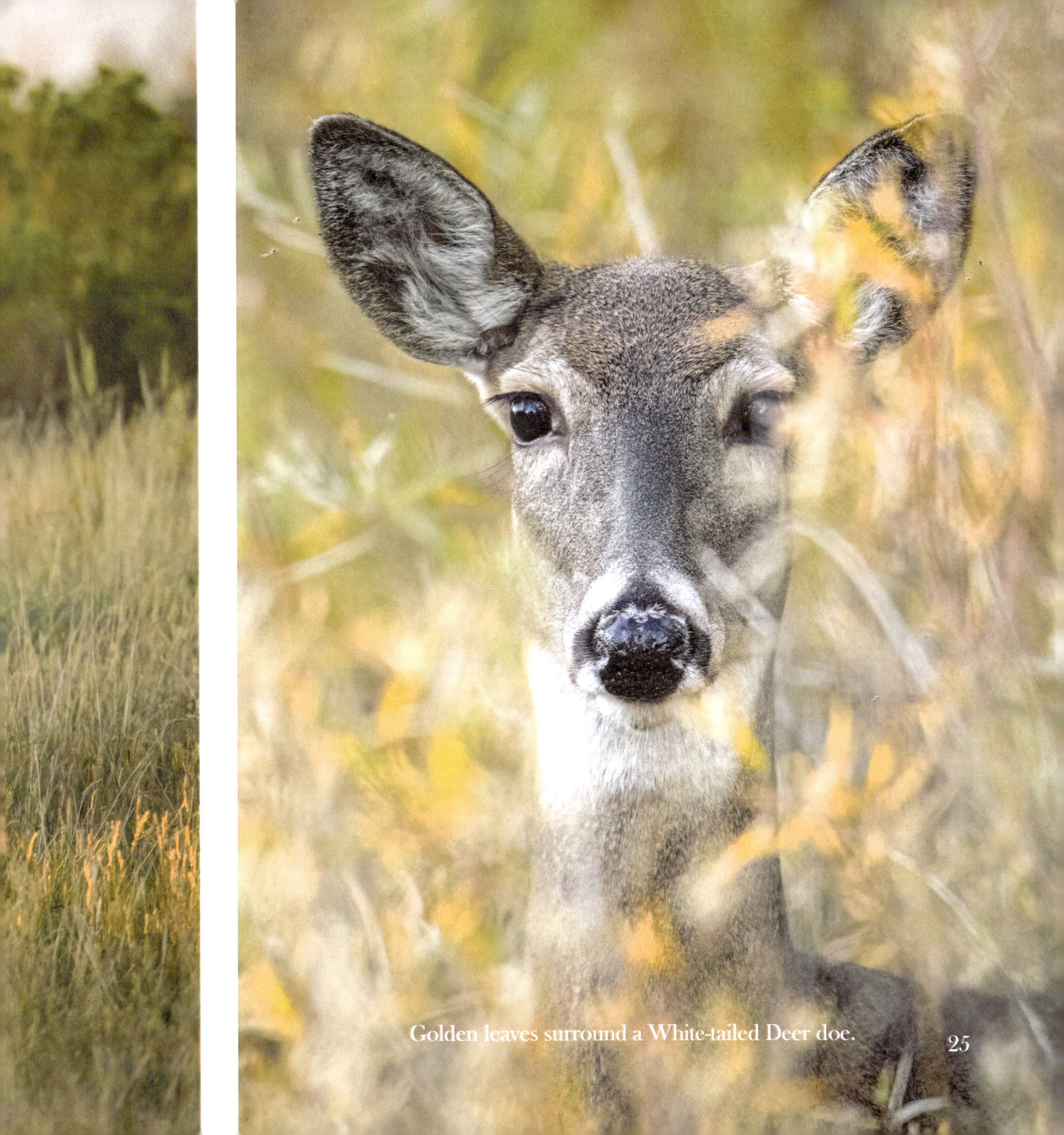

Golden leaves surround a White-tailed Deer doe.

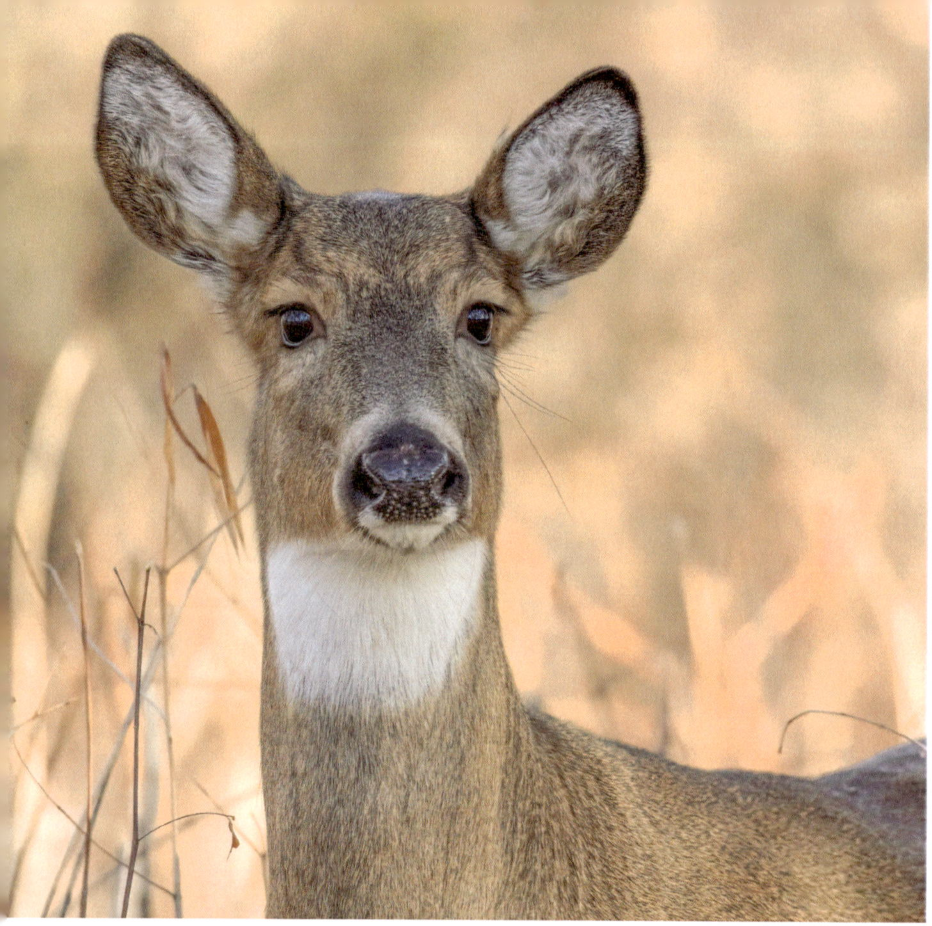

Many things in life come down to those beautiful brief moments.

Sometimes, for a few moments, beautiful light and beautiful deer come together right before your eyes.

As a photographer, these brief moments make all of the waiting, the scouting, the challenging weather, and all the missed shots, worthwhile.

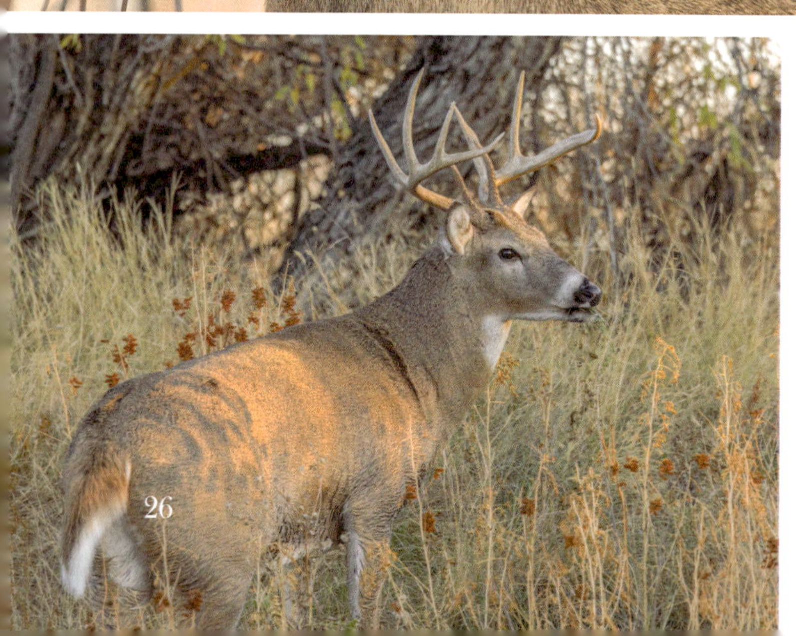

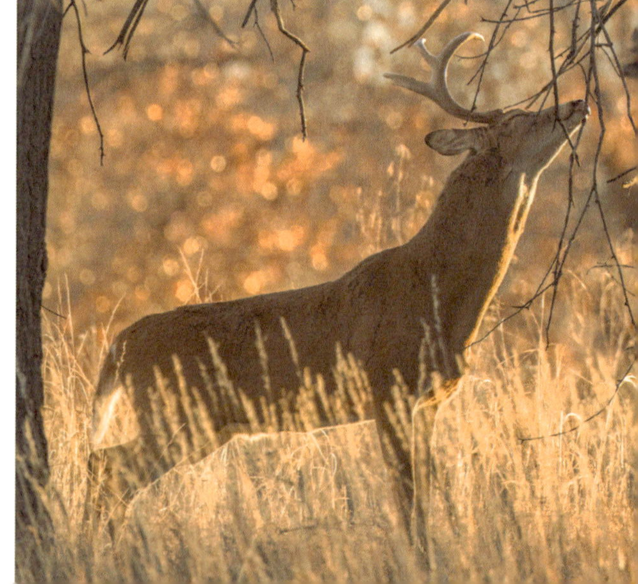

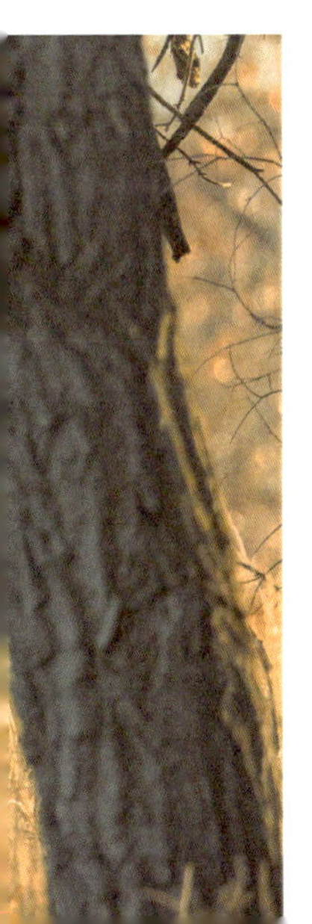

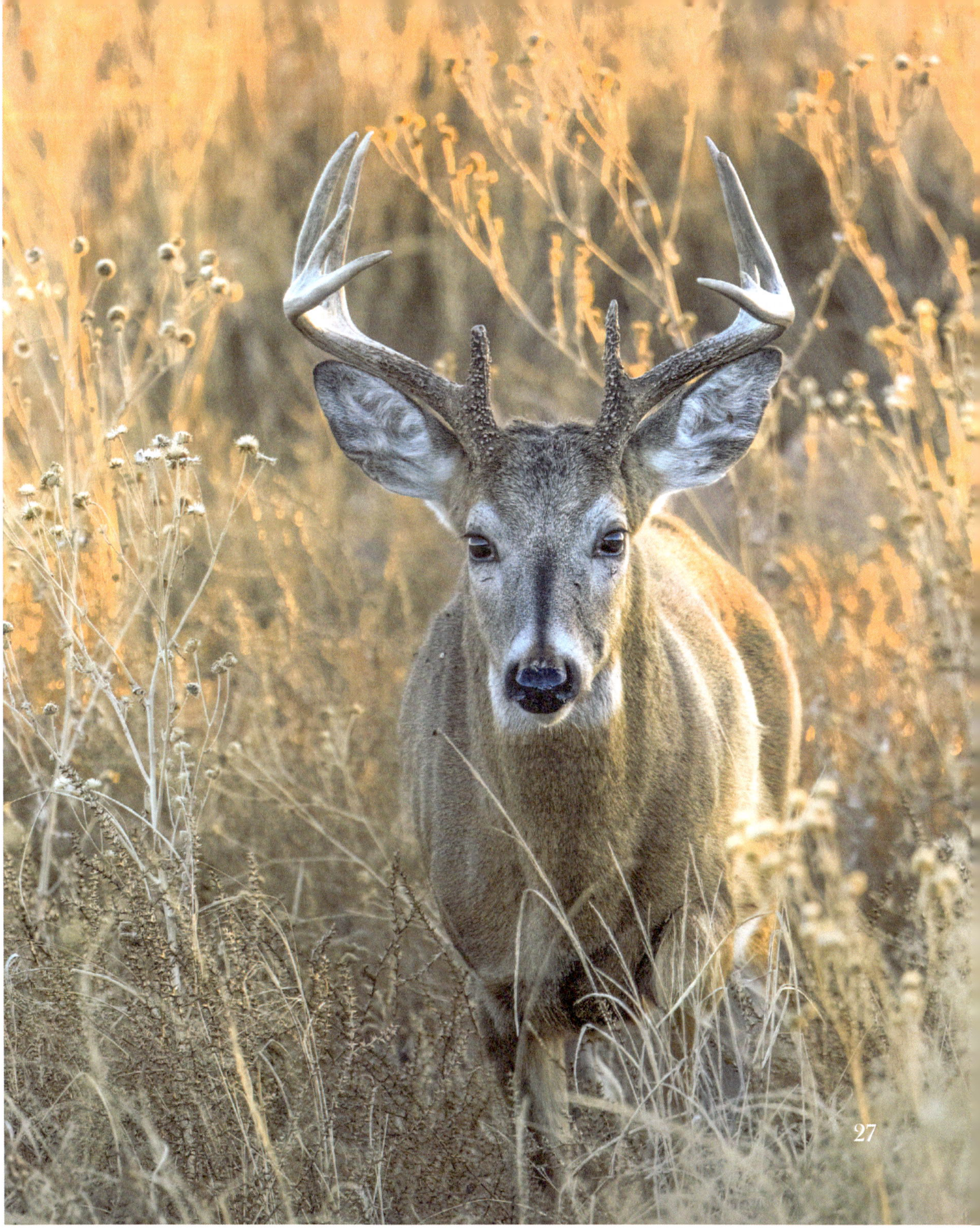

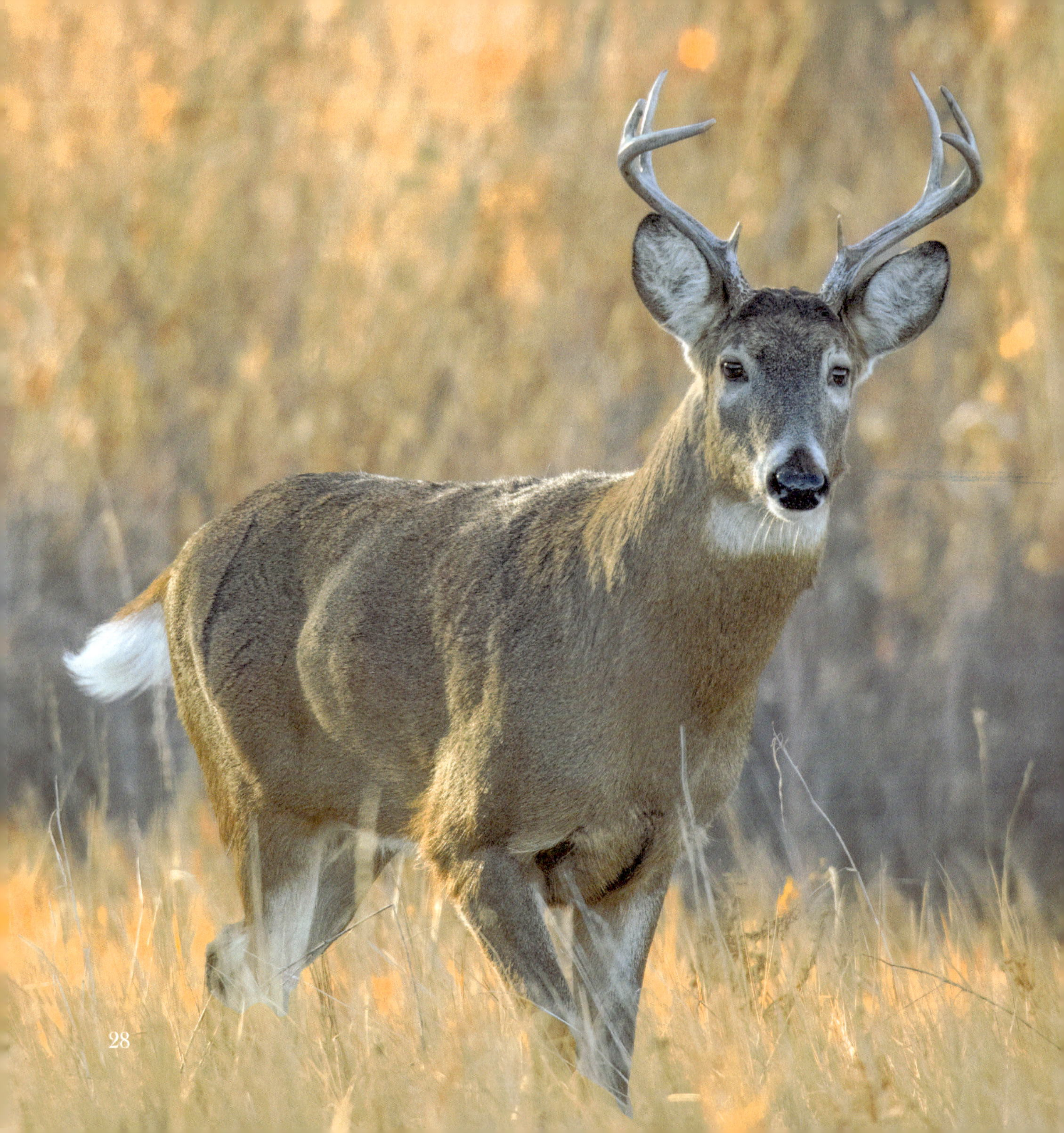

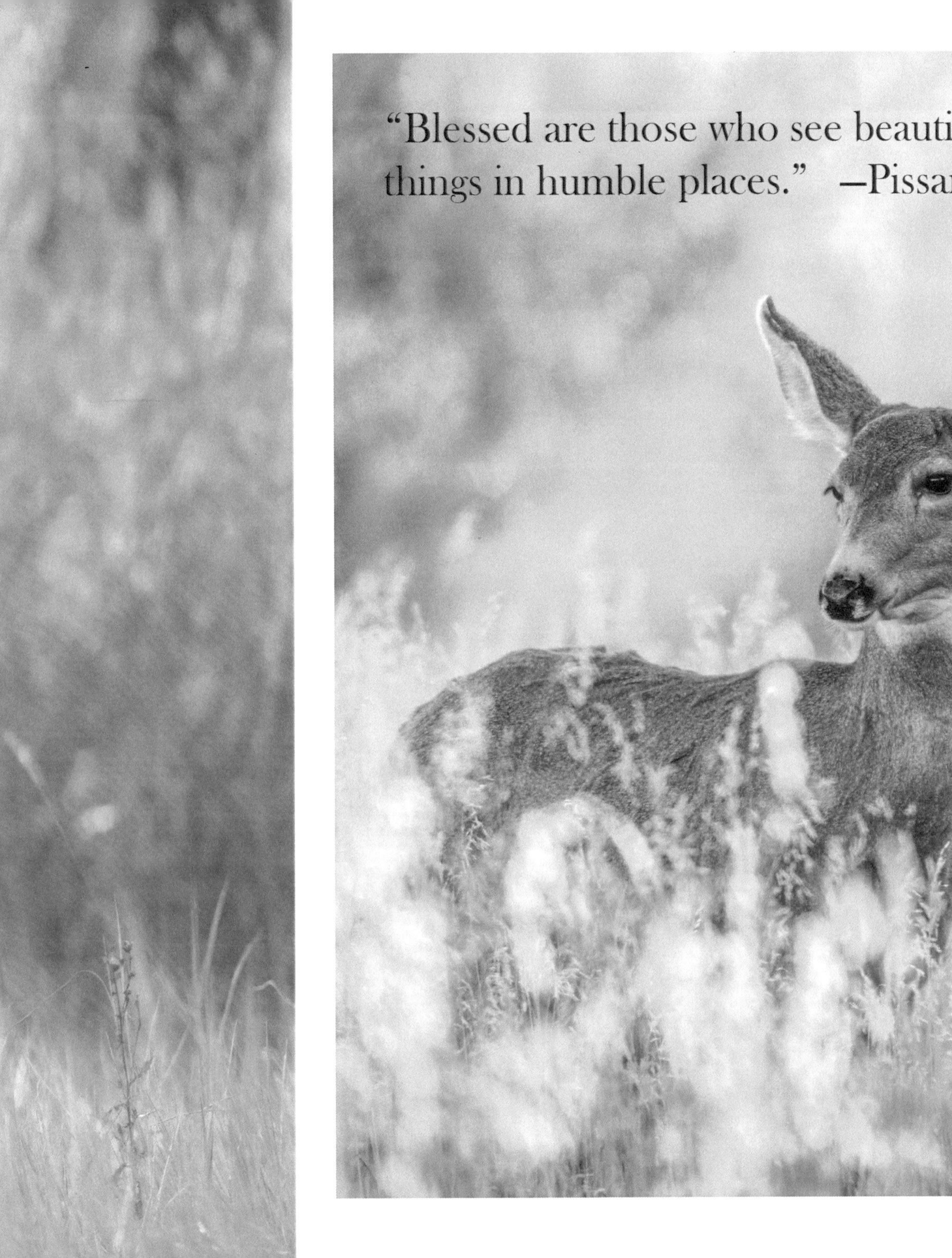
"Blessed are those who see beautiful things in humble places."   —Pissarro

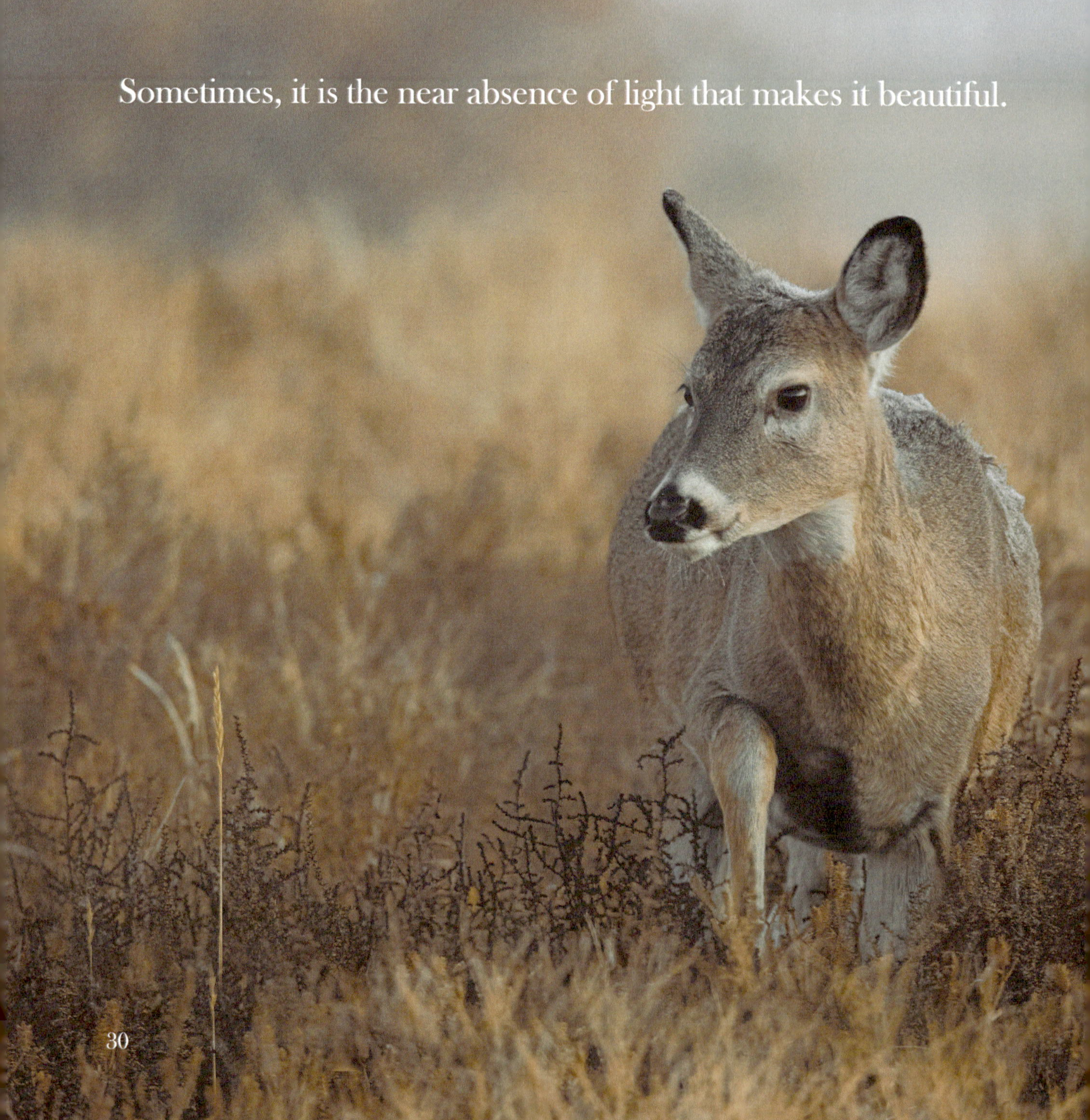
Sometimes, it is the near absence of light that makes it beautiful.

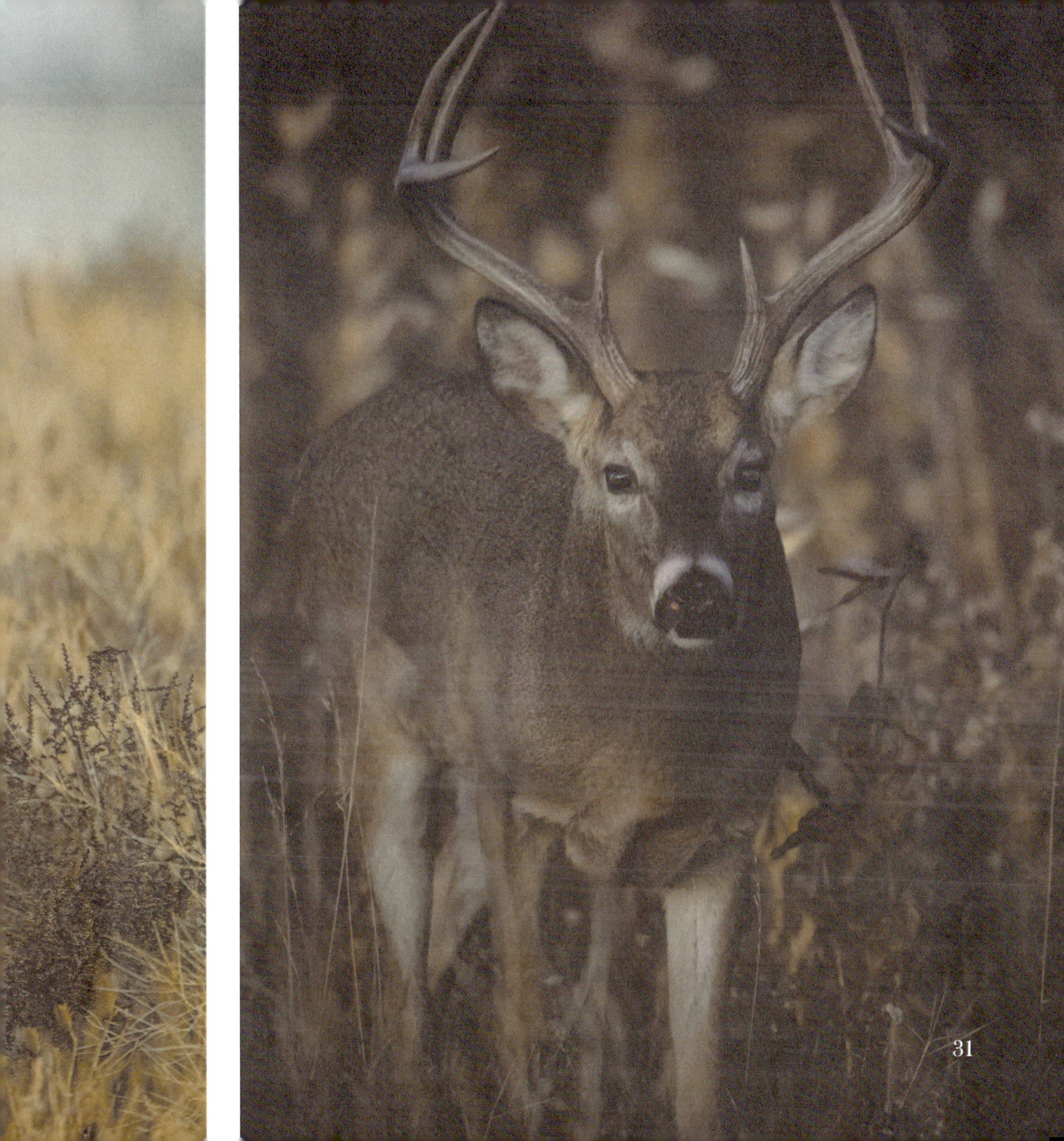

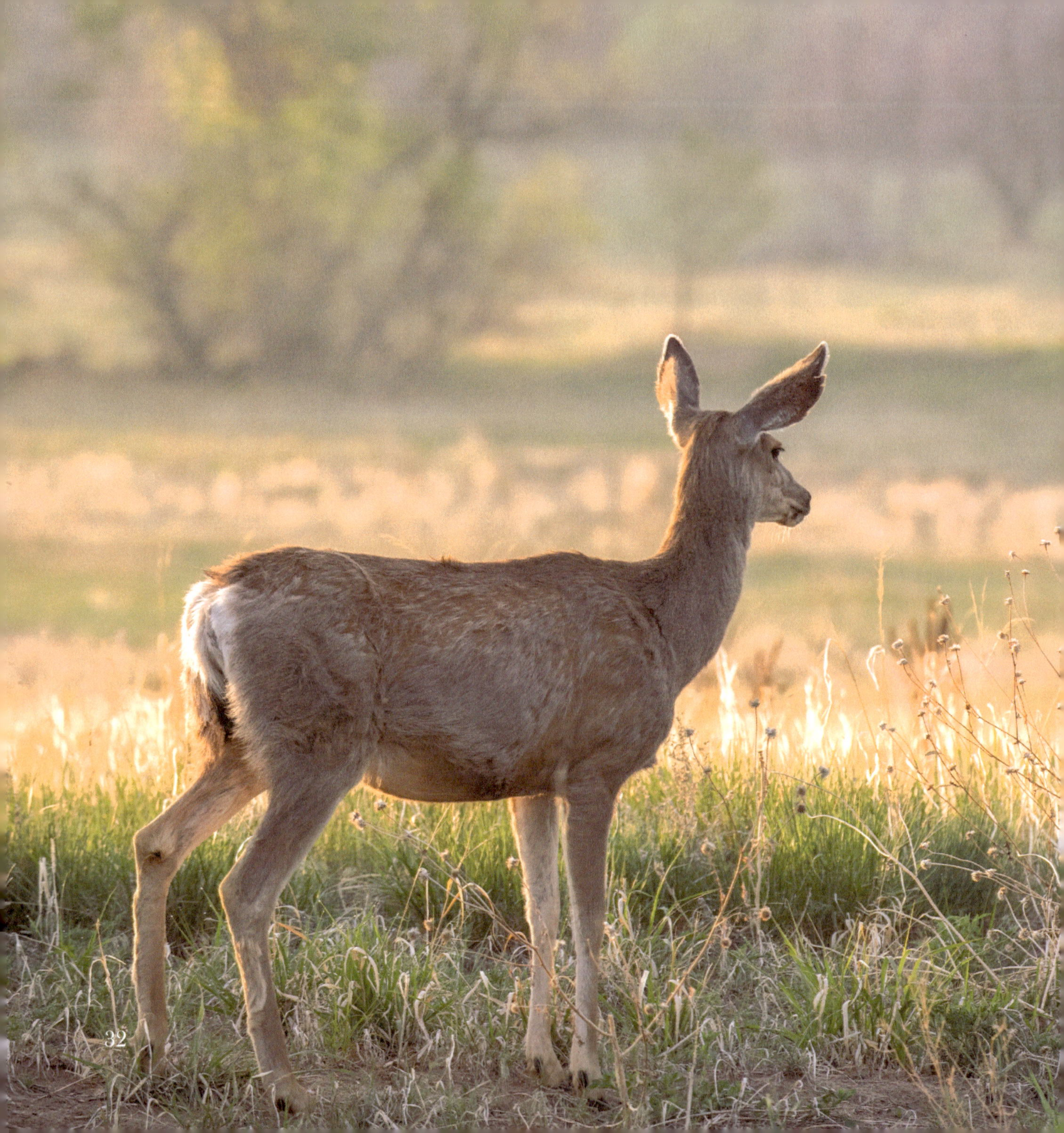
32

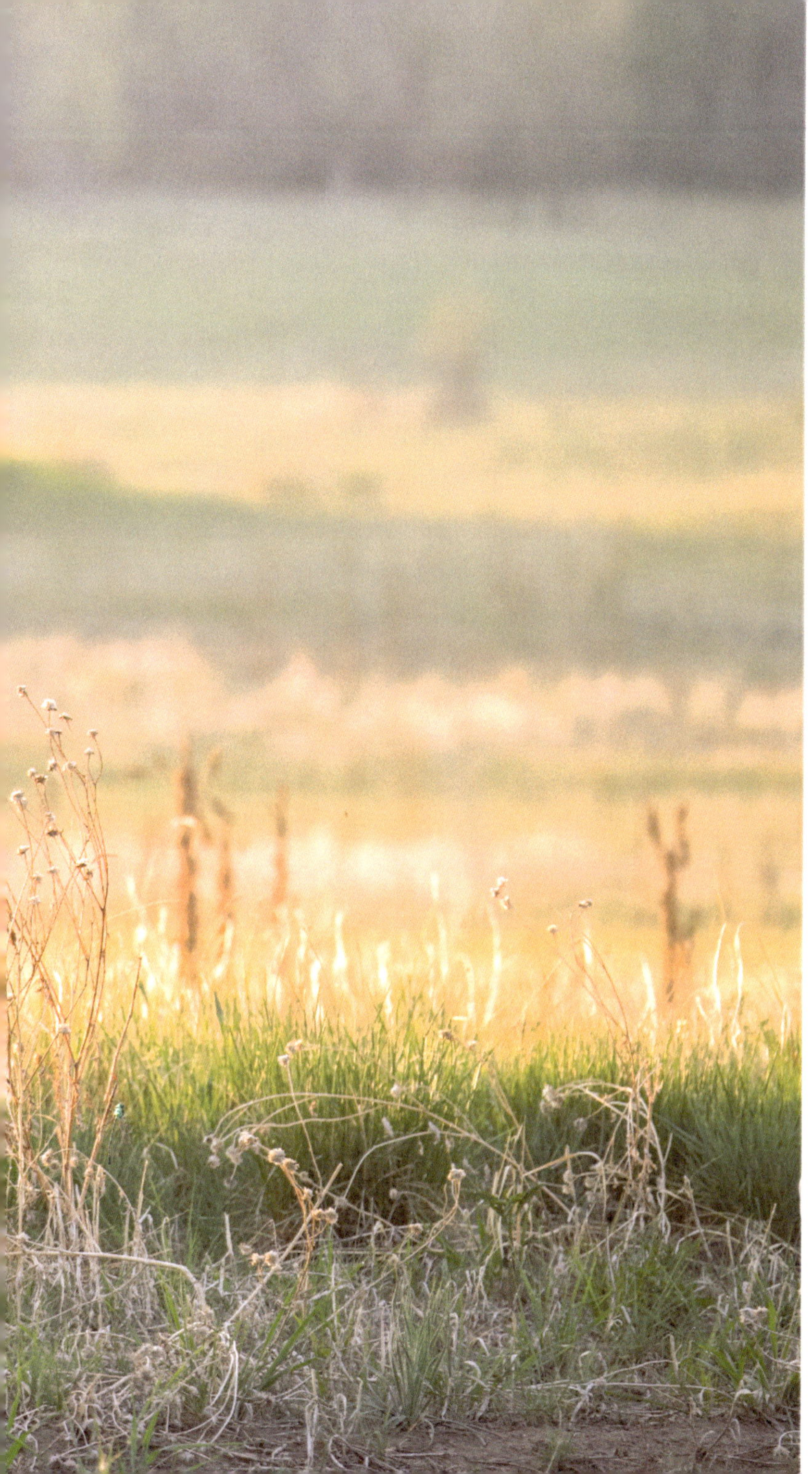

"It's never
too late to
be what you
might have
been."

—G. Eliot

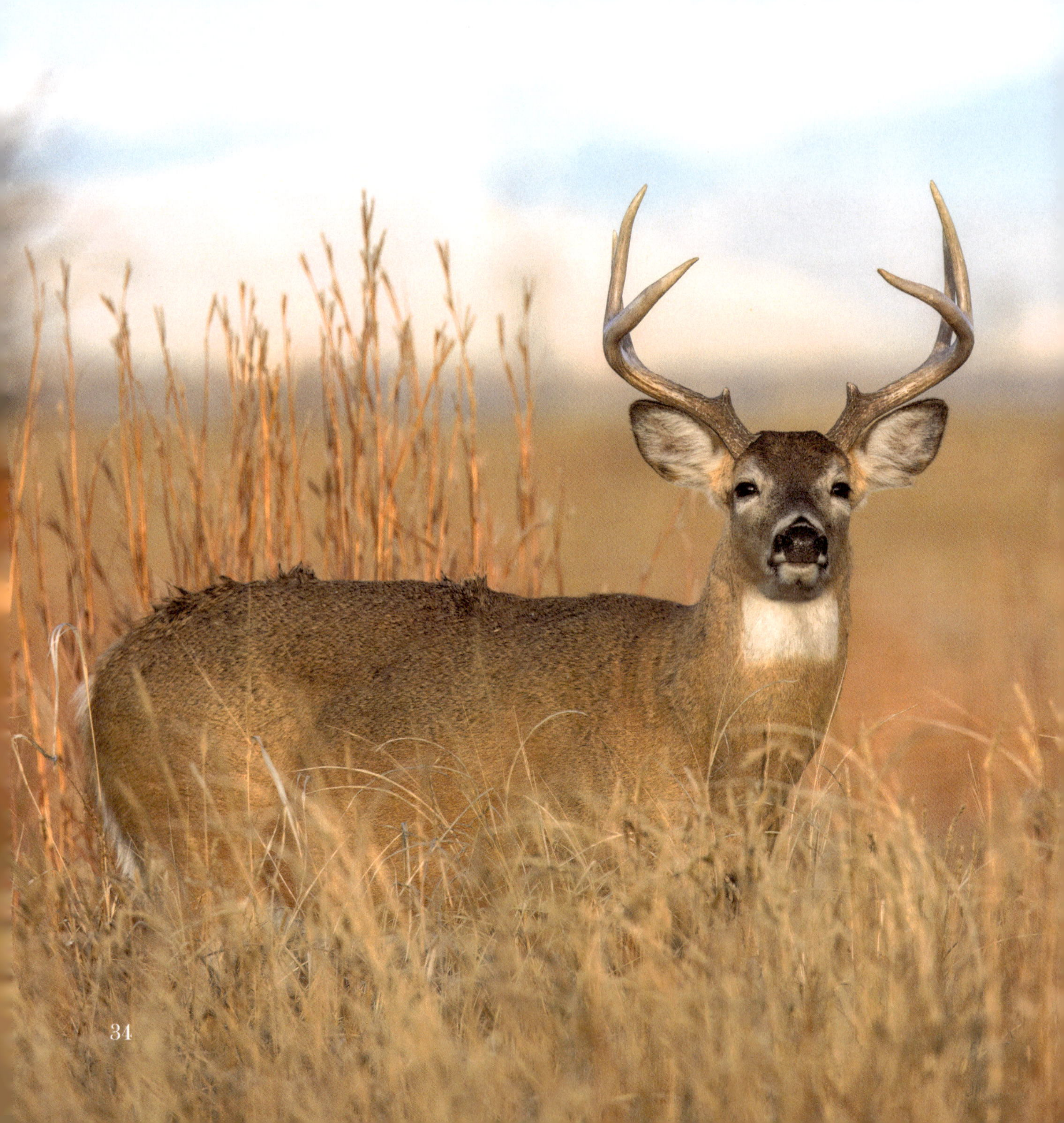

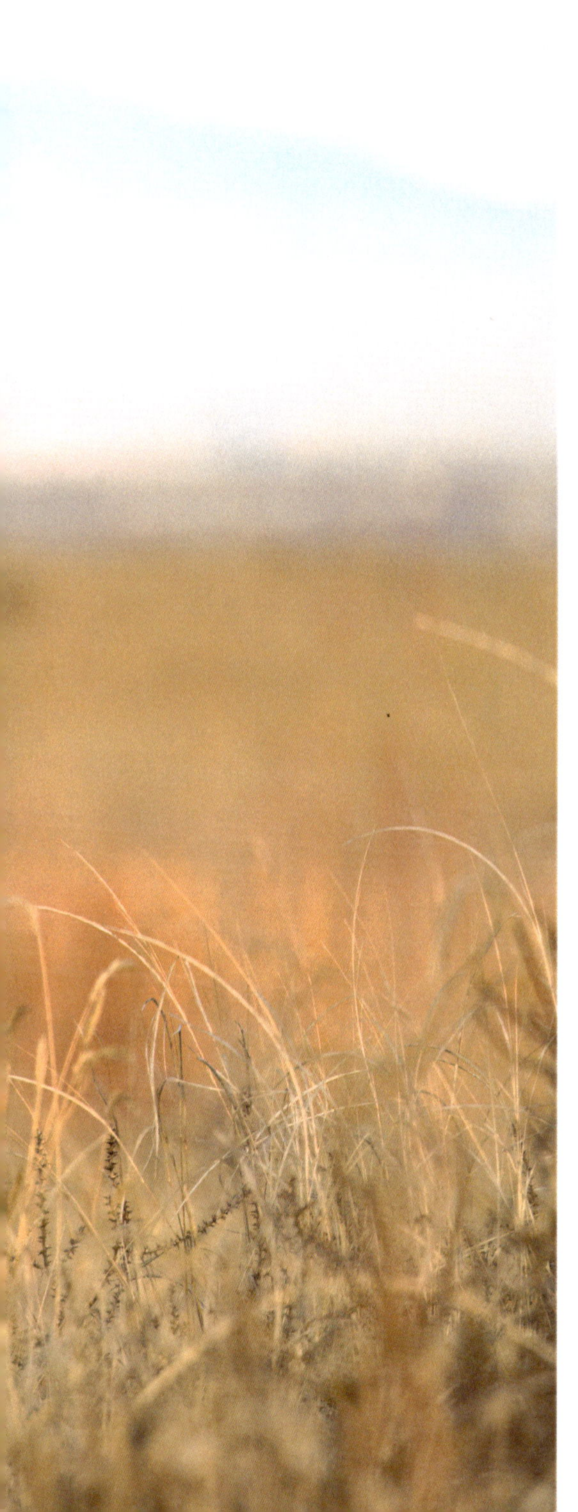

Autumn

Autumn in Colorado
is all about extremes.

One day it is bright,
warm, and sunny. And
the next day it is cold and wet.

But no matter the temperature,
the colors are beautiful!

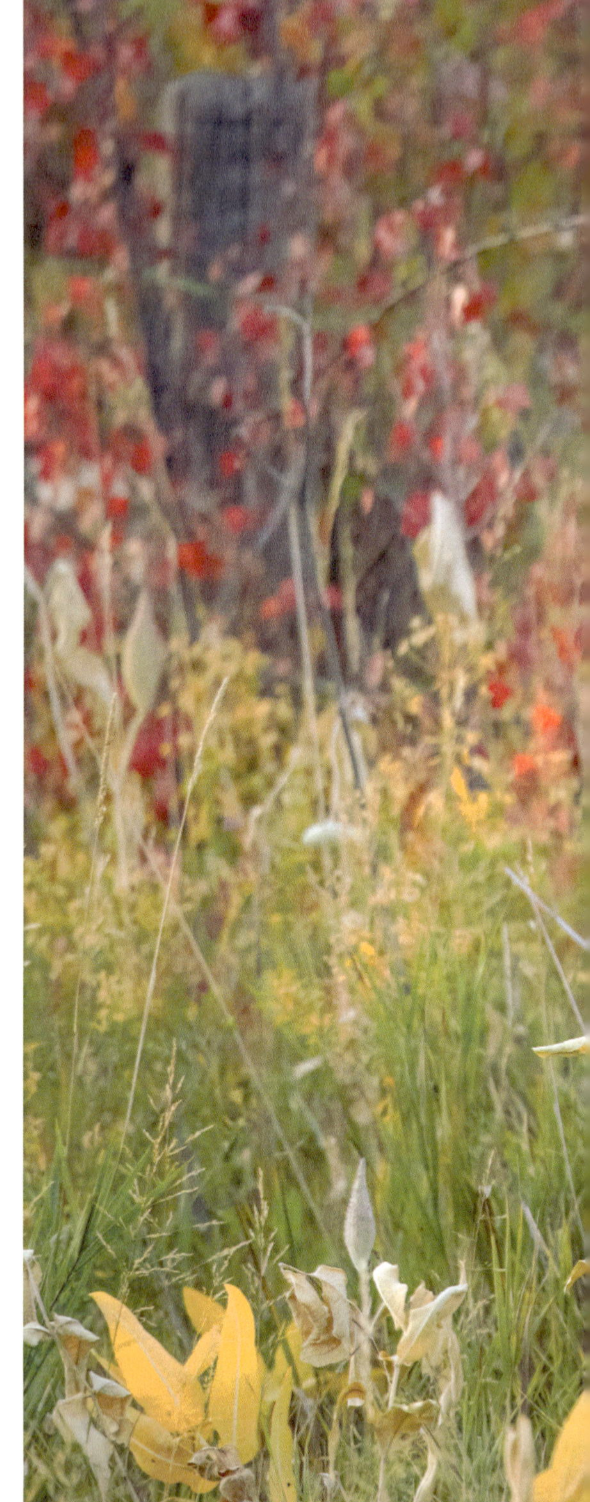

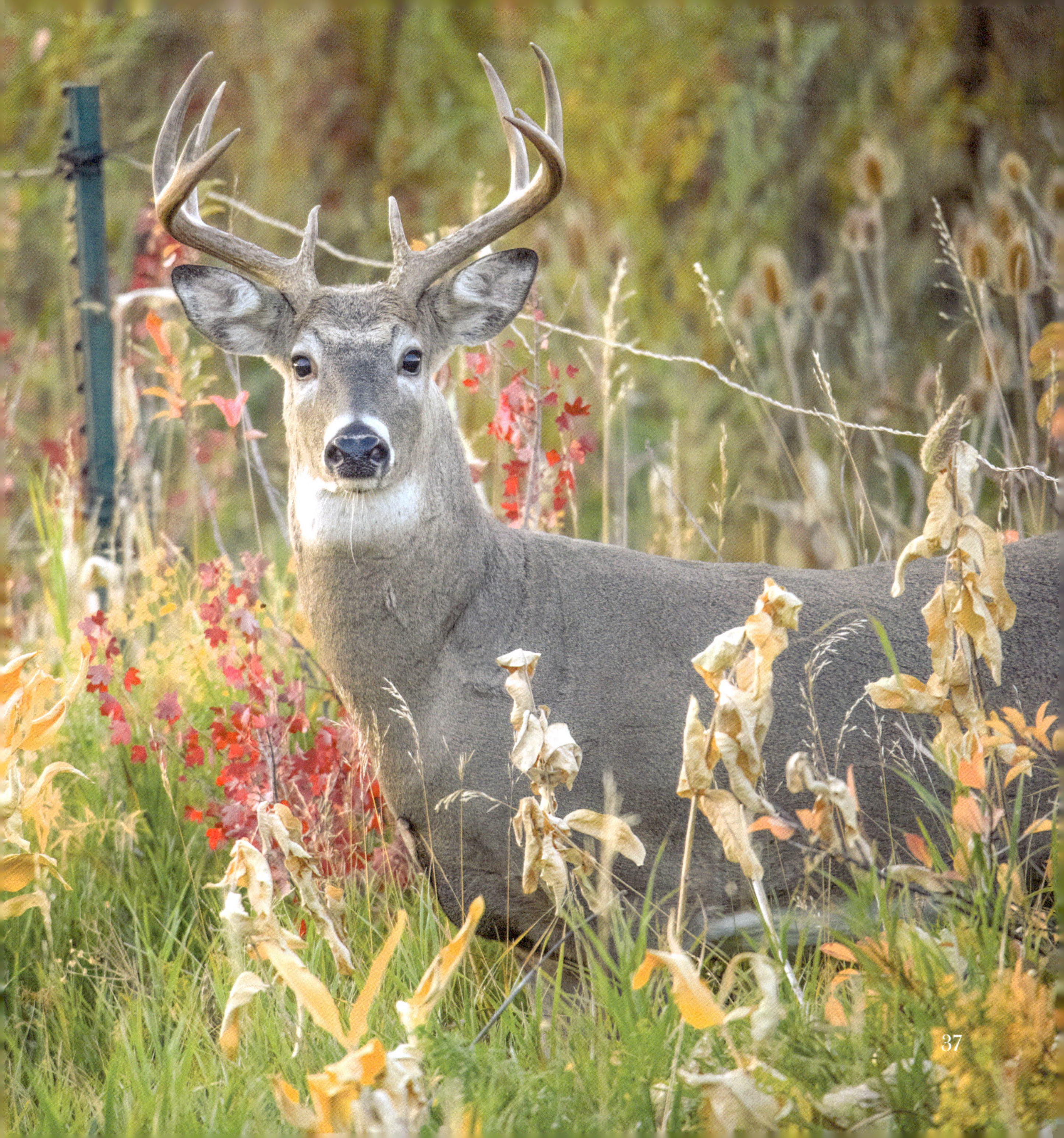

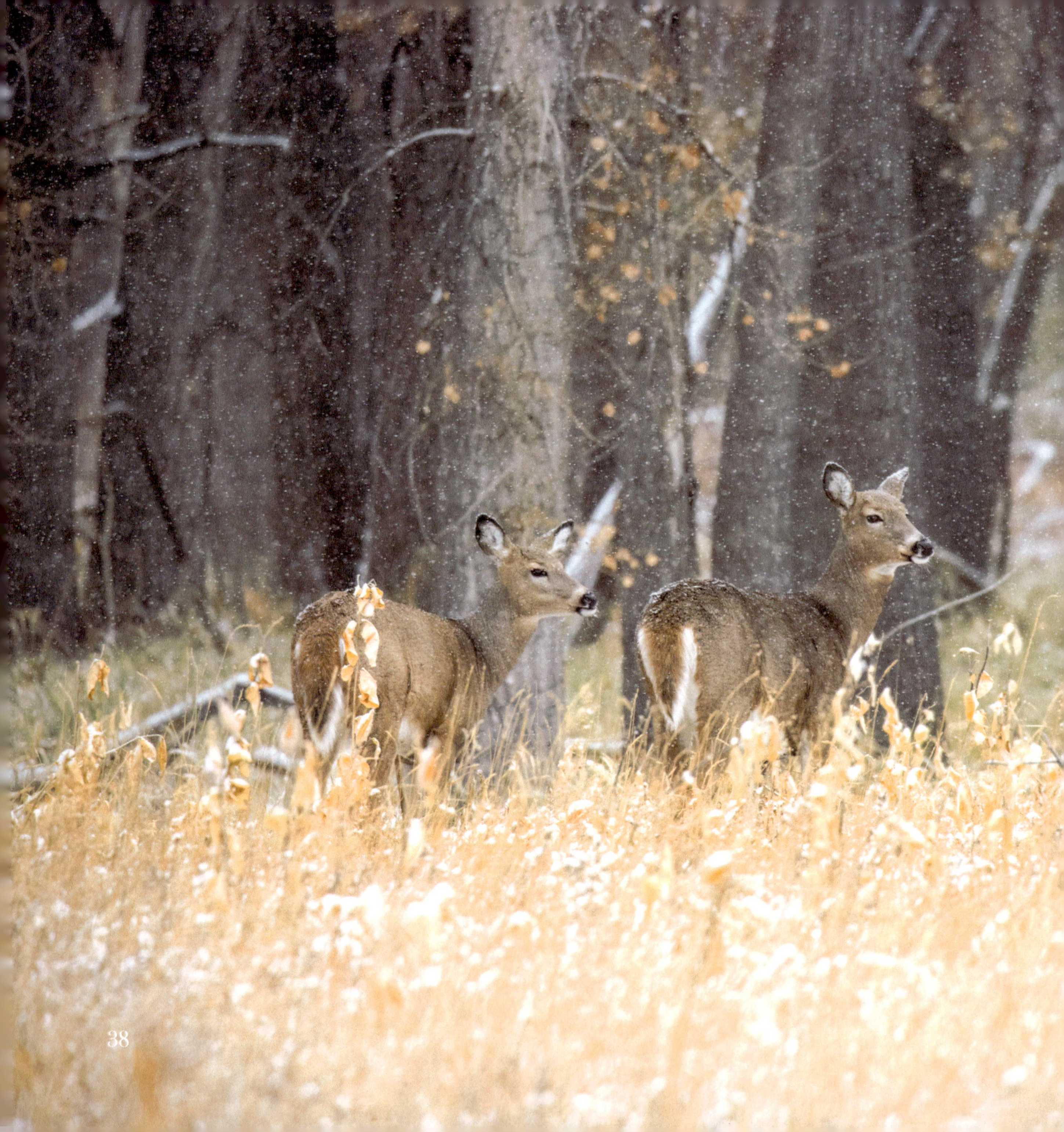

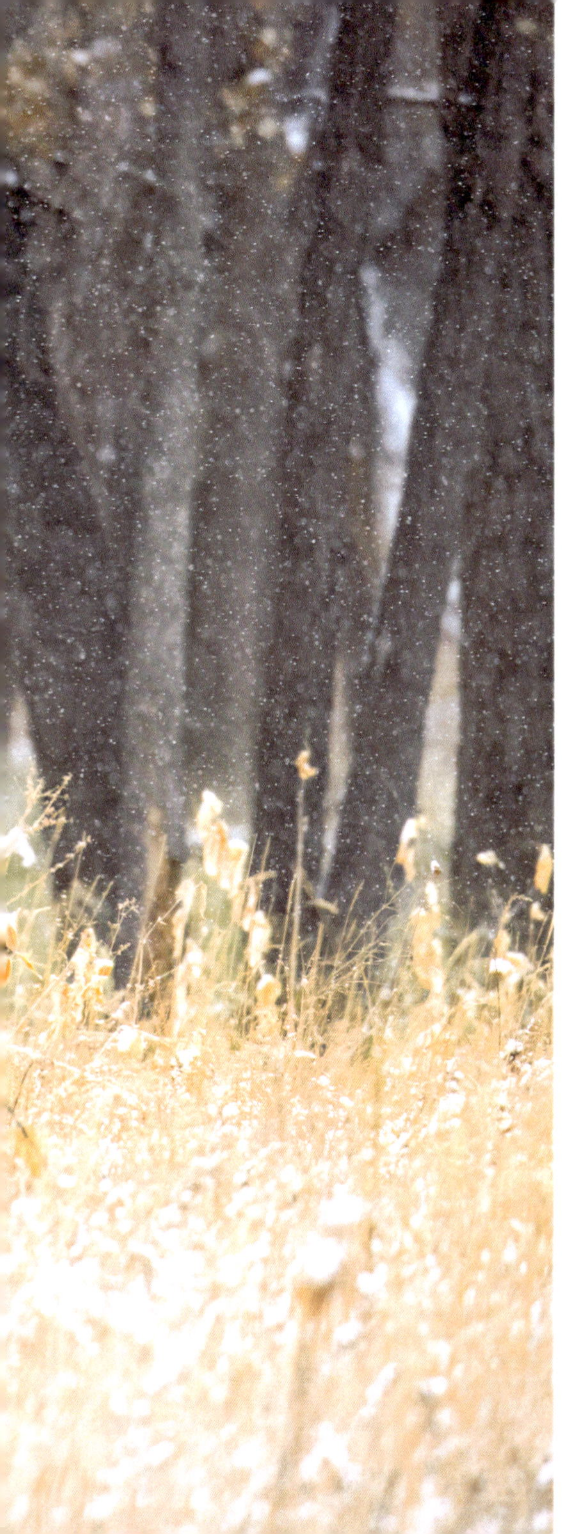

Two White-tailed does on a snowy autumn day.

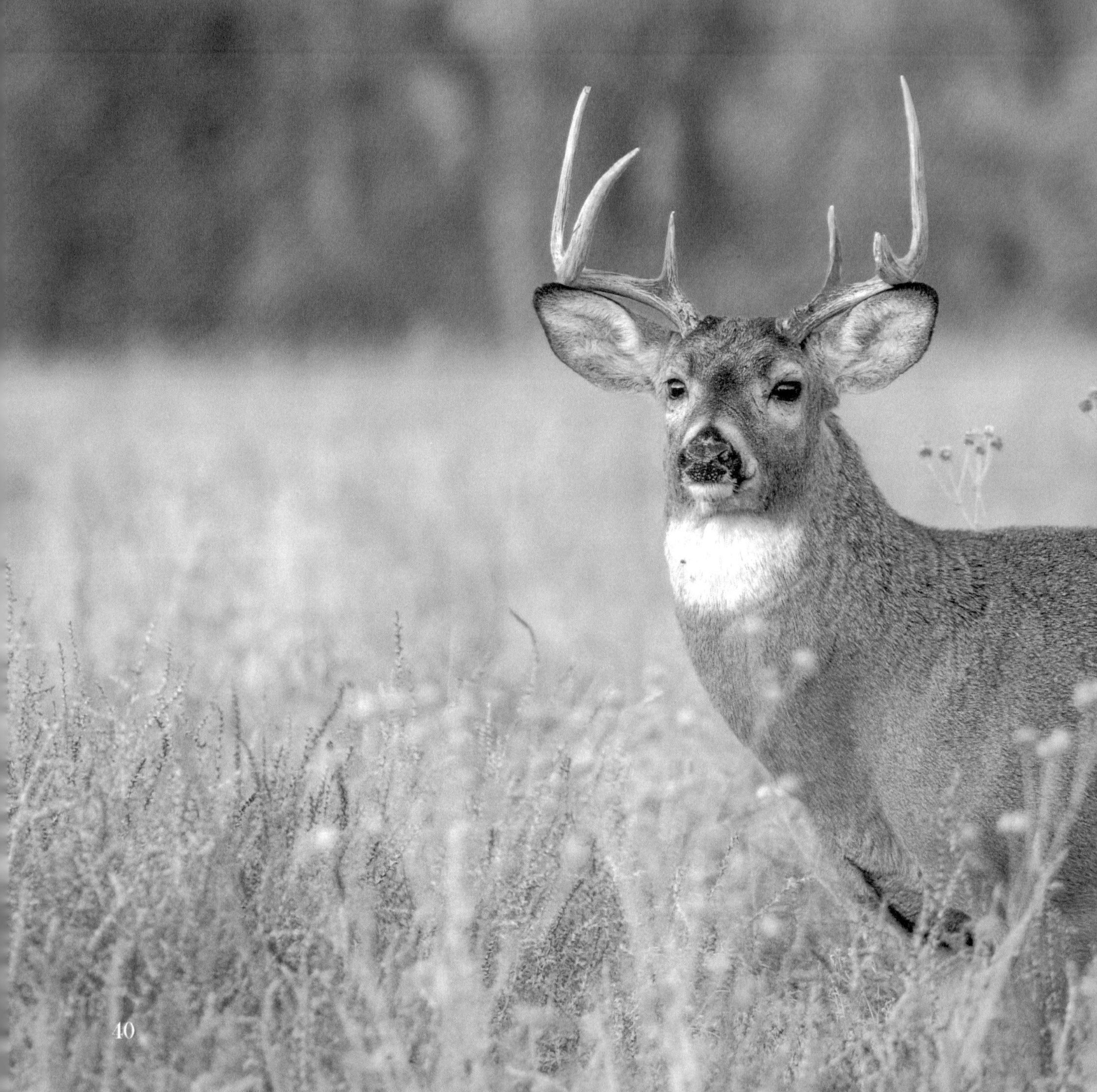

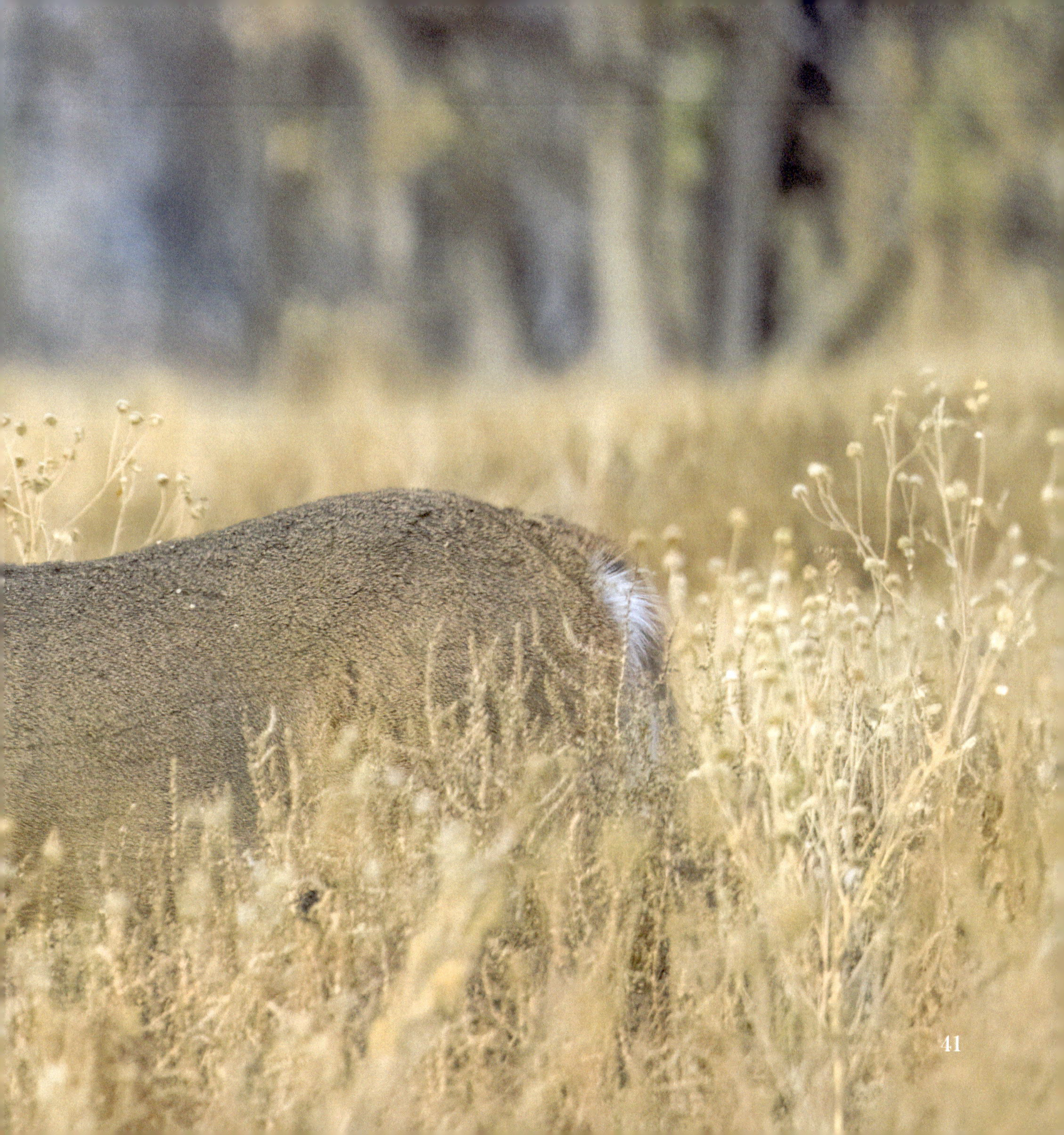

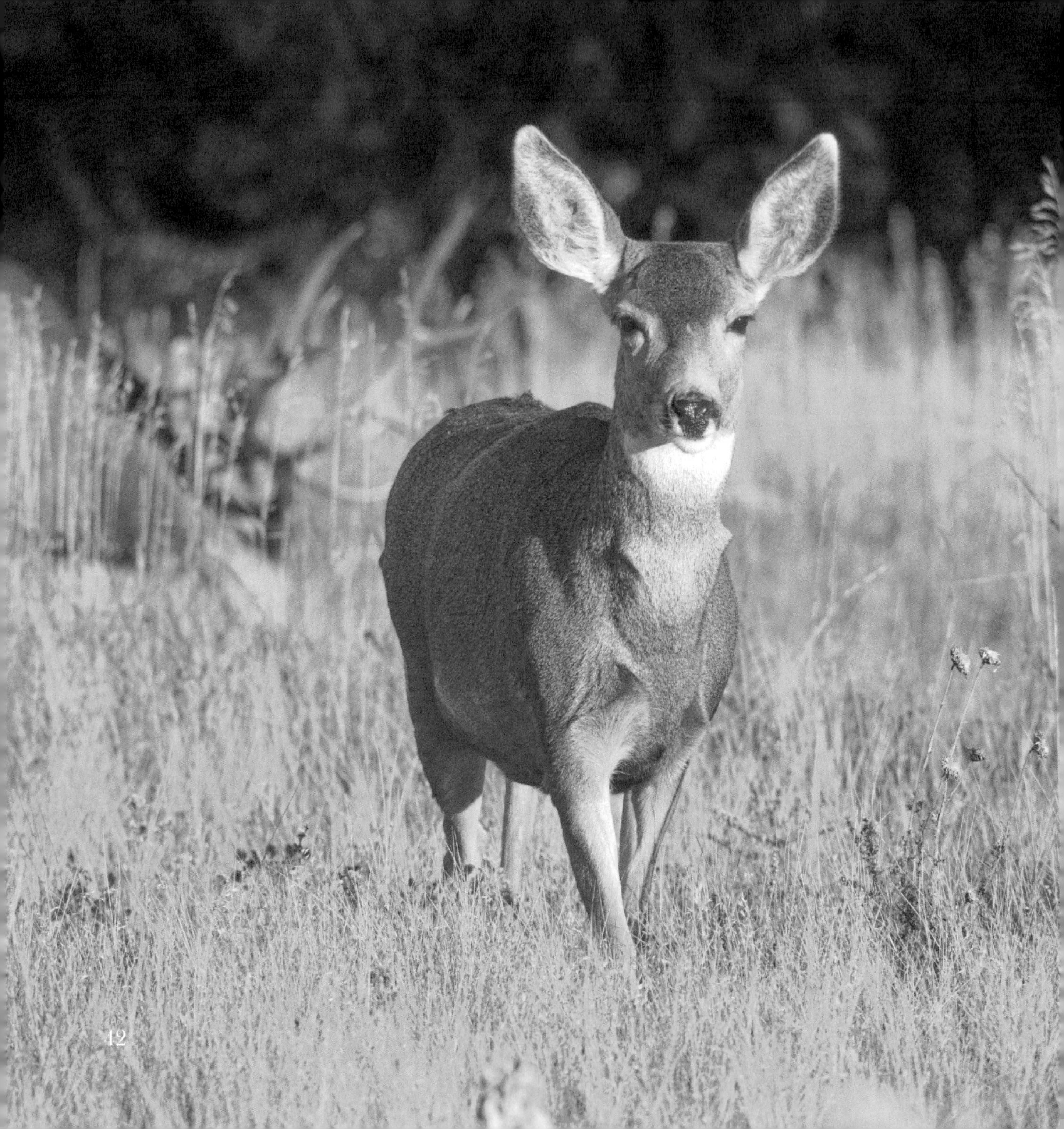

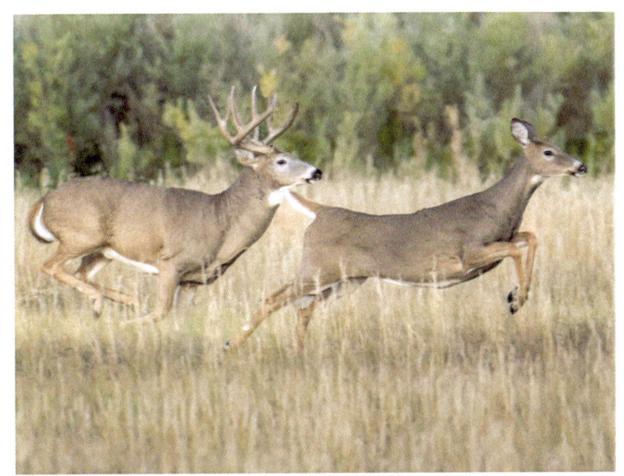

Autumn is also the time of the rut, or breeding season. The bucks will strive to gain dominance over other bucks either by intimidation or by fighting.

Both males and females are only able to breed during this time of year.

Does choose their mates and will usually choose a dominant buck because of perceived good genetics.

A doe instinctively knows that a dominant buck may improve a fawn's chances of survival.

Not all bucks may breed during the rut, but most does will be bred. During this time, a doe has two breeding cycles, twenty-eight days apart.

Throughout the rut, both bucks and does will run extensively. Some are chasing and some are being chased.

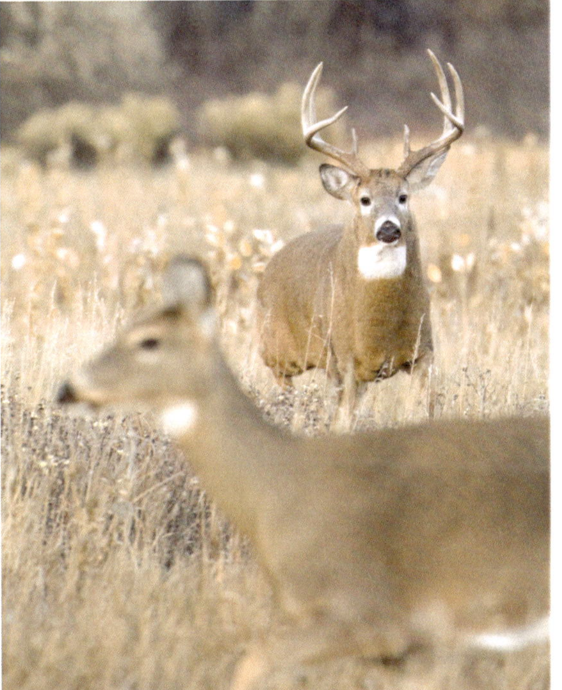

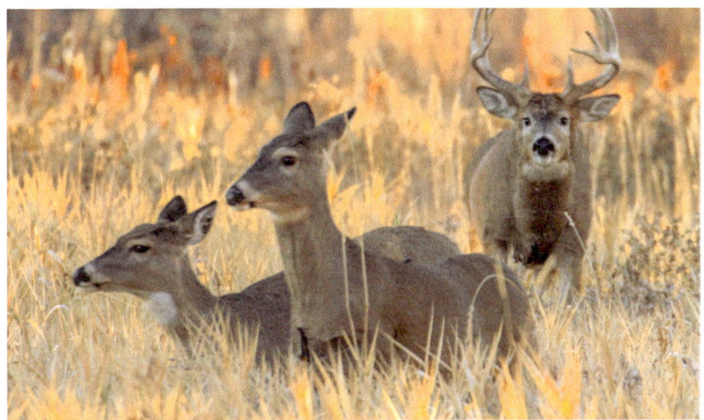

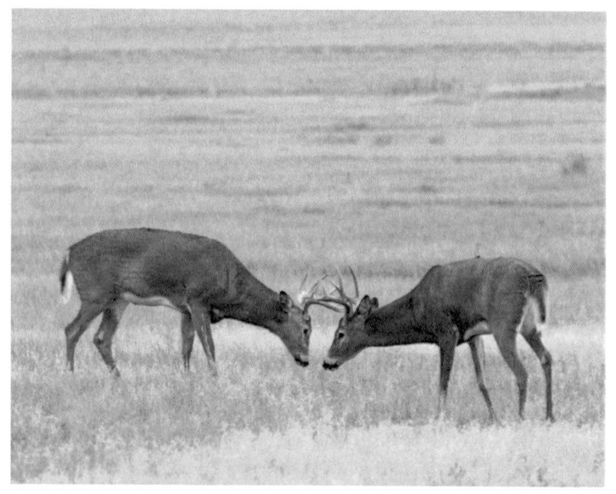

The rut is very hard on the bucks and fighting other bucks can be deadly.

Antlers are broken off either from fighting or from rubbing them on branches and trees.

Bucks spend little time eating or sleeping during the rut and they may travel many miles in a day. Bucks can lose up to thirty percent of their body weight during this time.

When the rut is over, the deer must endure the winter. If it's a harsh winter, bucks may not survive. Their lower body weight, rut injuries, and ease of food availability are all factors in their rut recovery.

44

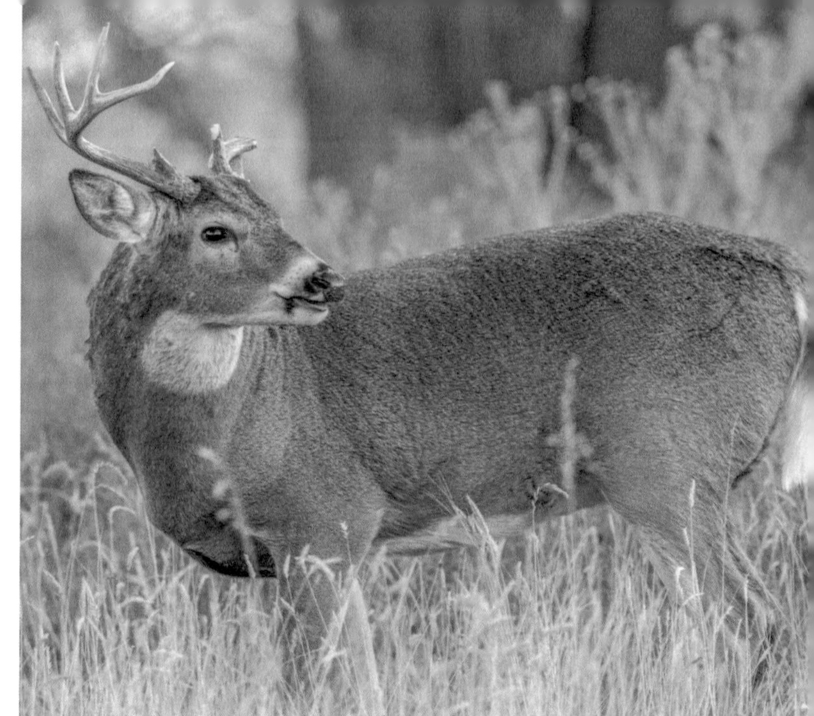

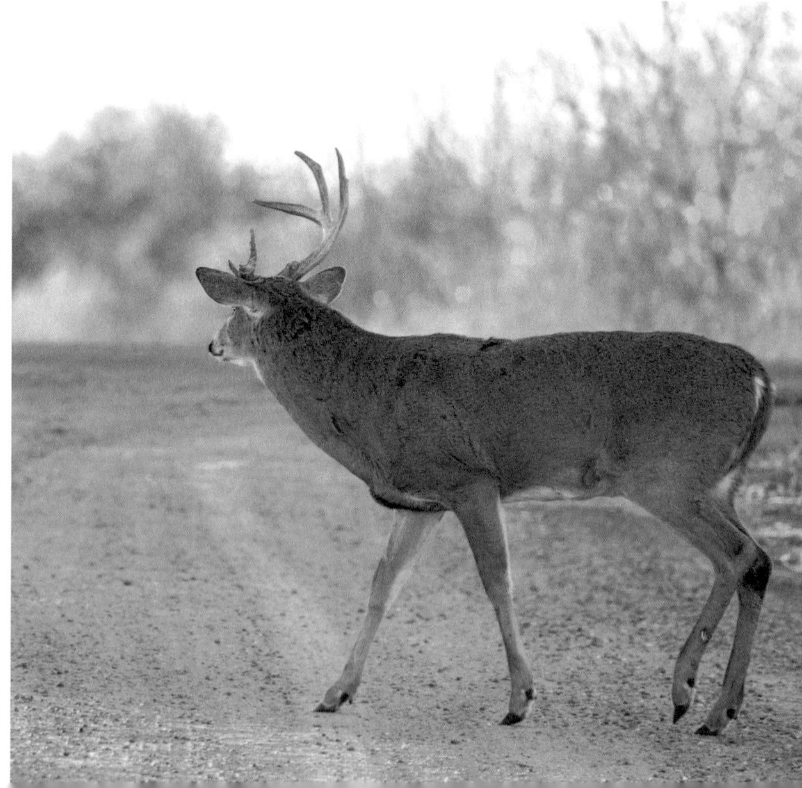

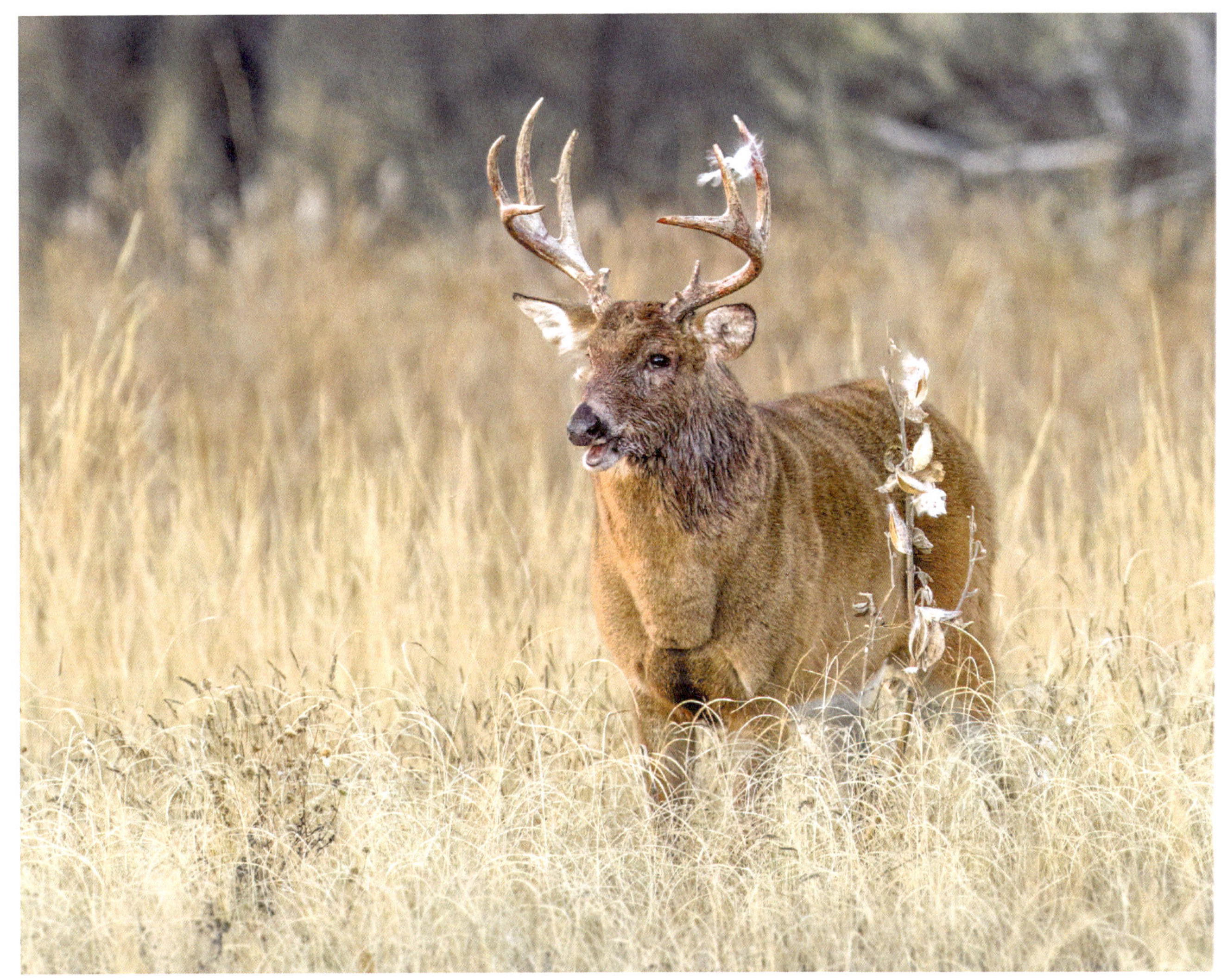

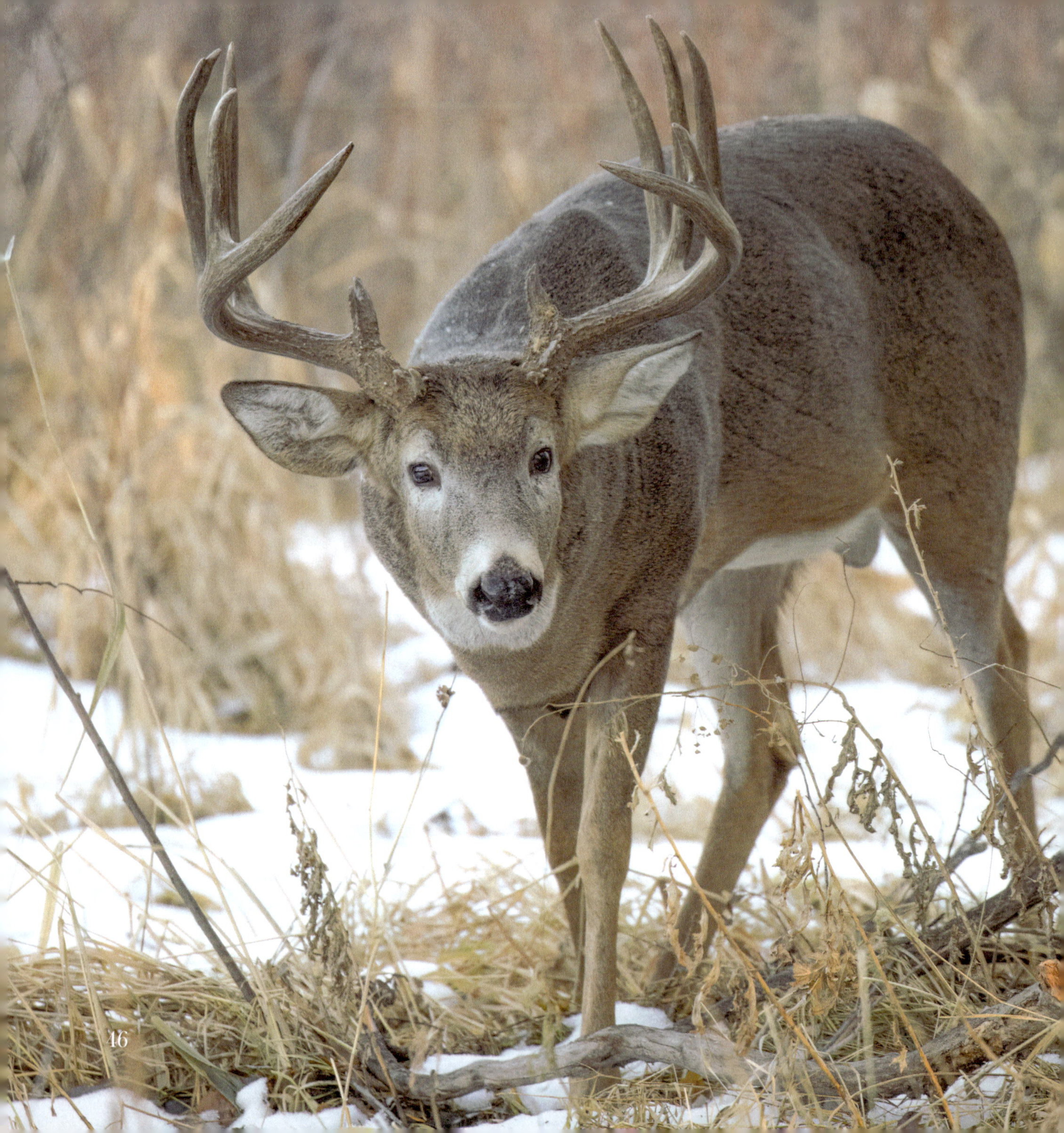

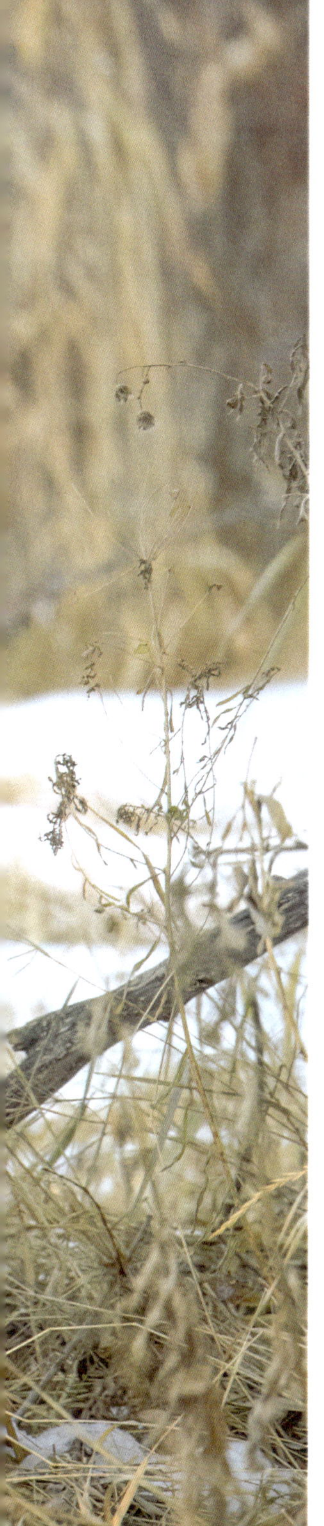

"Above all else,
guard your heart,
for everything you
do flows from it...

Let your eyes look
straight ahead;
fix your gaze directly
before you.

Give careful thought
to the paths for your
feet and be steadfast
in all your ways."

—Proverbs 4:23-26

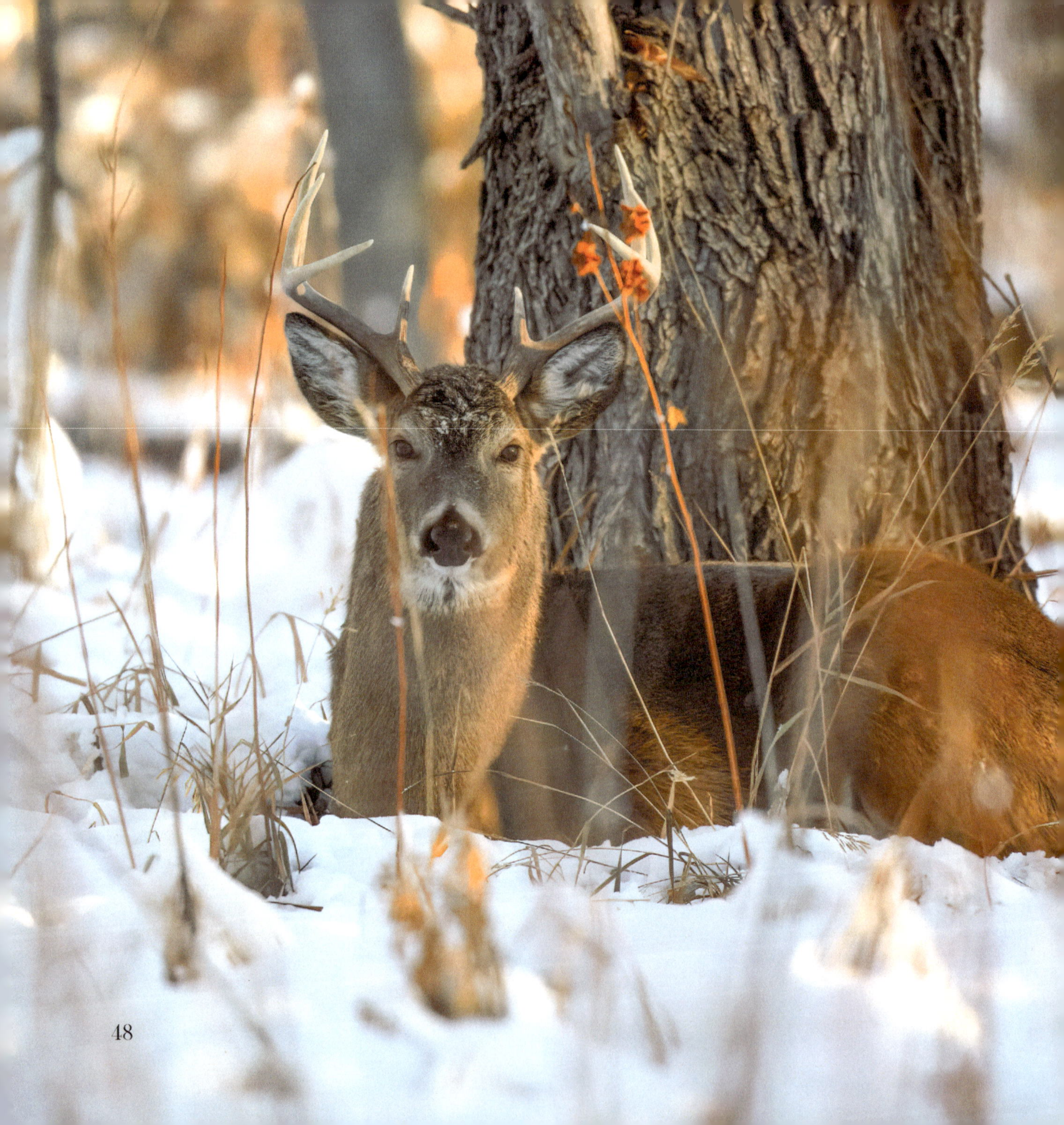

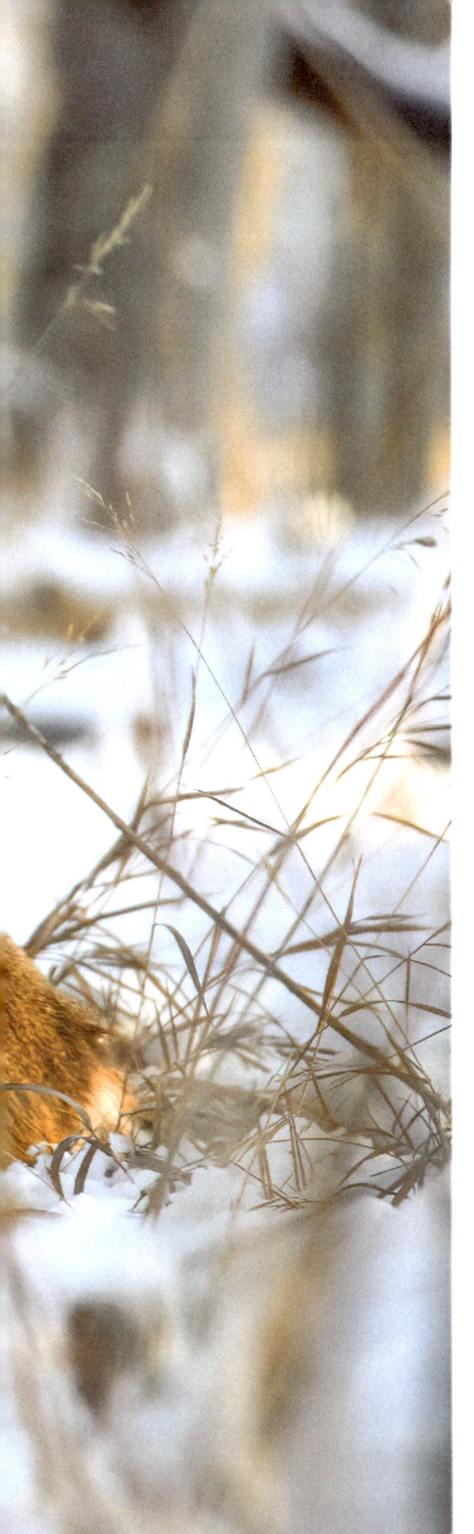

Winter

"If you truly love
nature,
you will find
beauty
everywhere."

—Van Gogh

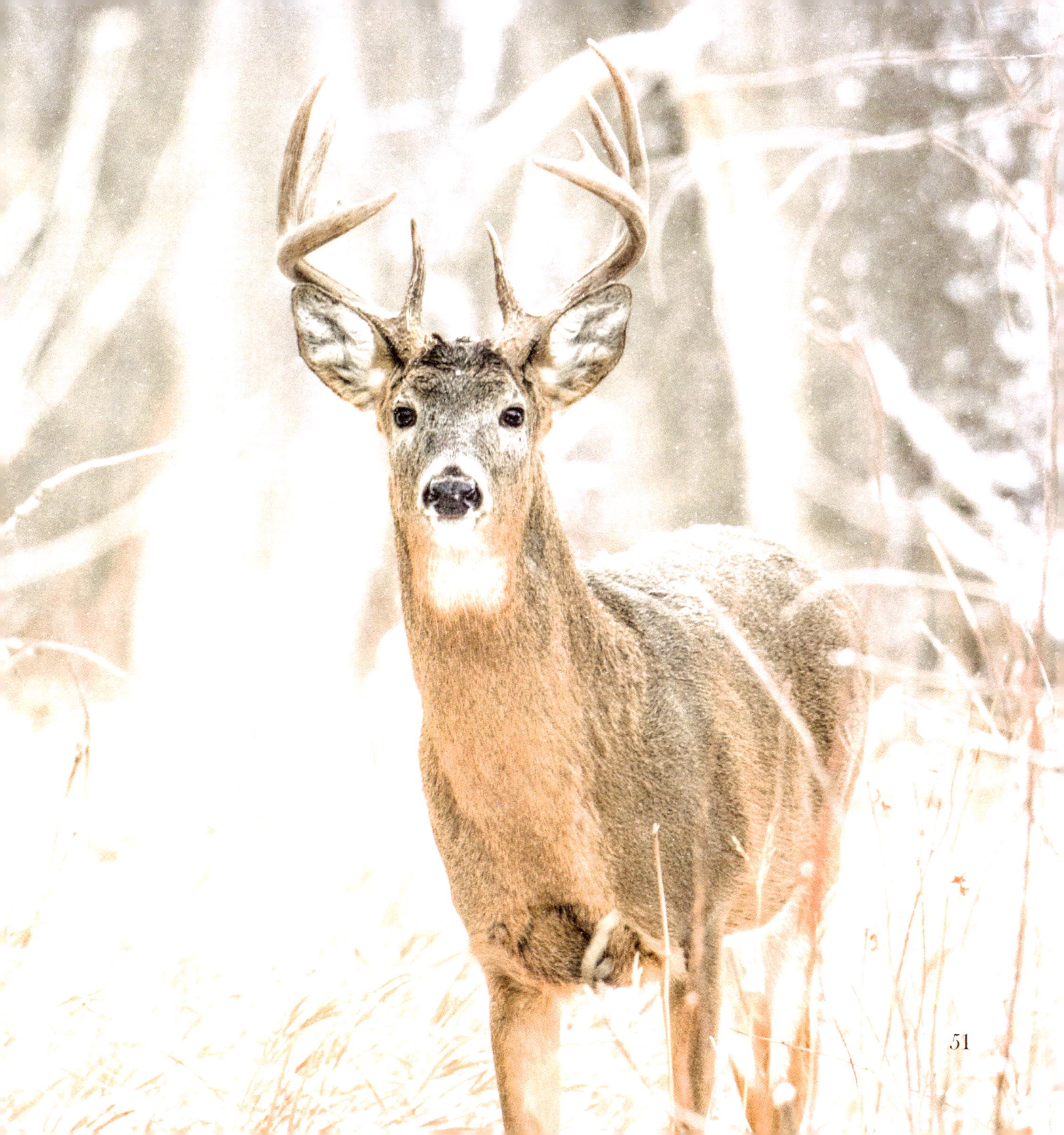

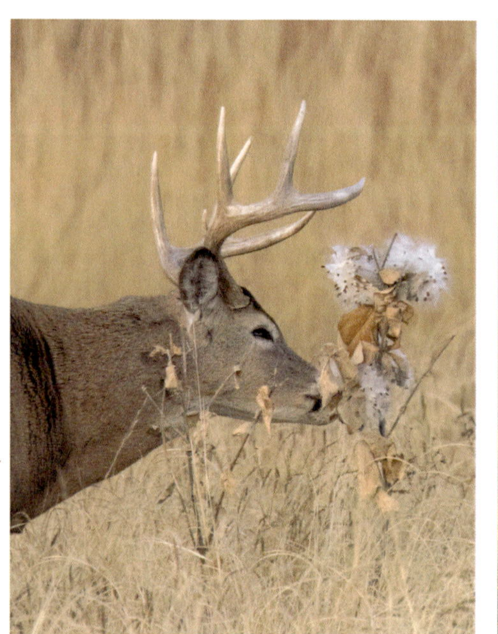 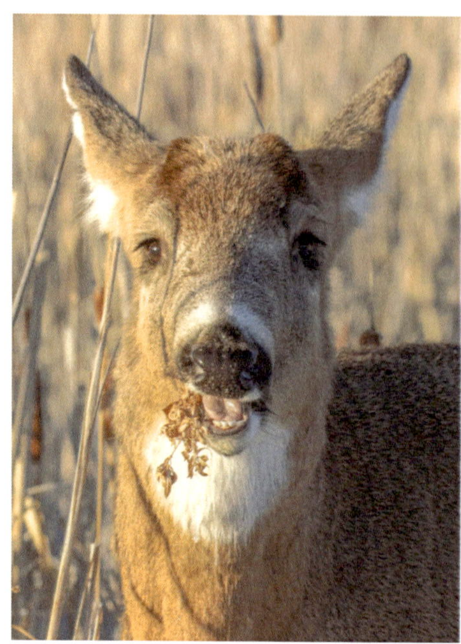 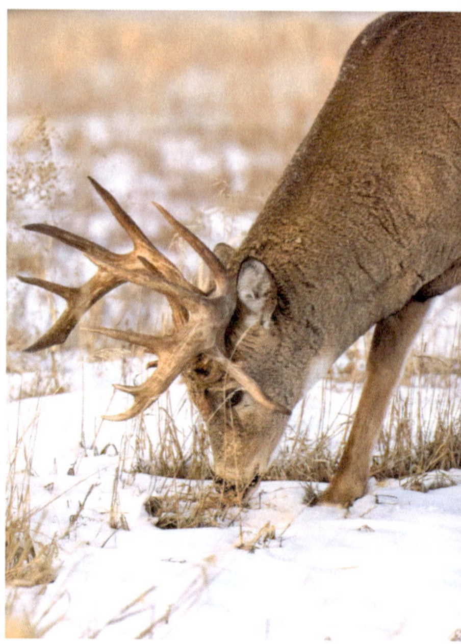

Deer are herbivores, for the most part, and heavy snow can make it difficult for them to find the grasses, twigs, and branches that make up their winter diet. They have a four-chambered stomach. As prey animals, deer need to eat quickly while out in the open and then chew and digest their food at a later time, when they are less vulnerable.

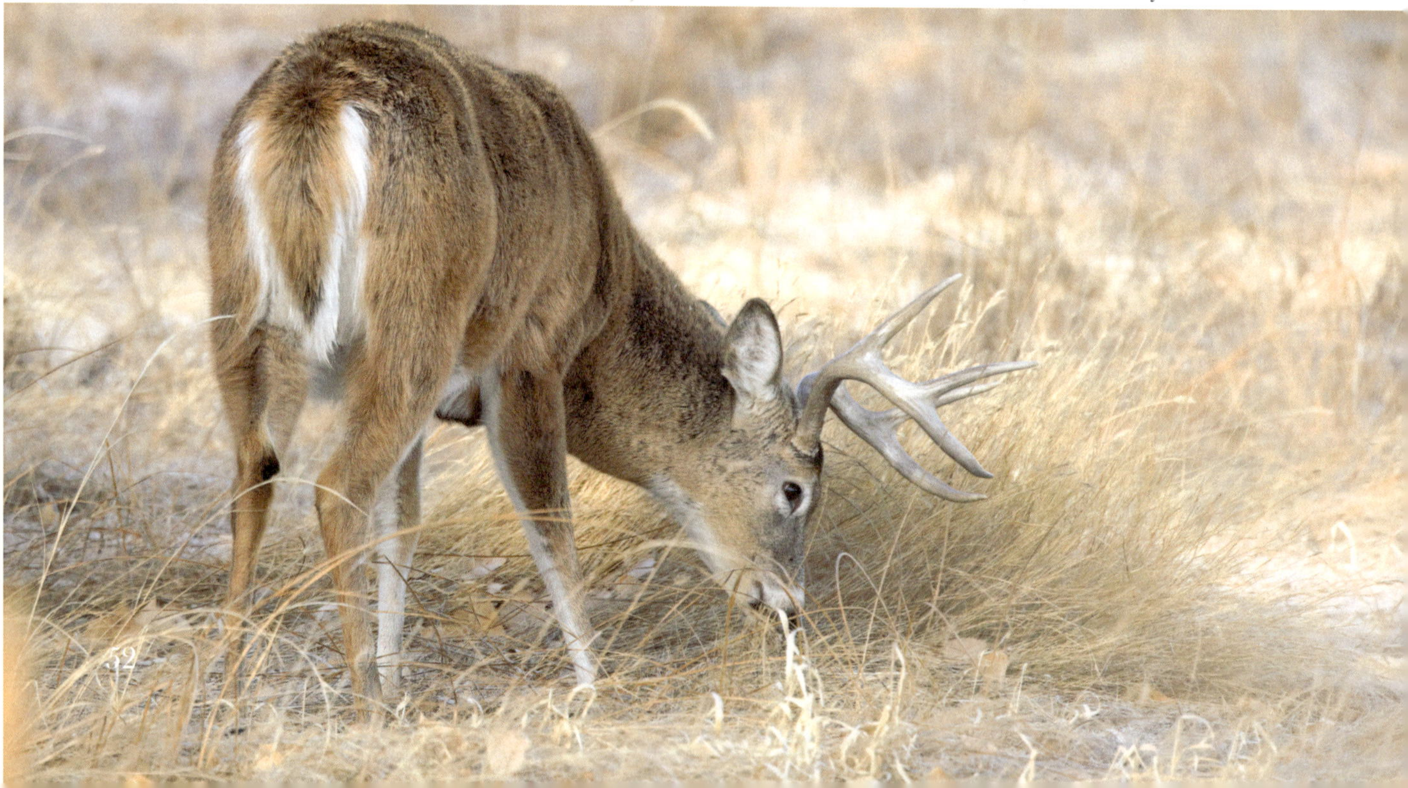

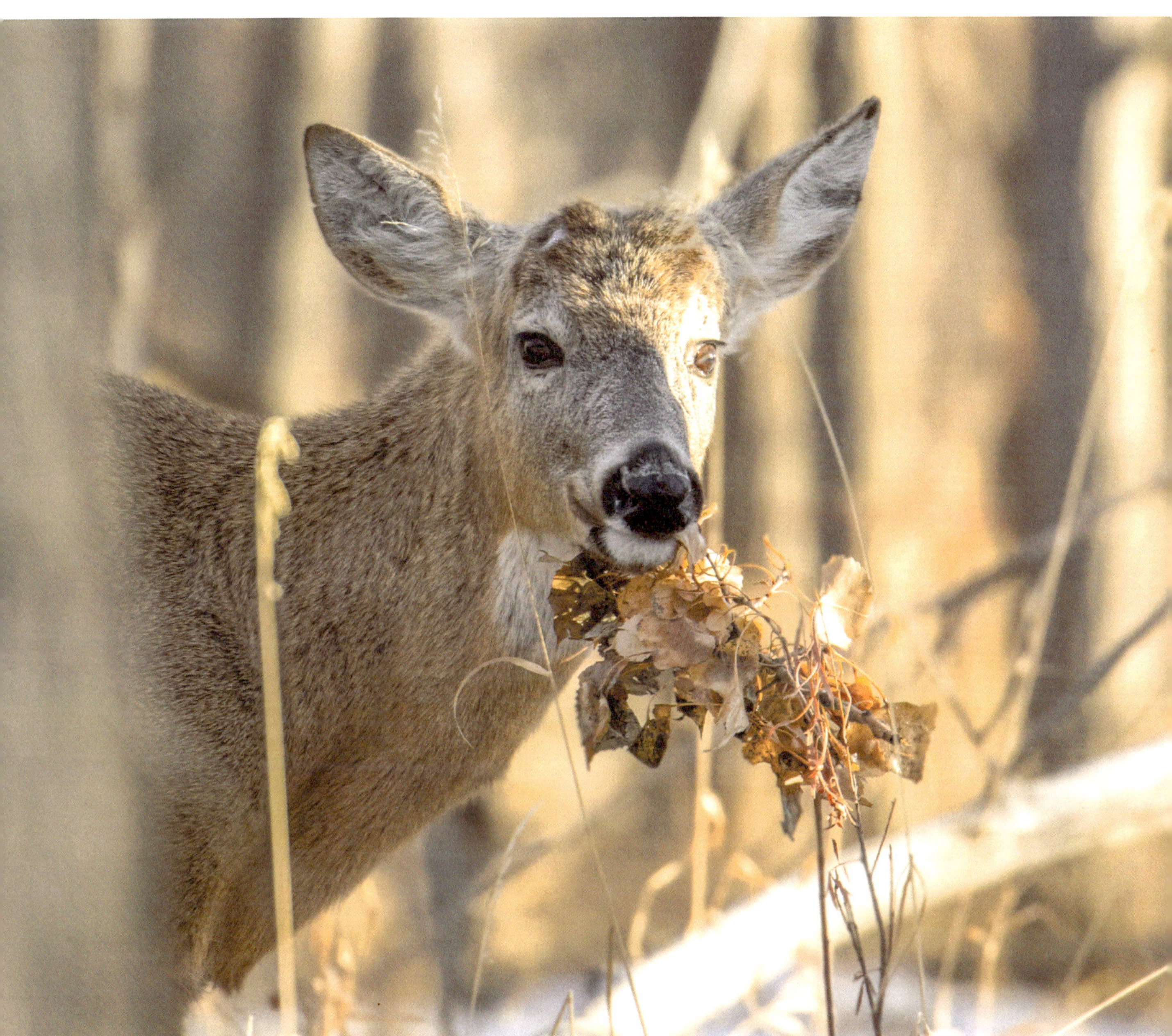

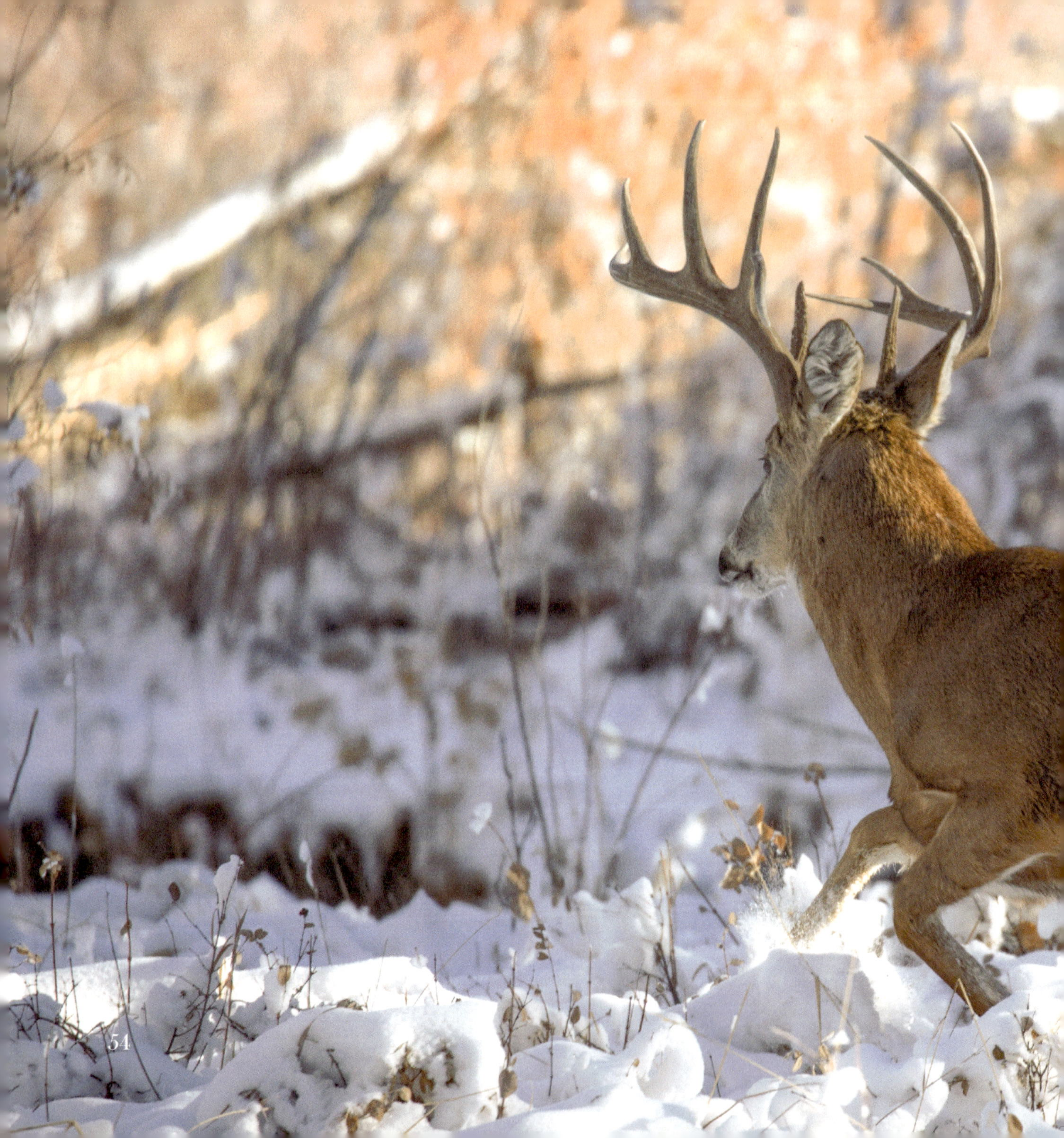

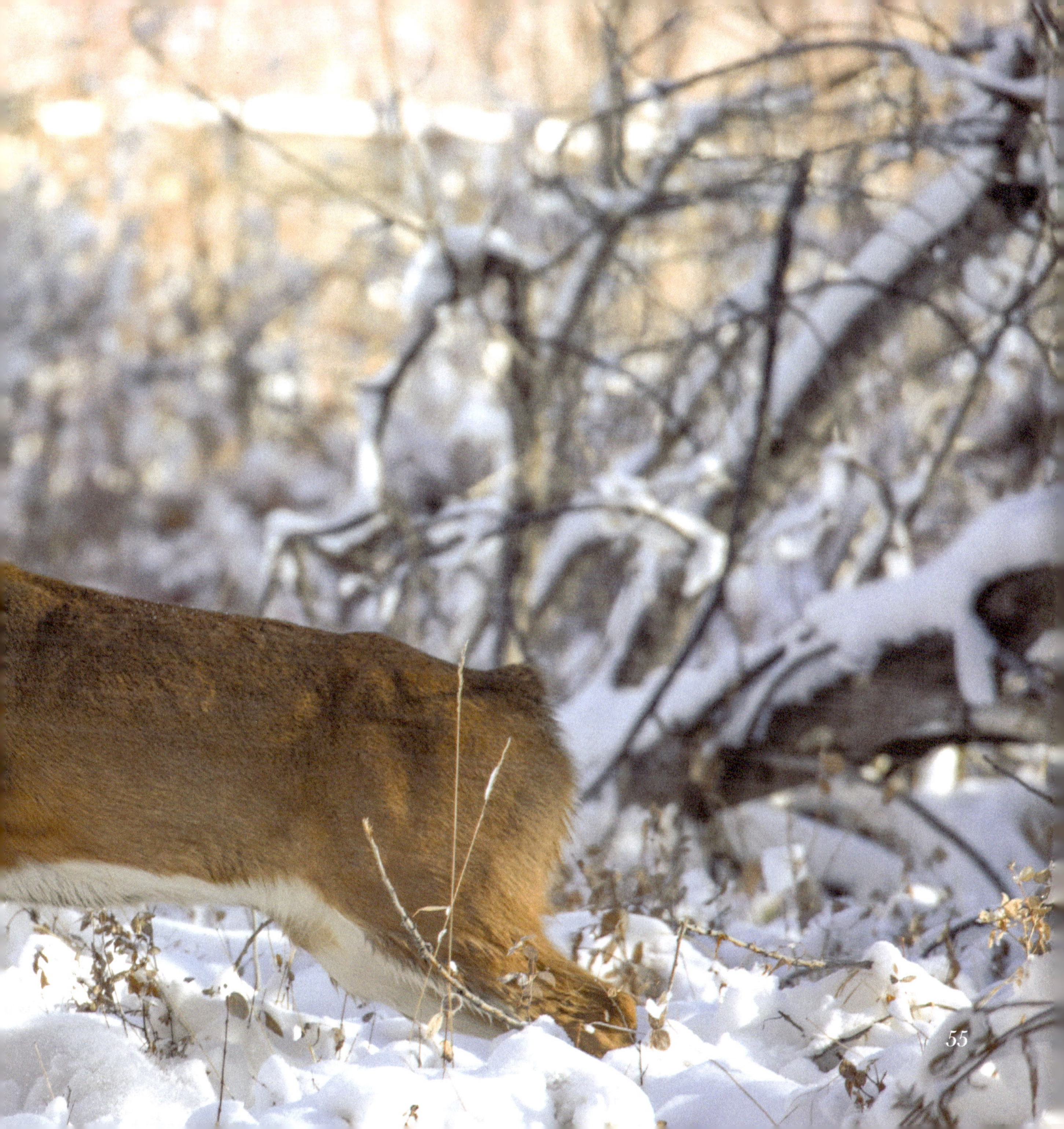

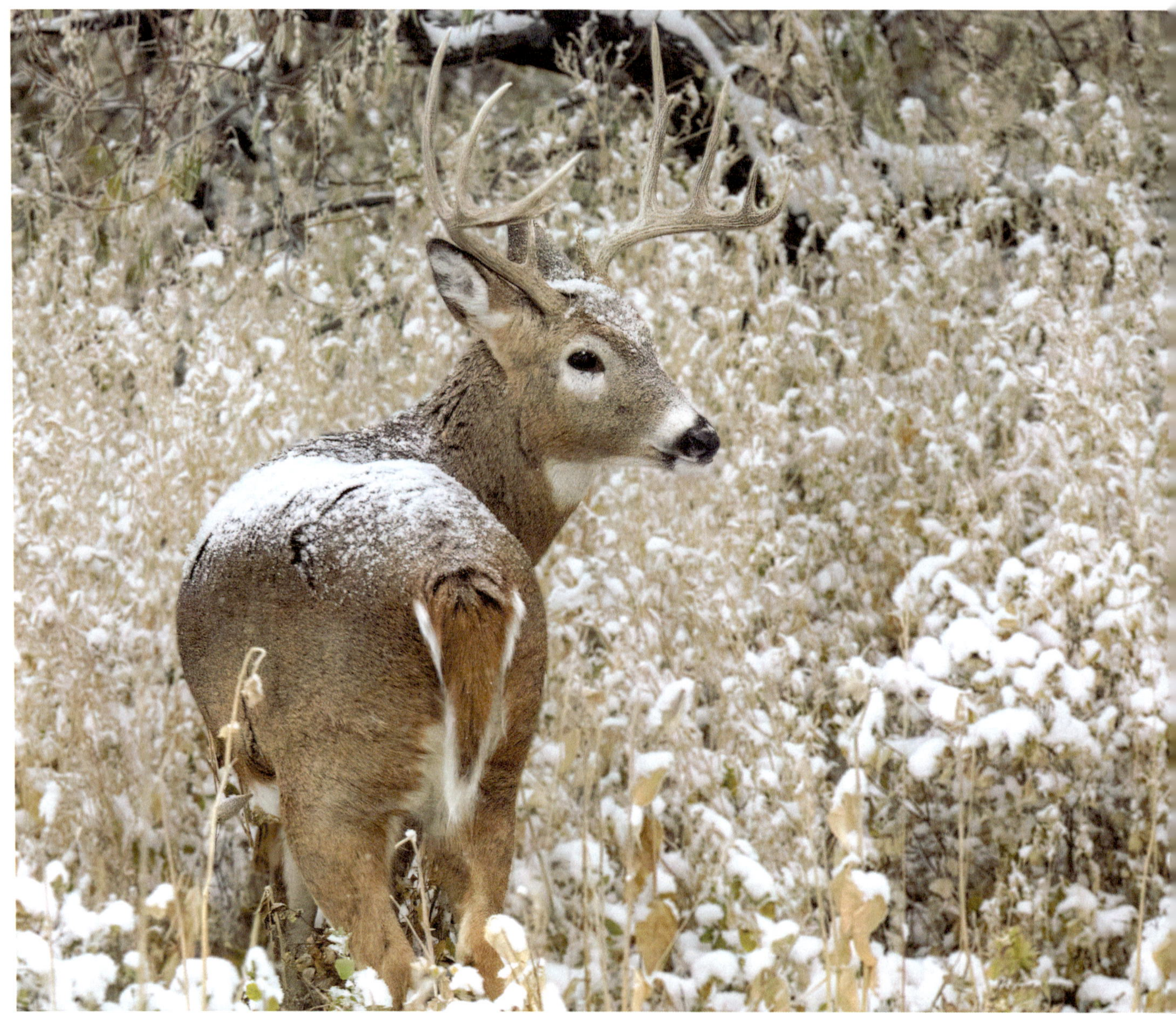

How do deer stay warm in the winter? Their winter coat is very thick and the top hairs are hollow. The hollow hair traps air. Oil from their glands help to repel water. This provides the necessary insulation against frigid temperatures.

56

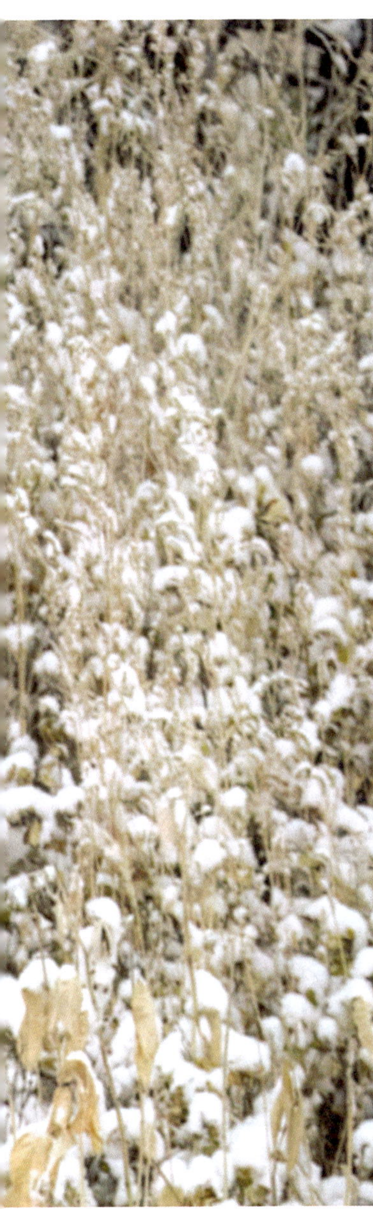

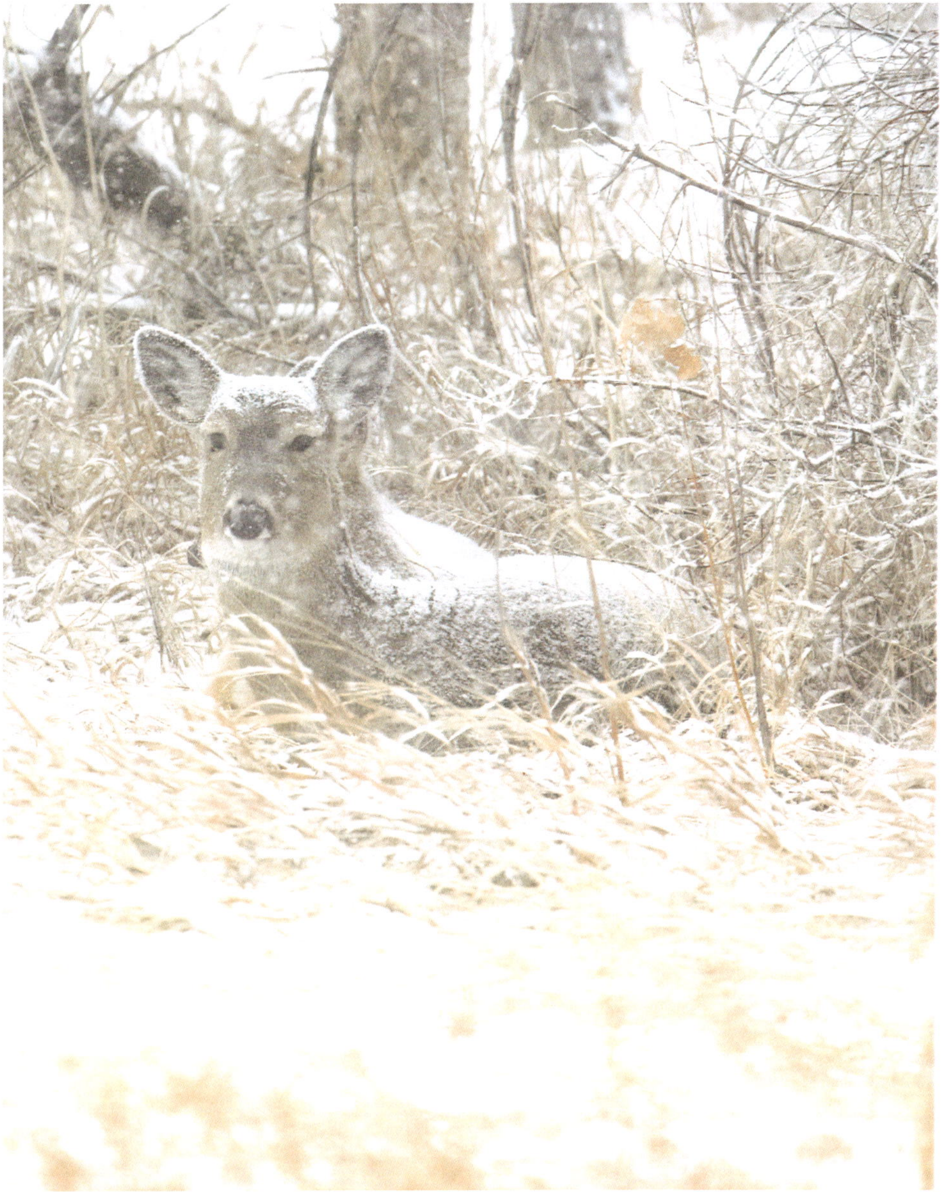

Deer will also limit their activity to conserve energy.

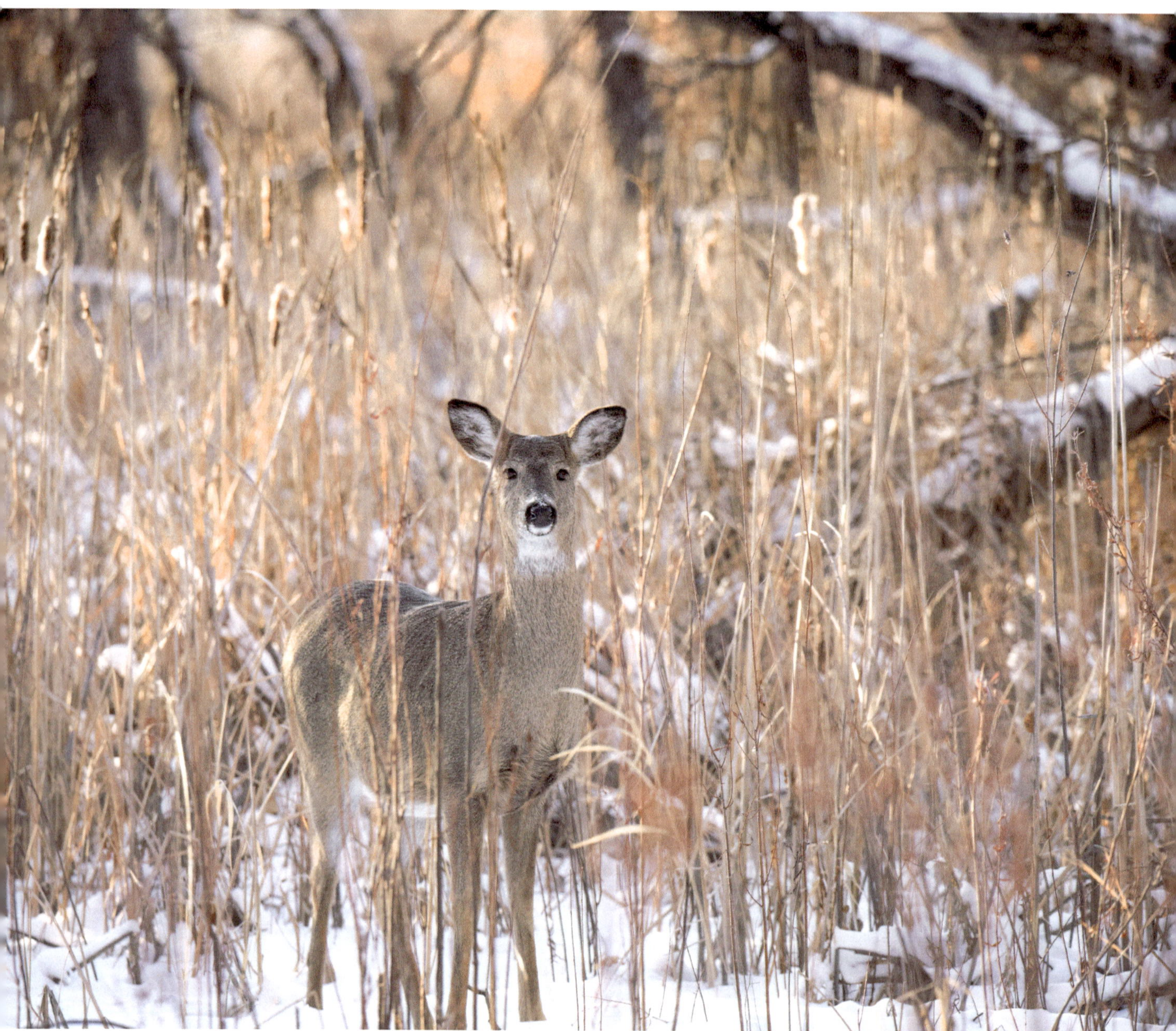

Deer utilize their snouts and hooves to brush snow off their food. If there is snow where they forage, there may also be snow on their noses.

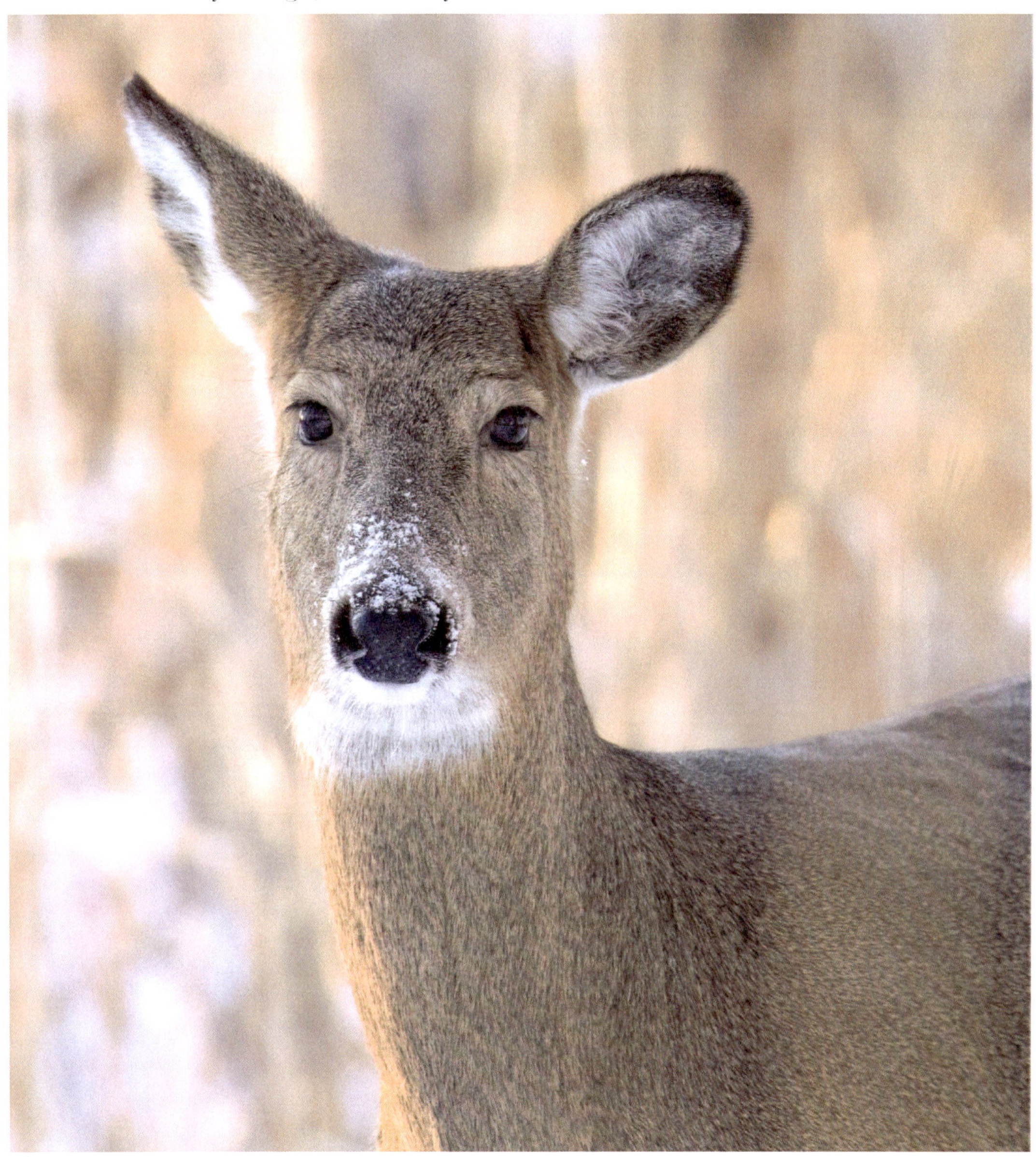

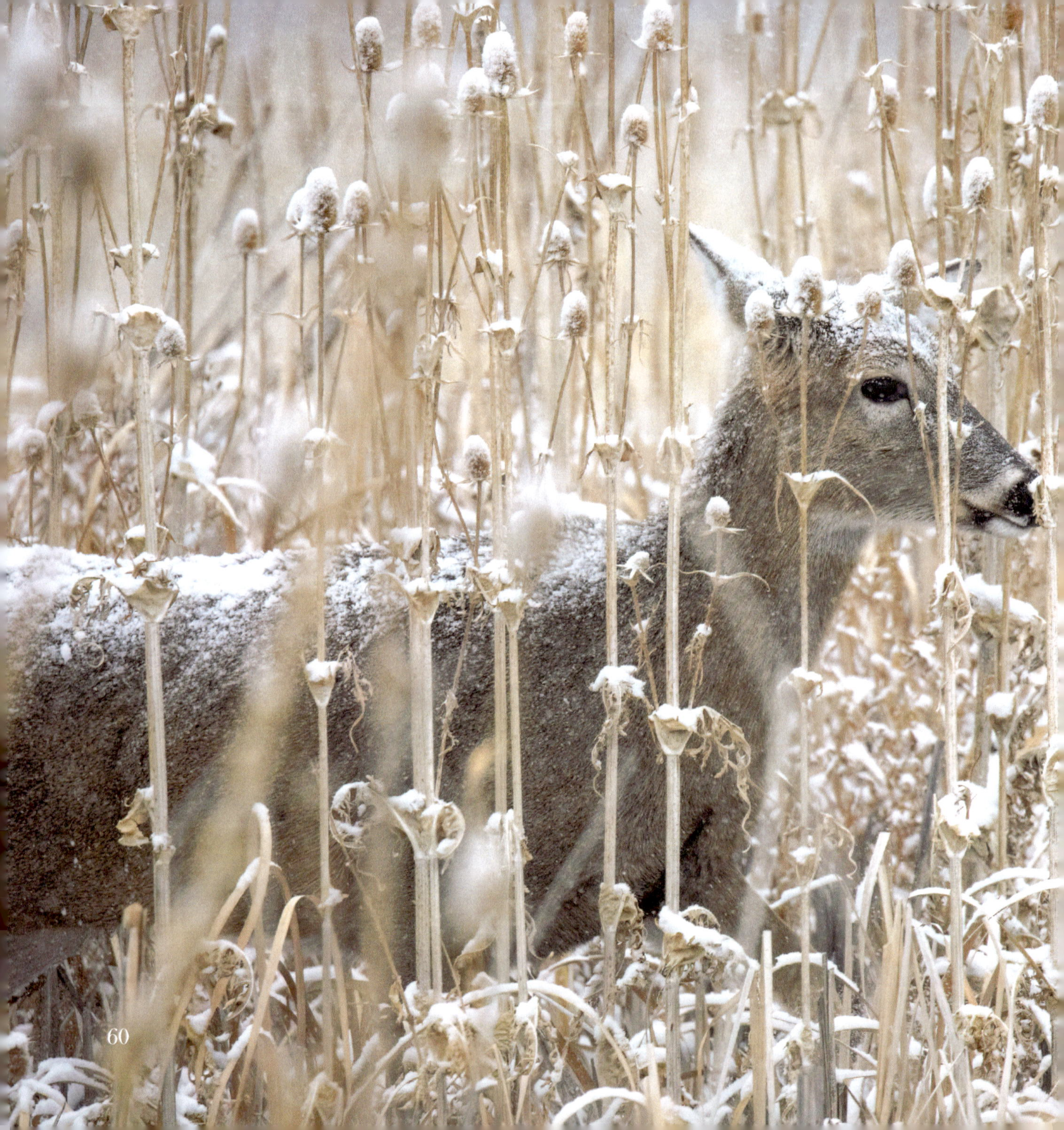

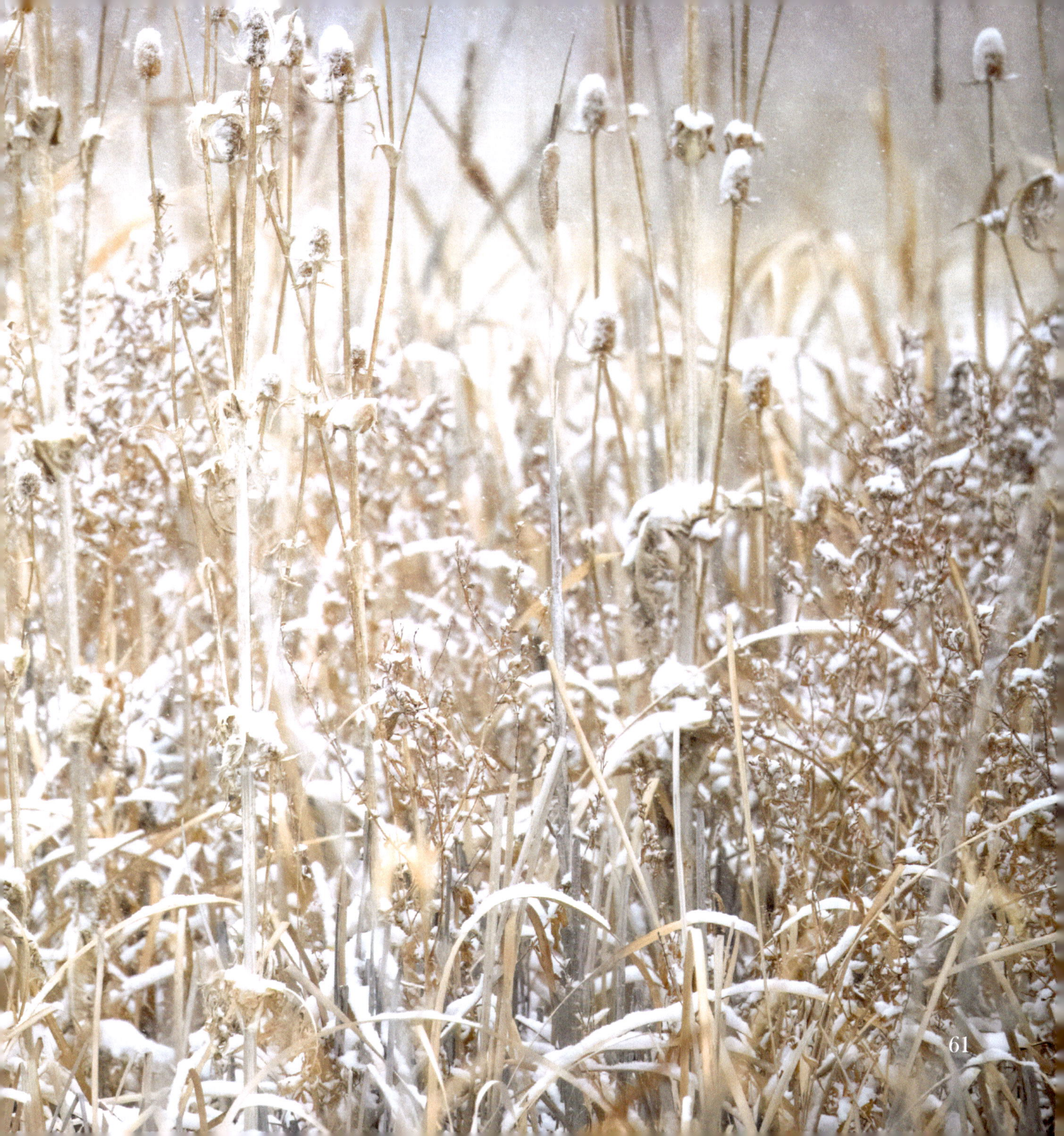

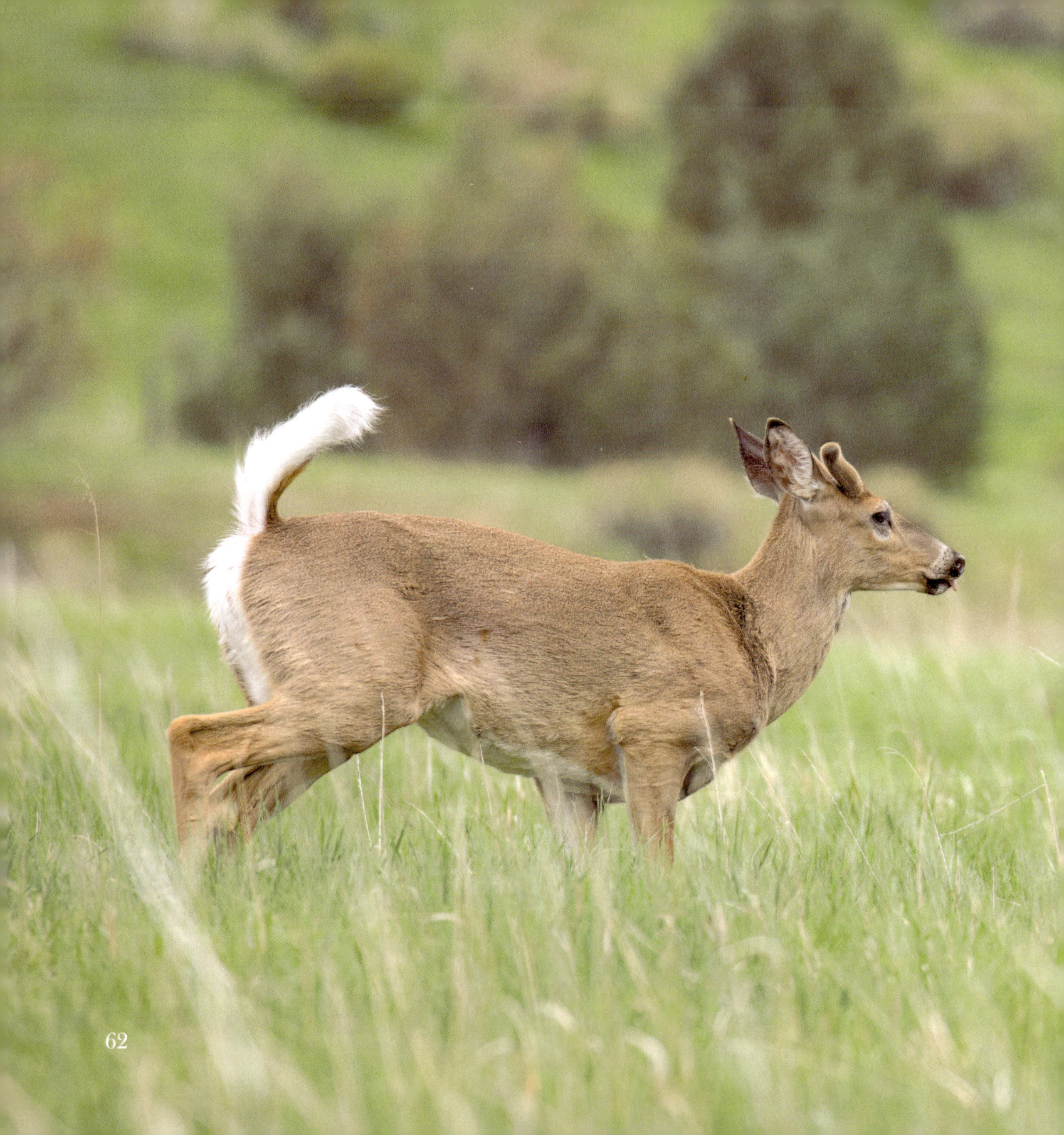

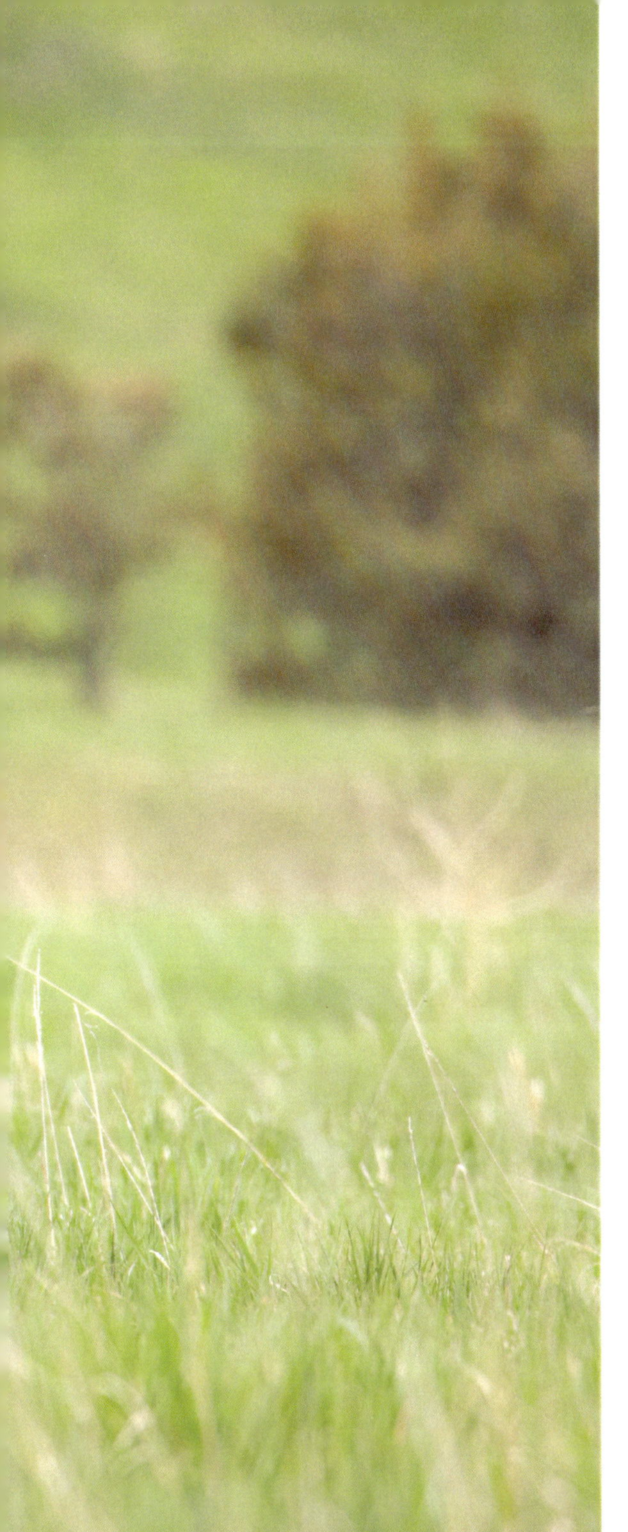

Spring

"To every thing
there is a season,
and a time to every
purpose under the
heaven."

—Ecclesiastes 3:1

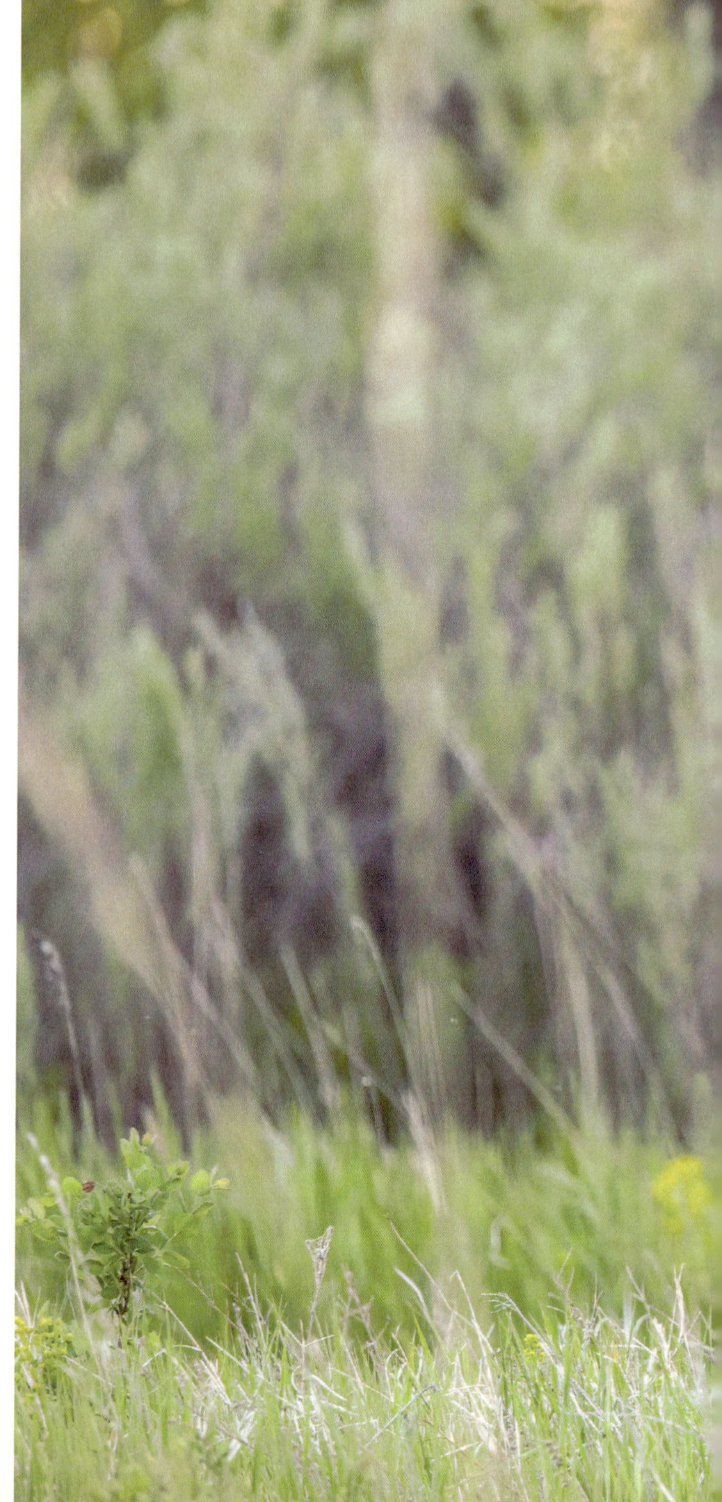

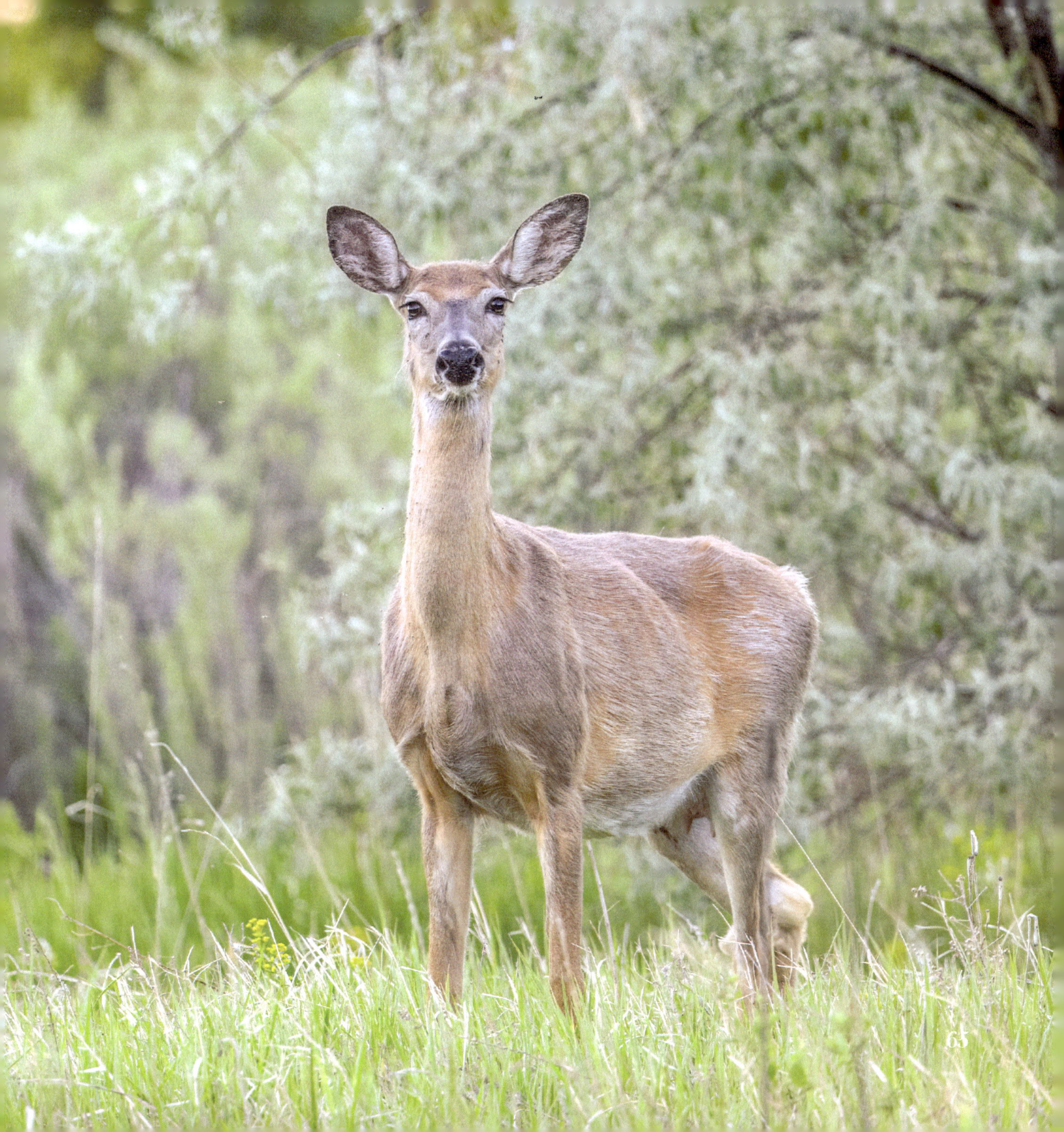

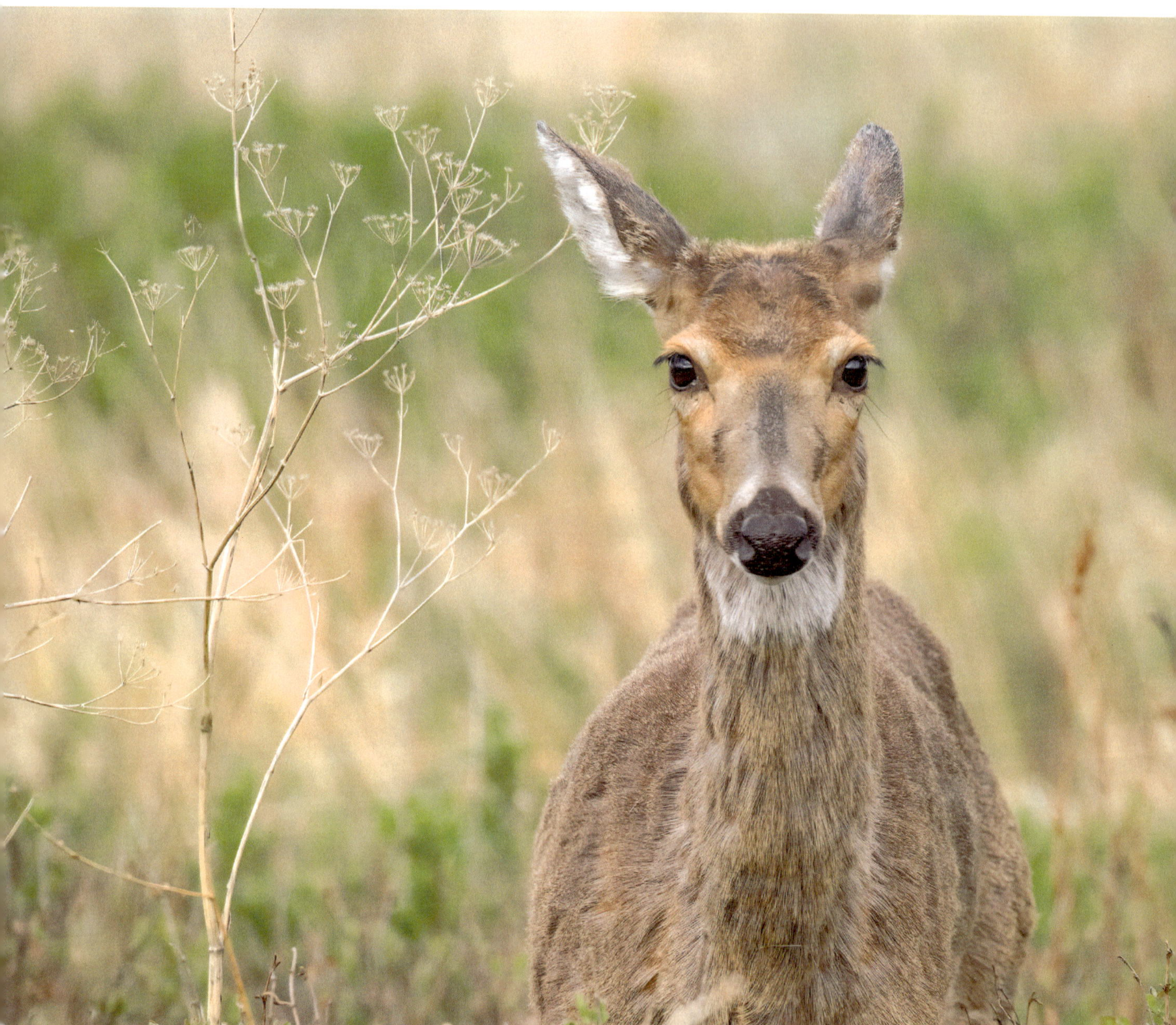

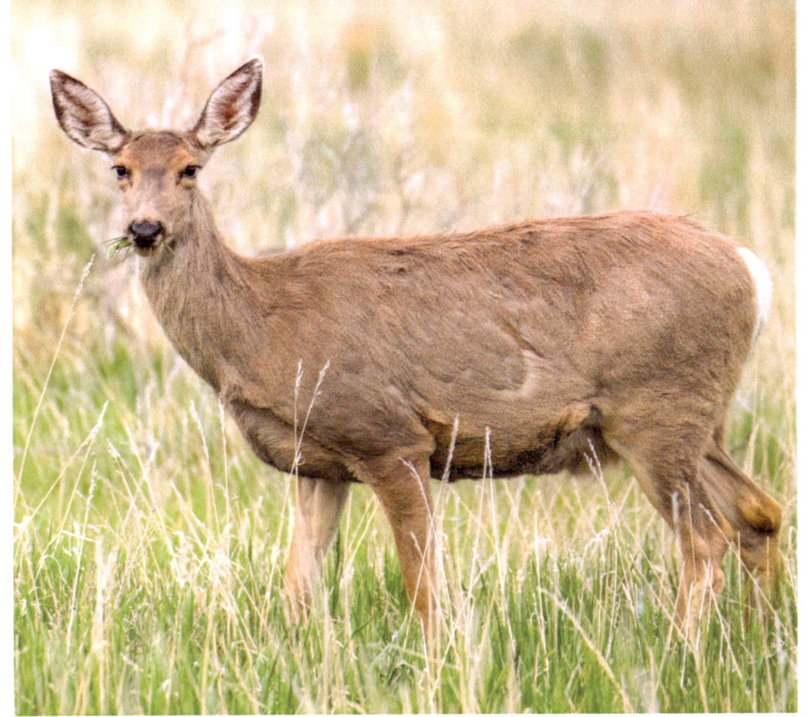

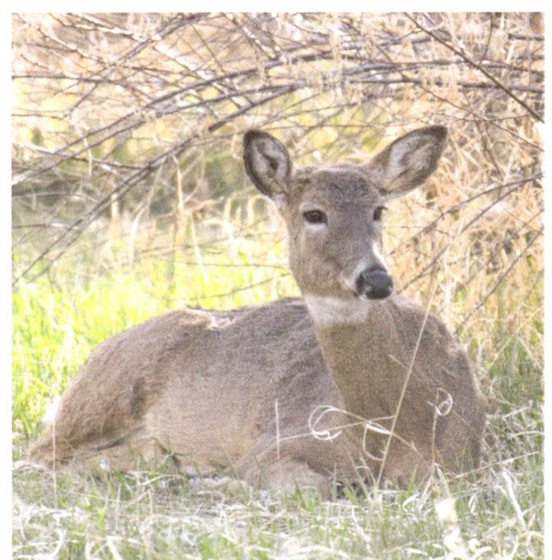

During the spring, does are in the last days of their pregnancies.

Grasses are starting to green and leaves are starting to bud.

In the late spring, deer will shed their winter coats. They may look a little scruffy at this time.

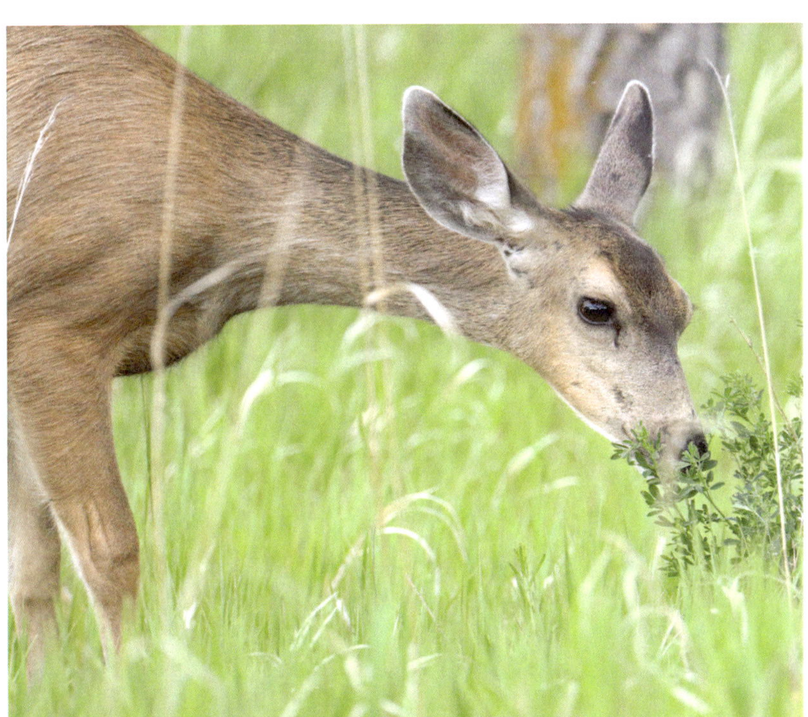

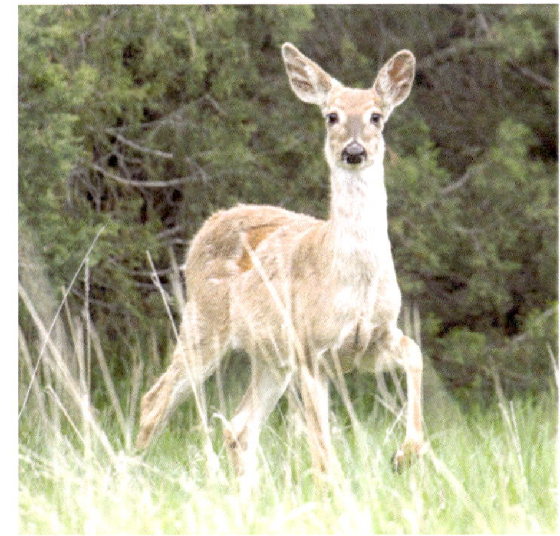

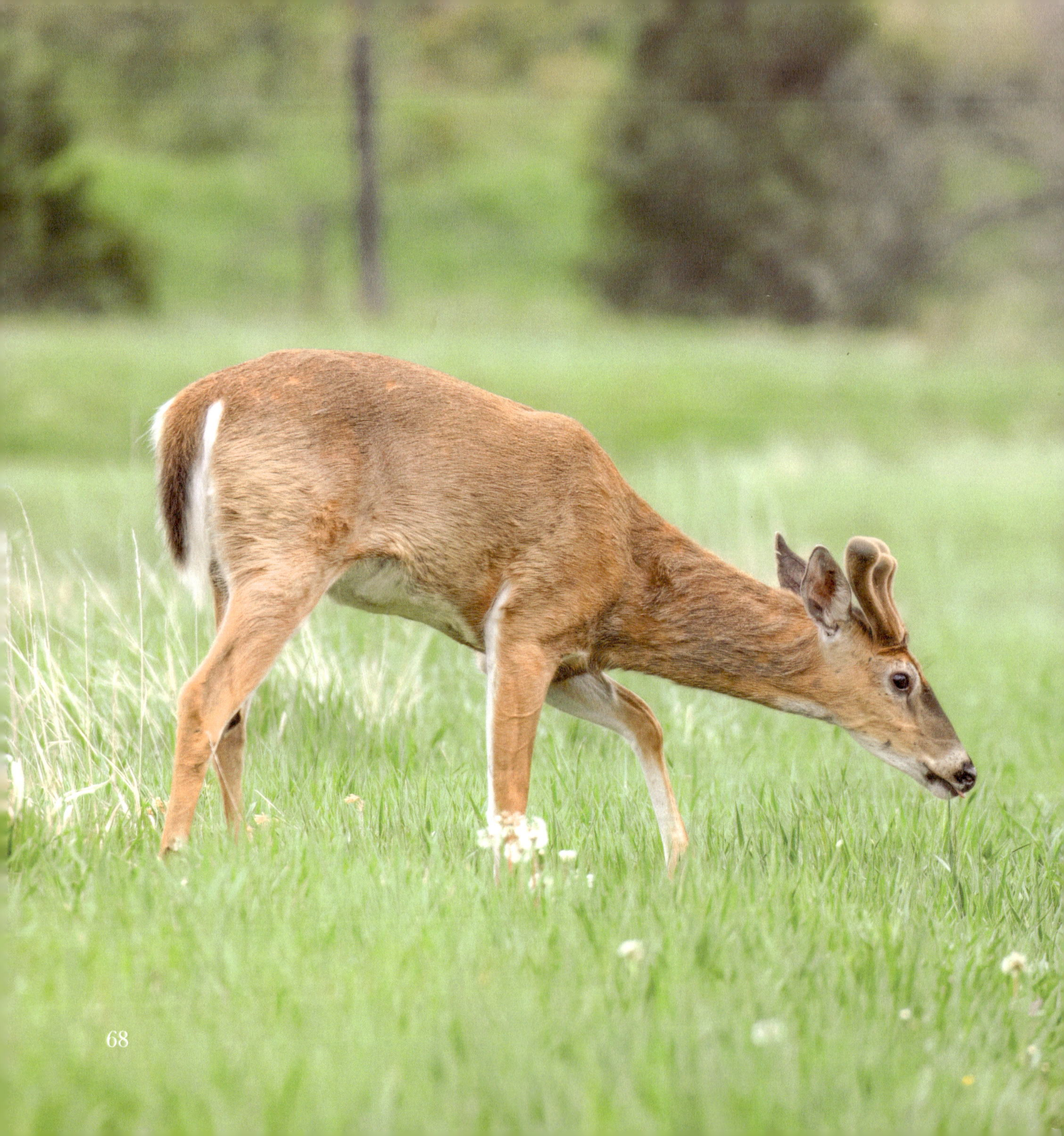

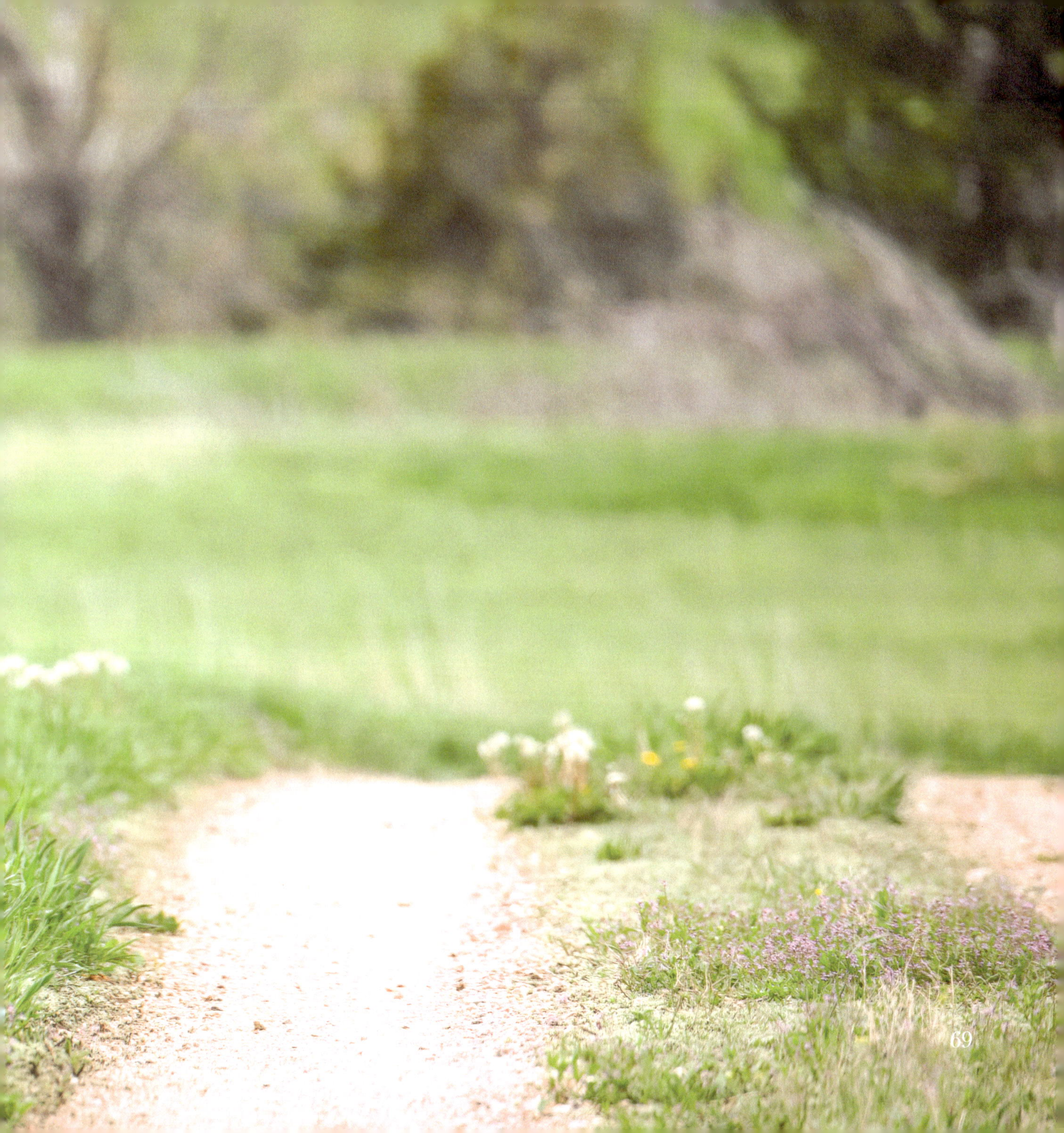

Male deer grow new antlers every year. During the new growth stage, a velvet-like skin covers and protects the soft tissue and blood vessels underneath.

Since the antlers are not yet hardened, they must be very careful not to damage them. This is a challenge for the bucks.

Their antlers grow quickly and are very itchy. They can scratch them, so they have to be careful. A damaged antler cannot be repaired during the growing period.

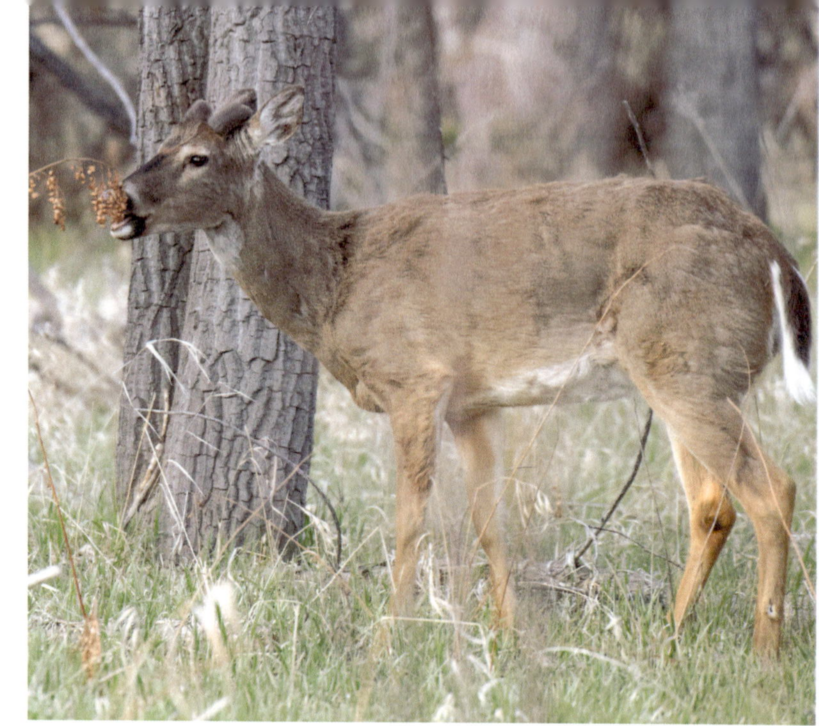

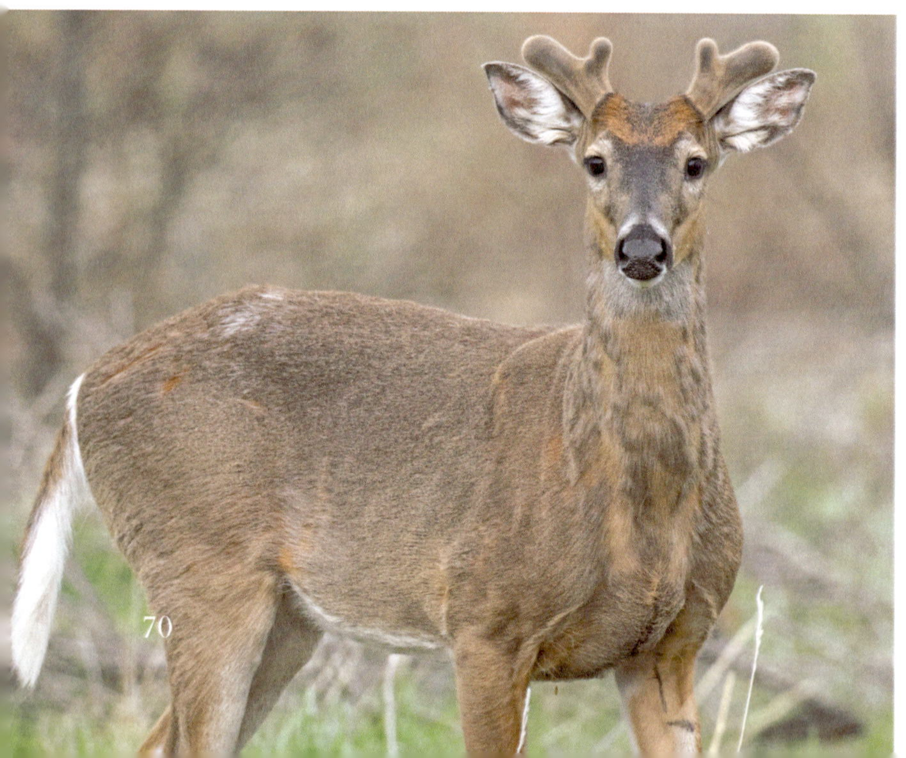

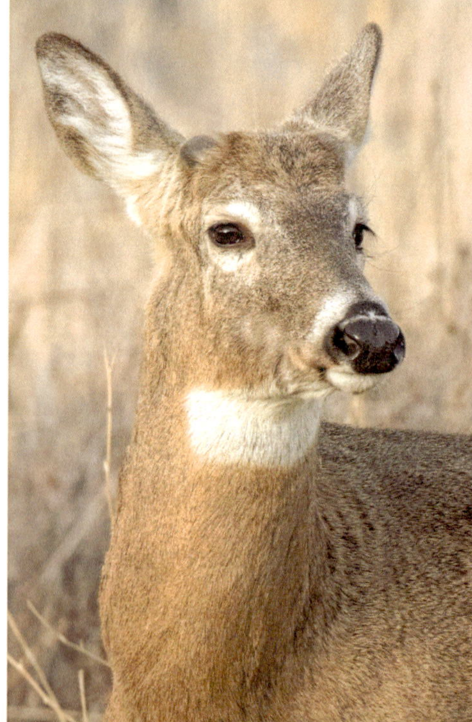

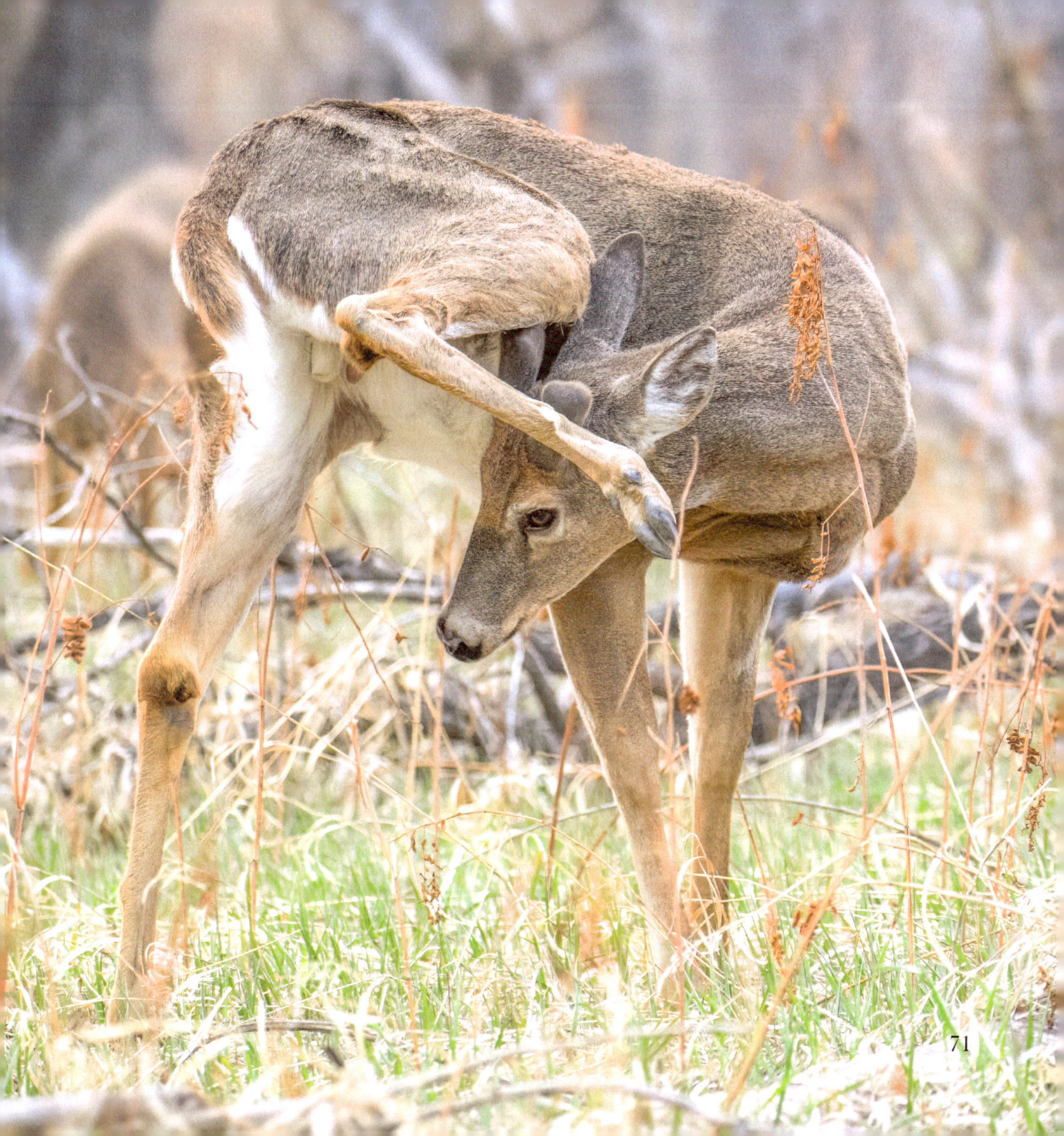

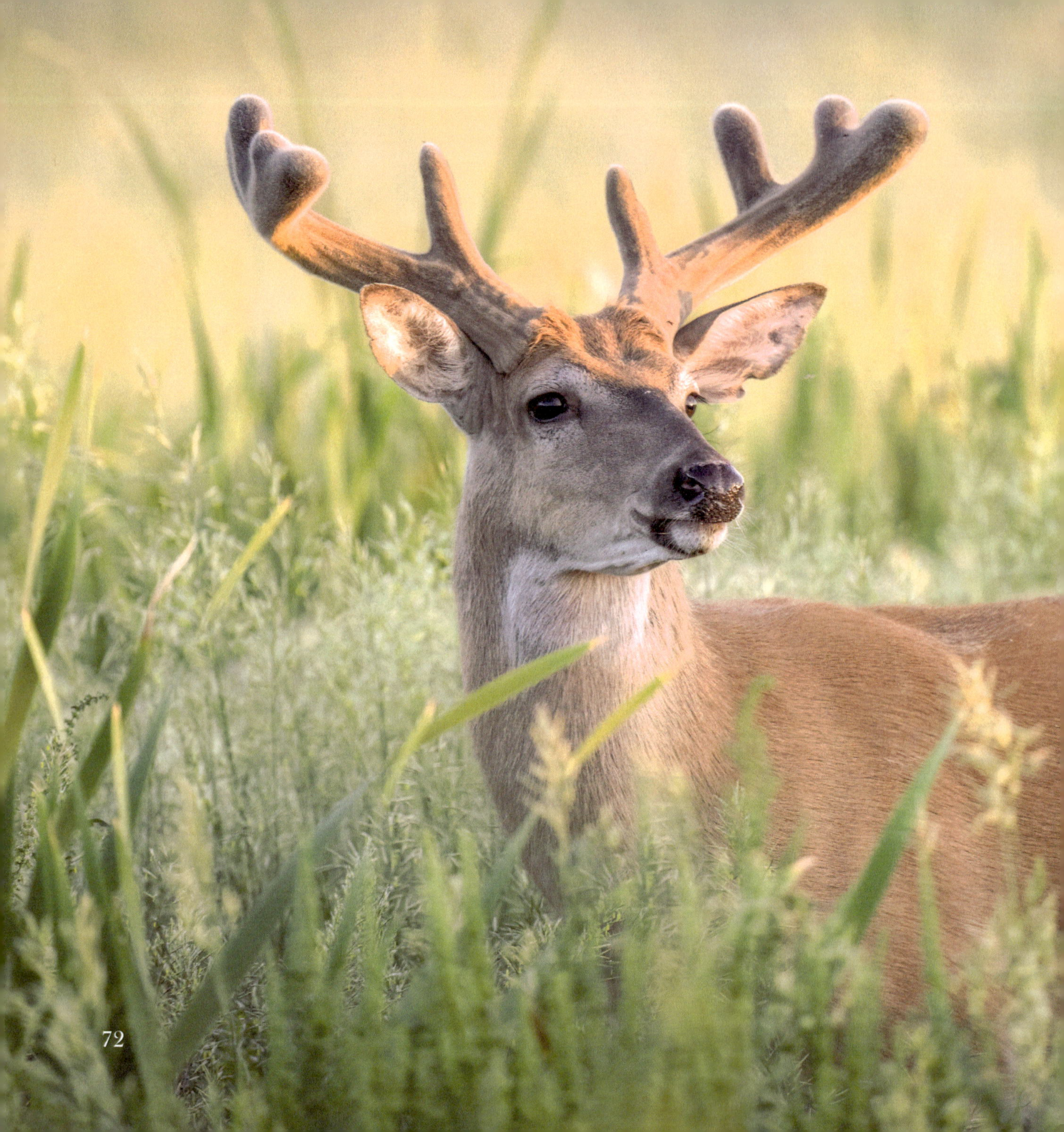

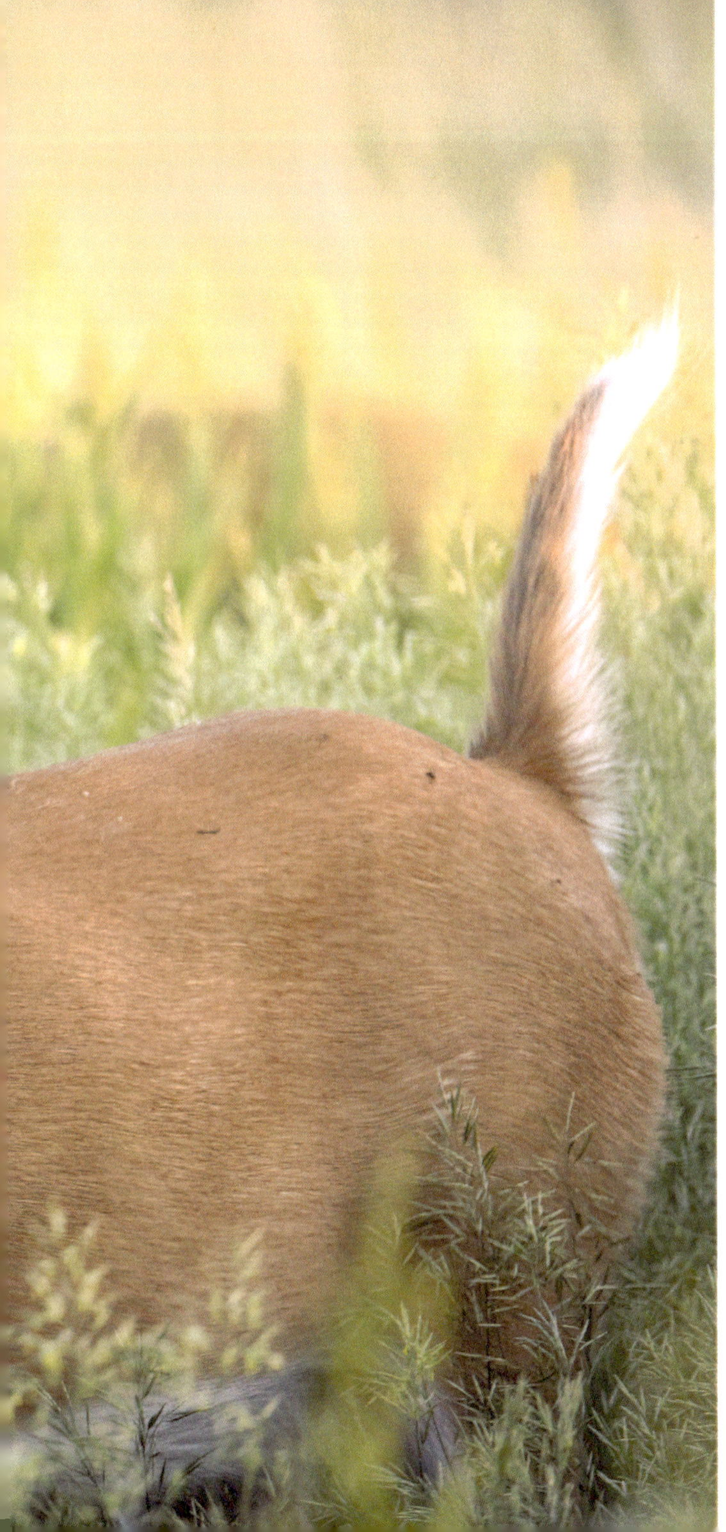

"Success
is not final,
failure
is not fatal:
it is the
courage to
continue
that counts."

—Churchill

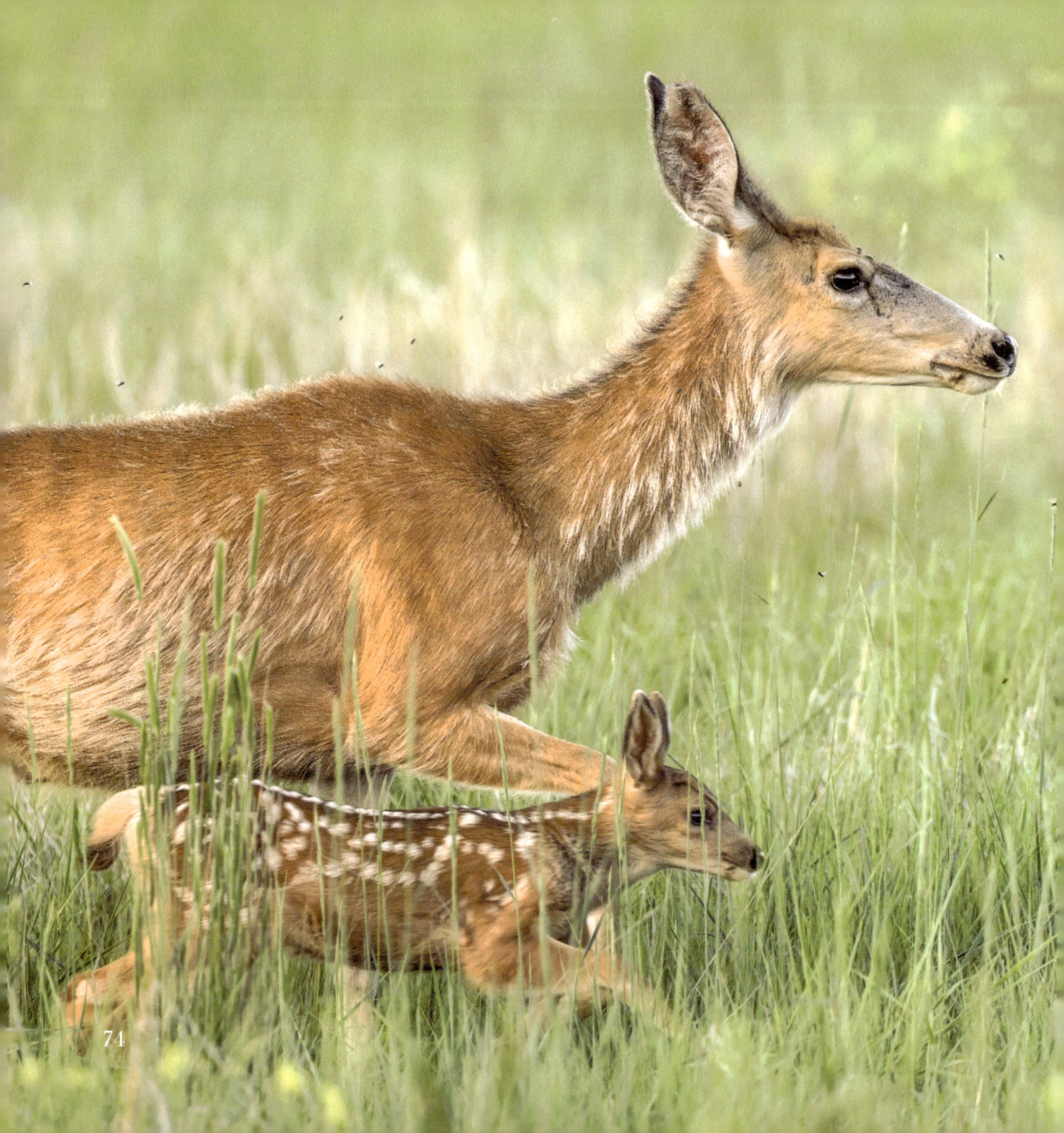

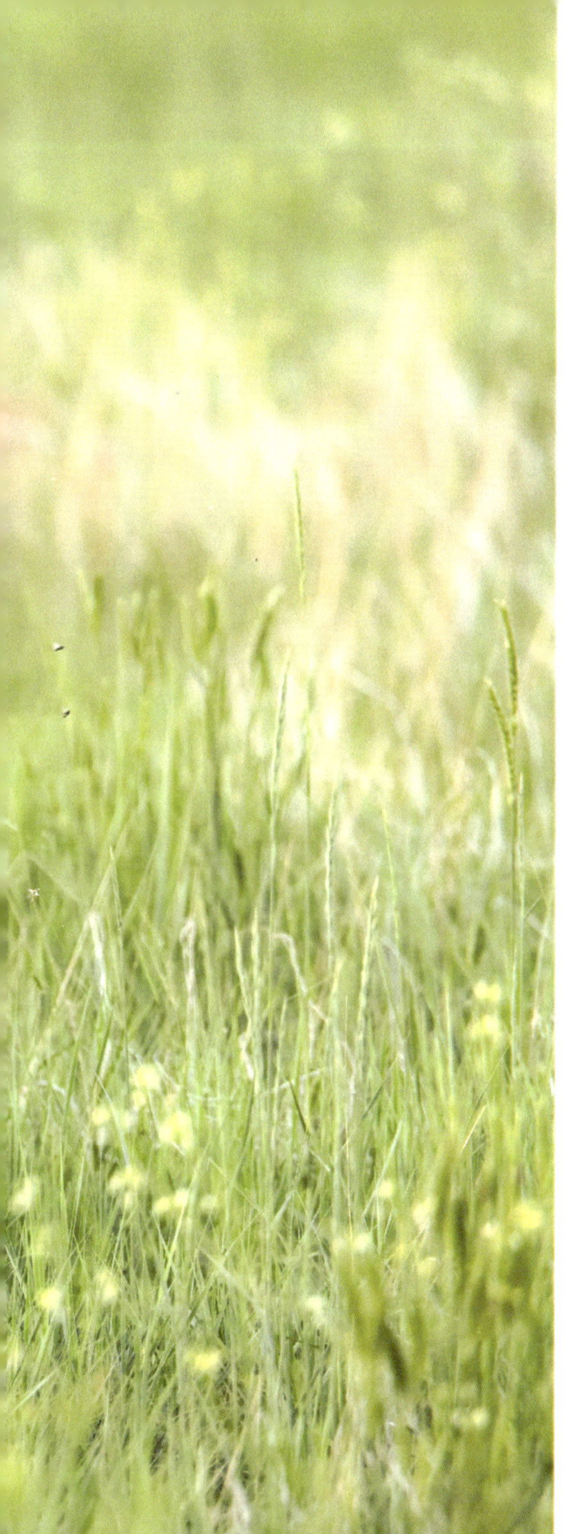

Summer

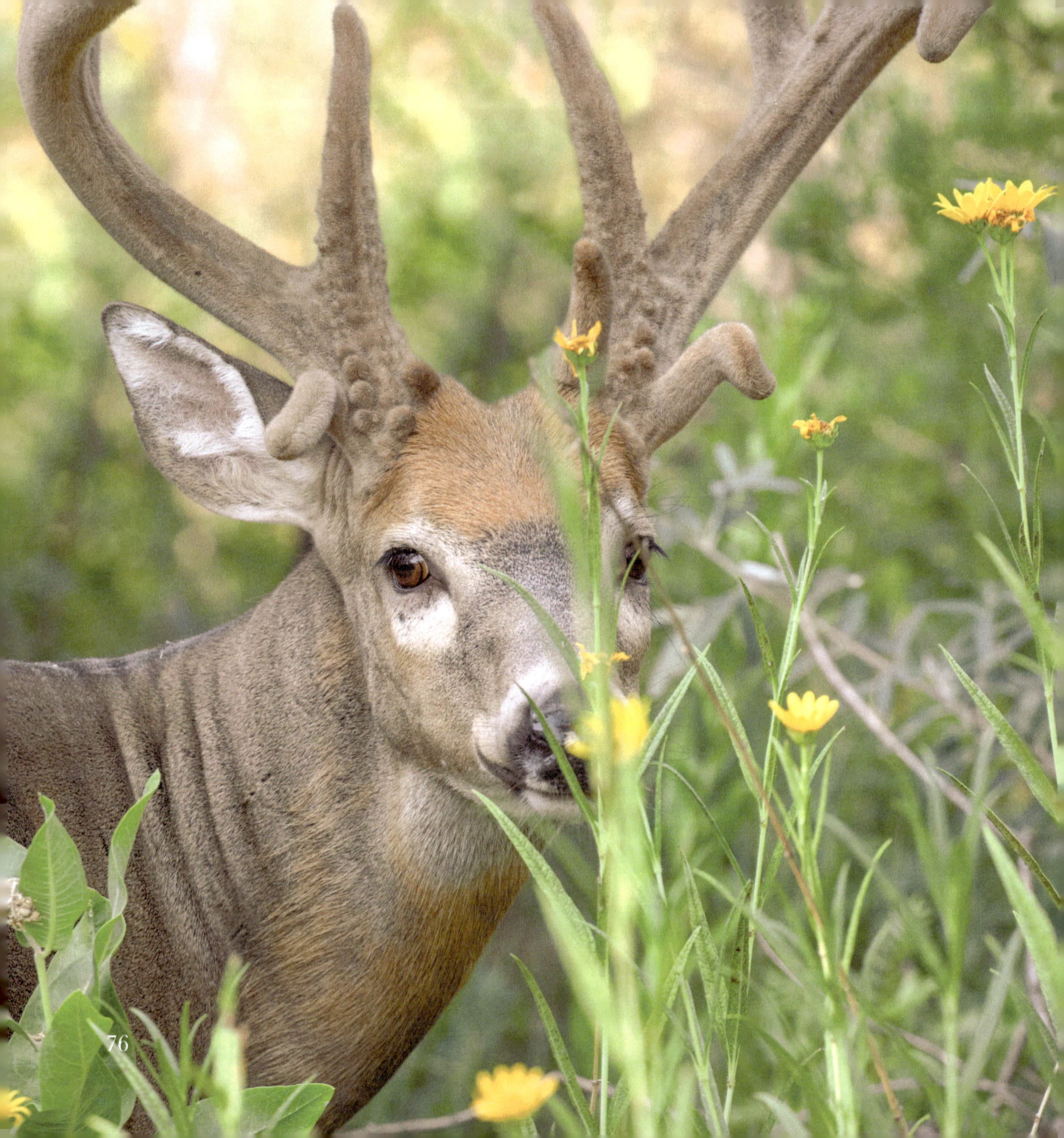

After the scarcity of food in the winter, summer is a time of recovery, growth, and preparation. Deer take this time to enjoy the availability of flowers, grasses, leaves, saplings, and more.

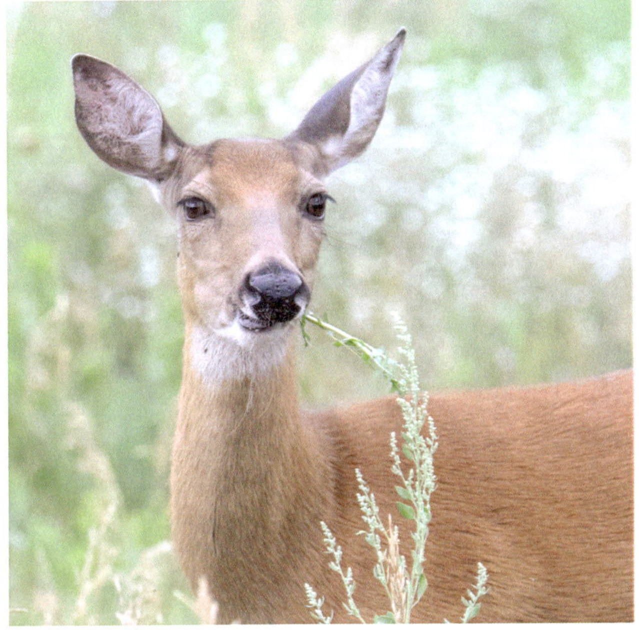

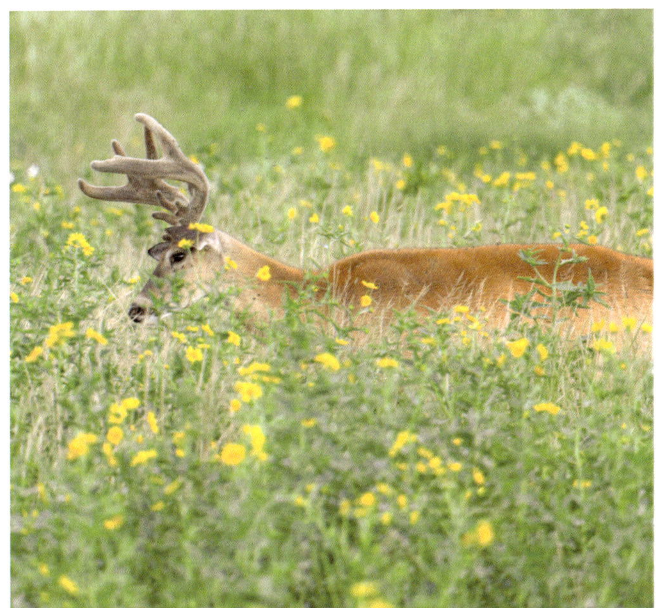

Their heavy fur has been replaced with a lighter and brighter summer coat.

The warm weather of summer also brings out the insects. Deer have to endure biting flies, mosquitoes, and ticks just to name a few. These insects may carry disease, and sometimes infection, and fur loss may occur.

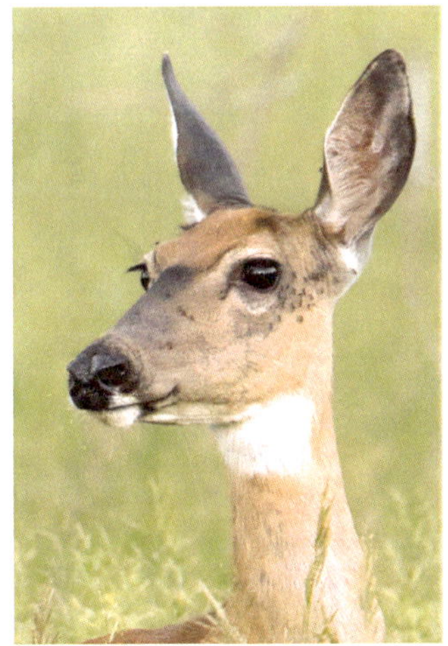

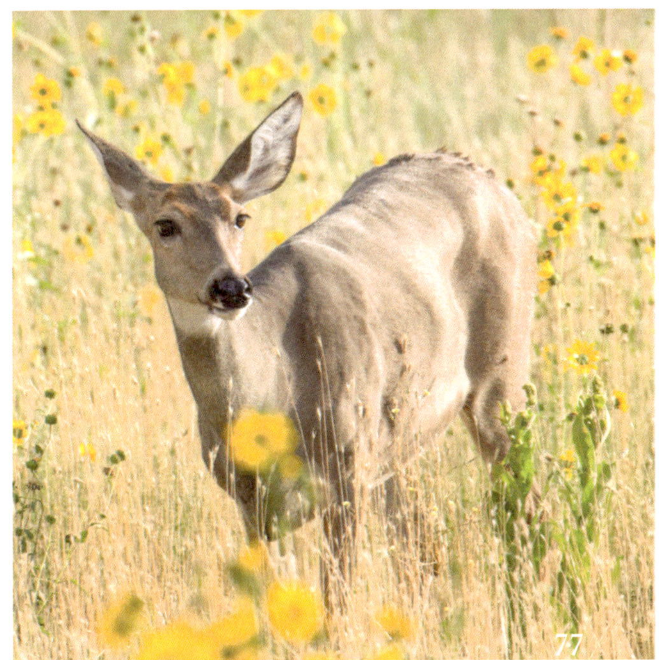

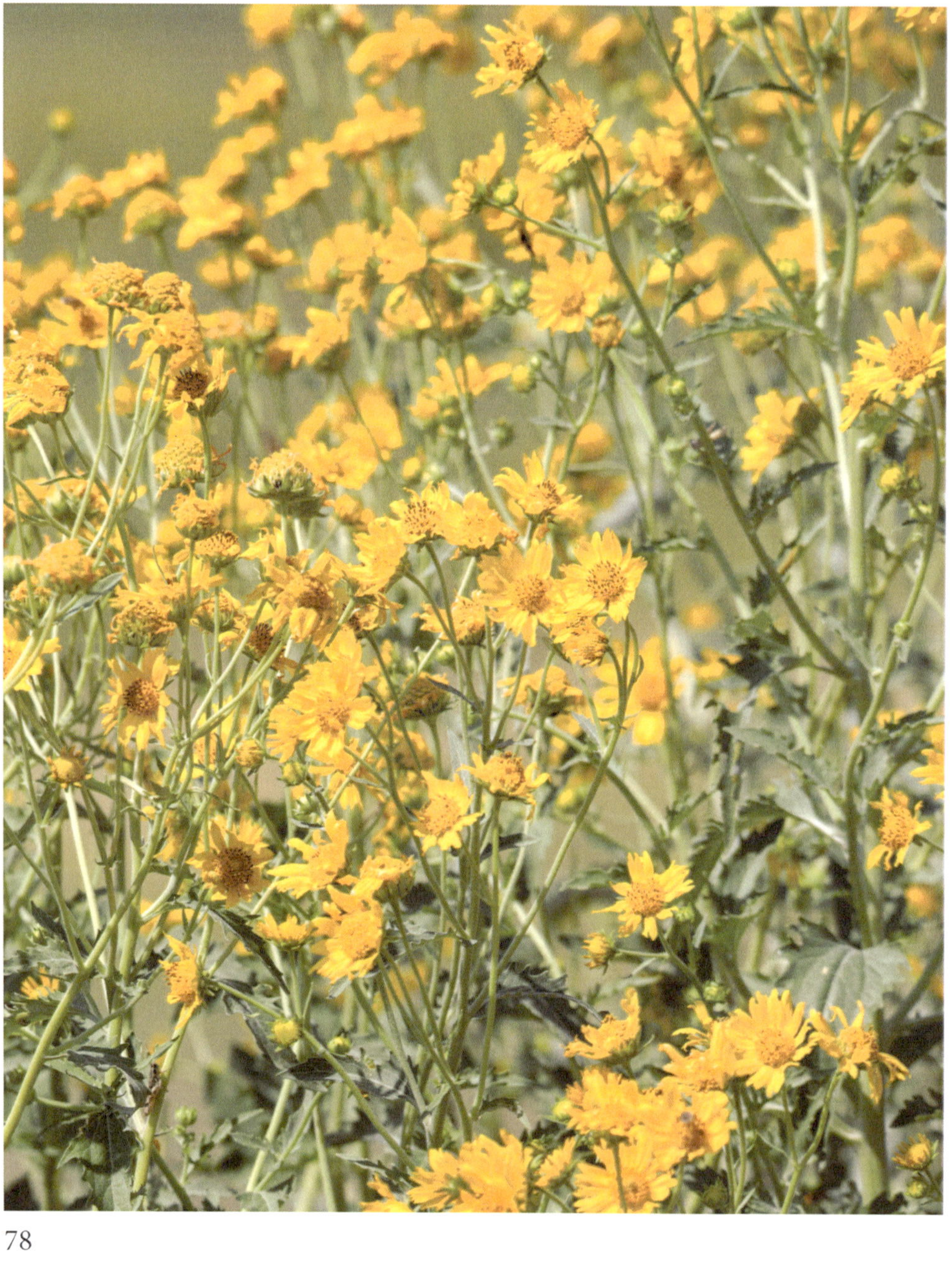

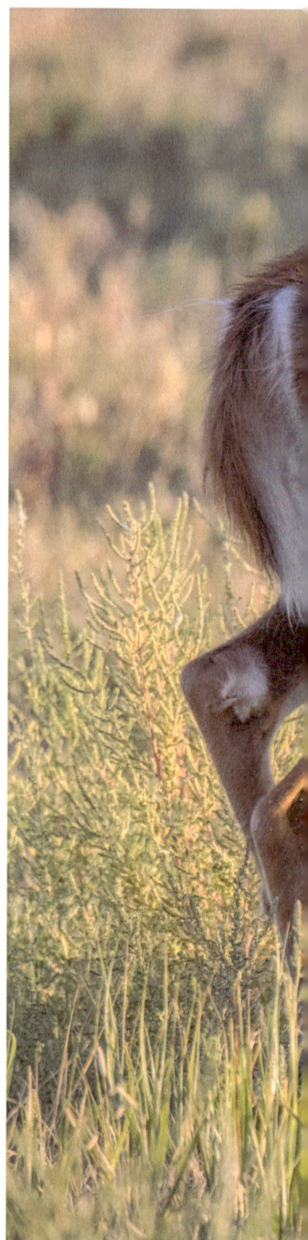

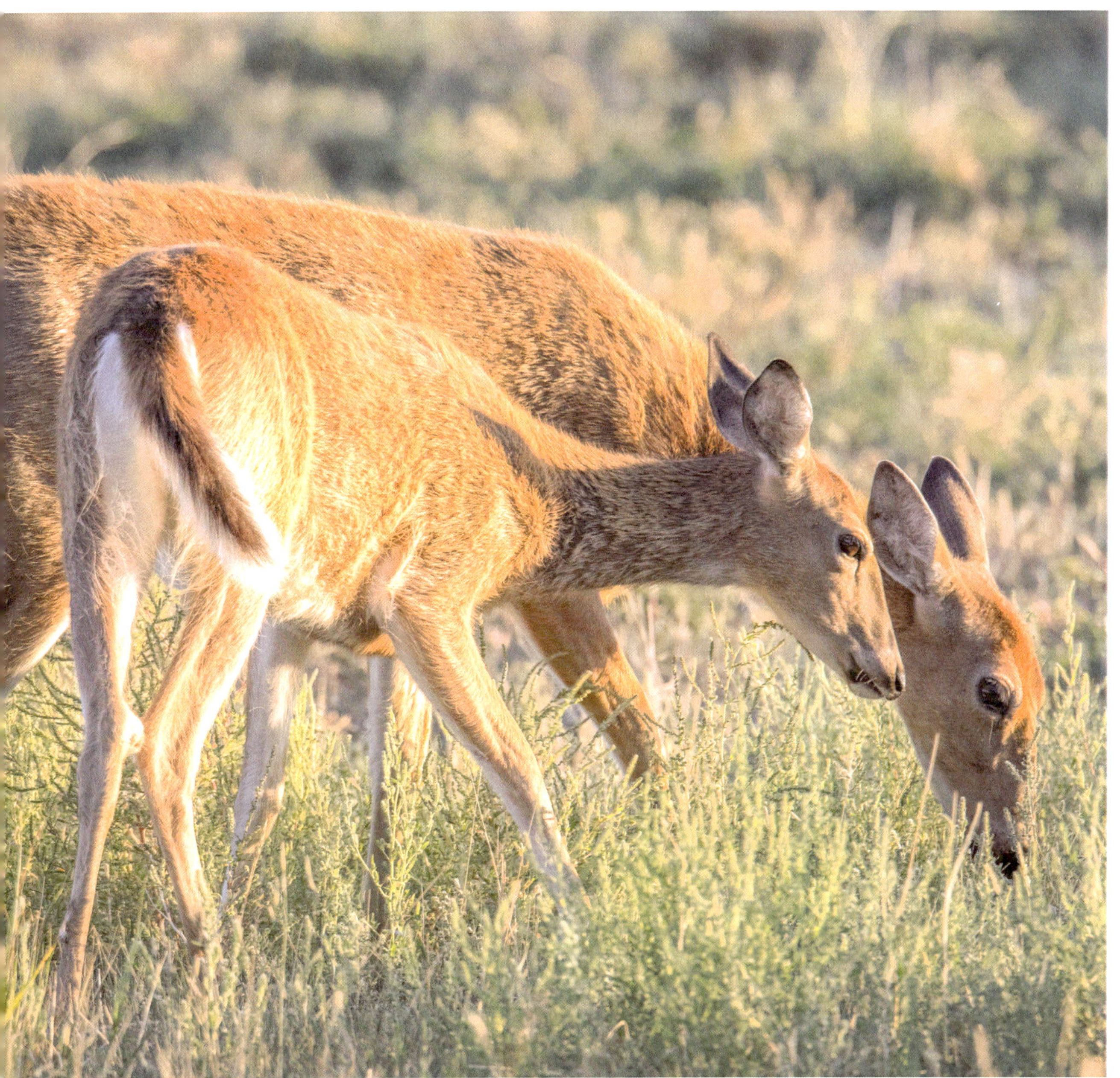

Fawns

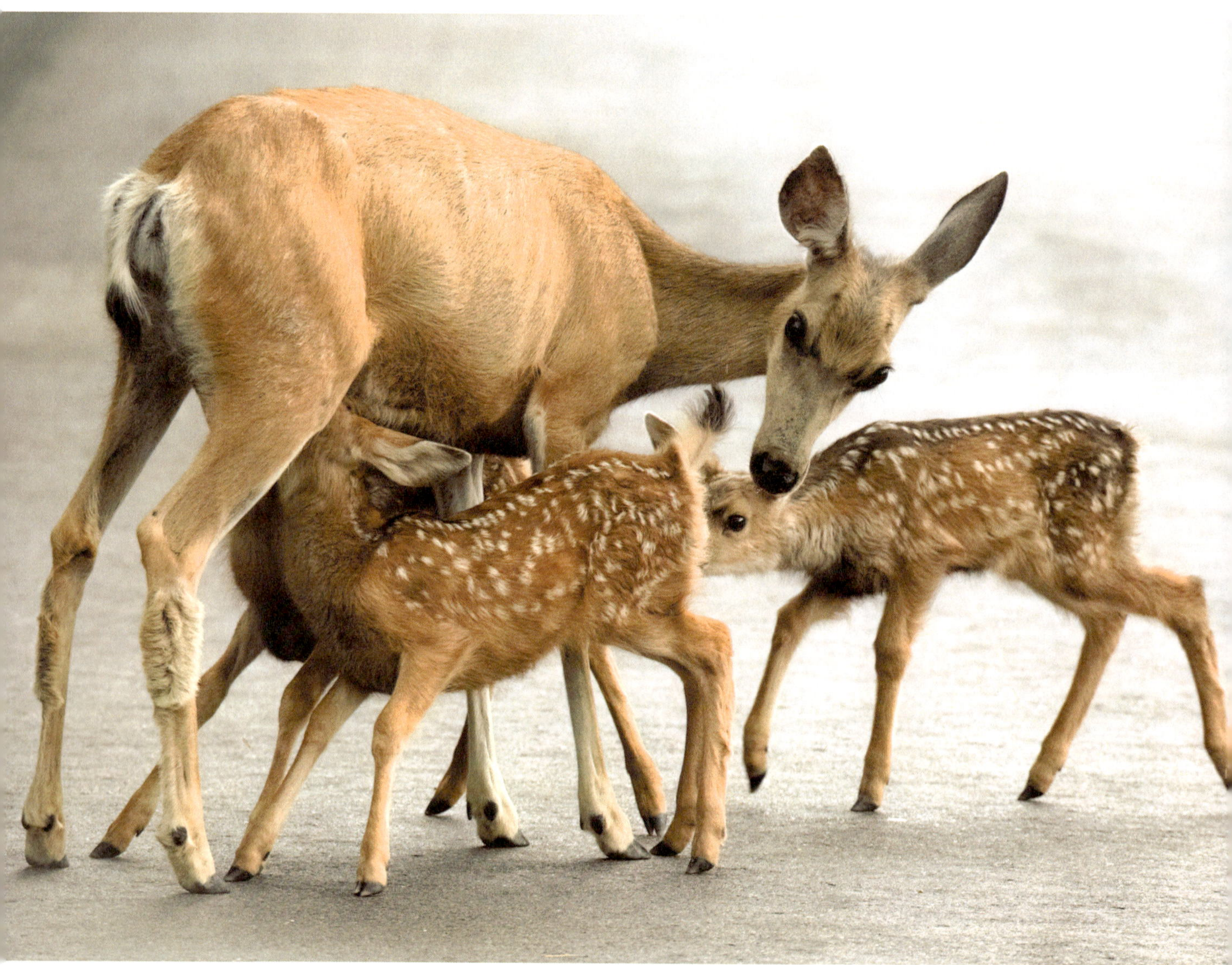

Fawns are born in late spring. The first few weeks of a fawn's life are crucial. They are most vulnerable to predators at this time. Fawns are born without a scent to help hide from predators. Their spots resemble dappled light, so they're very hard to see while laying in the shade. They will lay still for hours as they wait for their mother to return.

When they are about three weeks old, they will join their mother. They are fast enough to run from most danger.

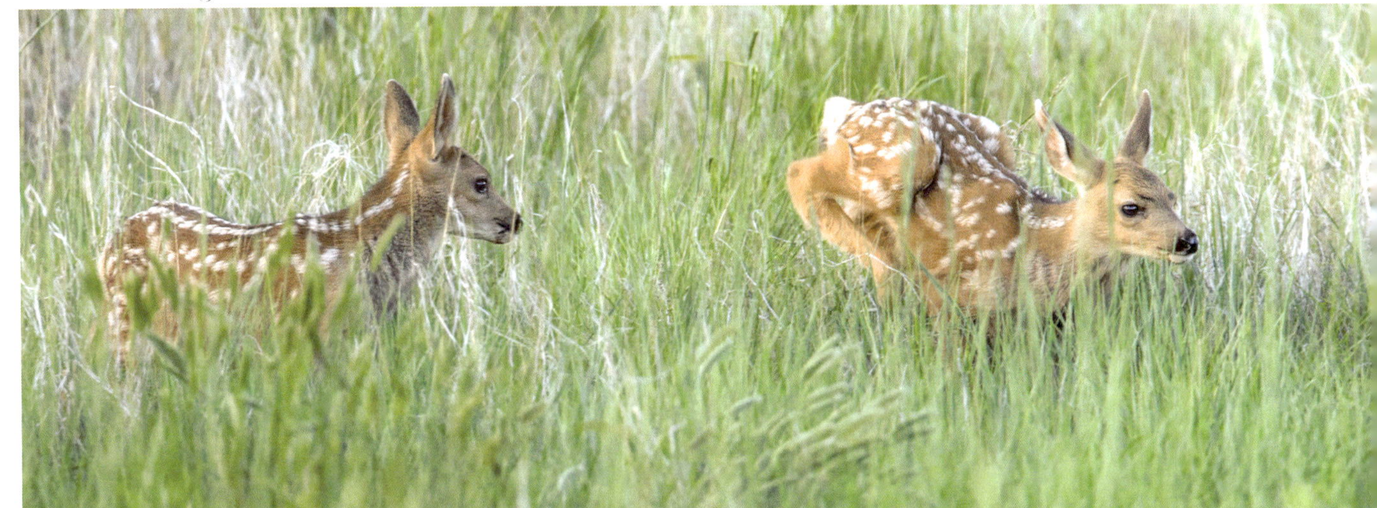

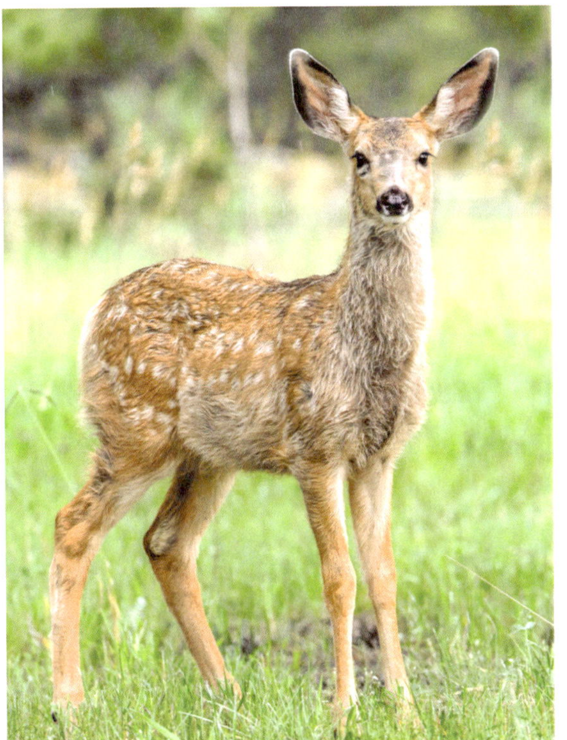

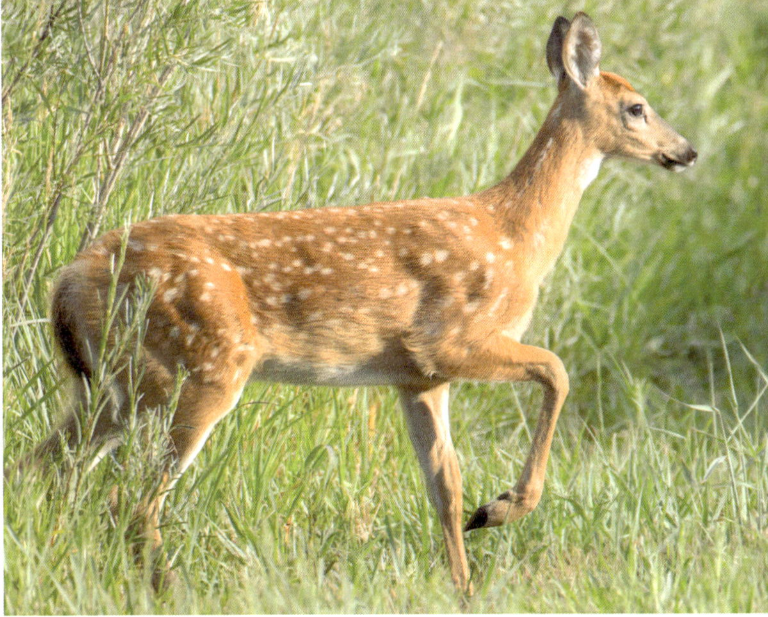

Toward the end of the summer, the fawn's protective spots will start to fade and their winter coats will start to grow.

81

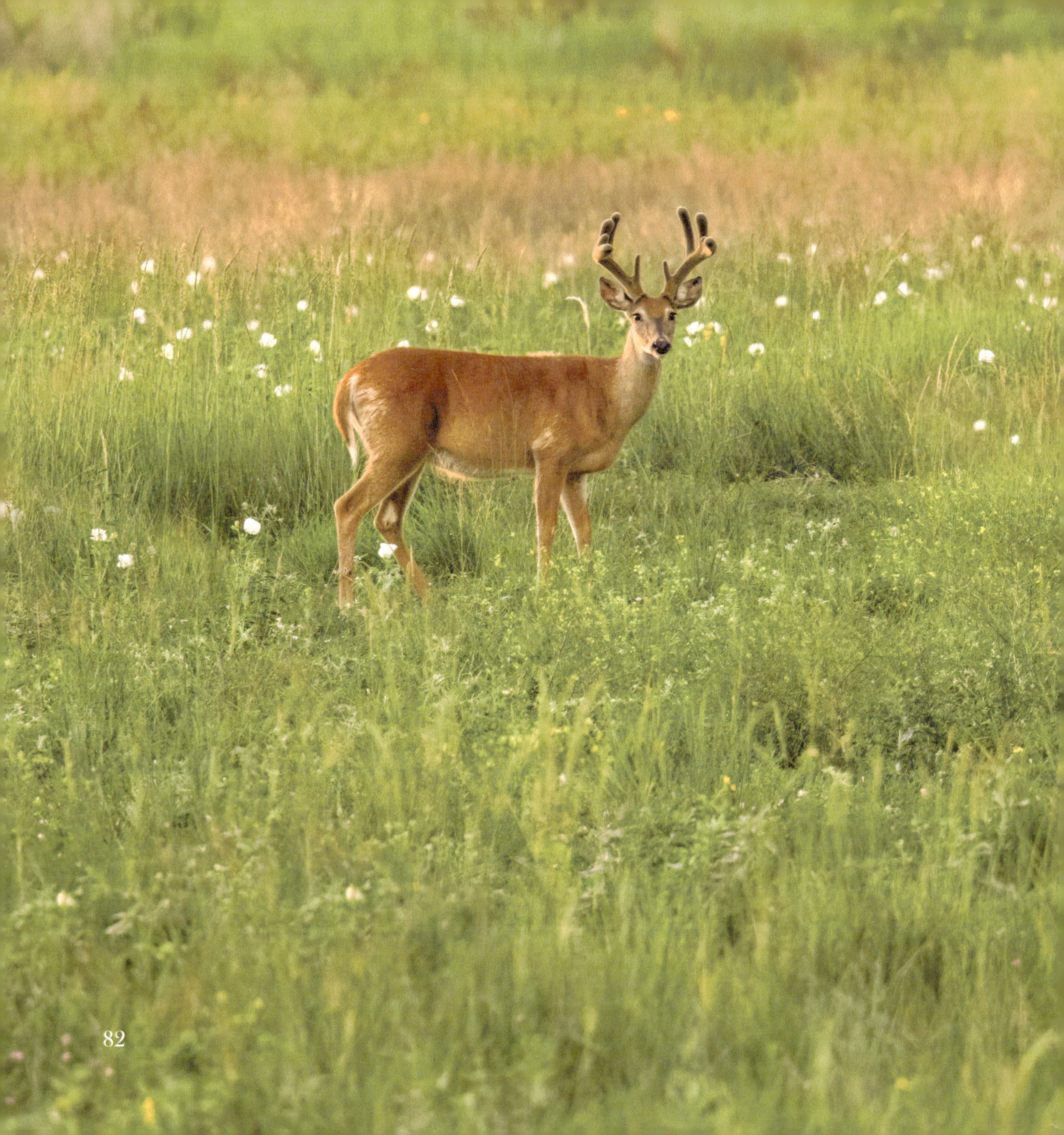

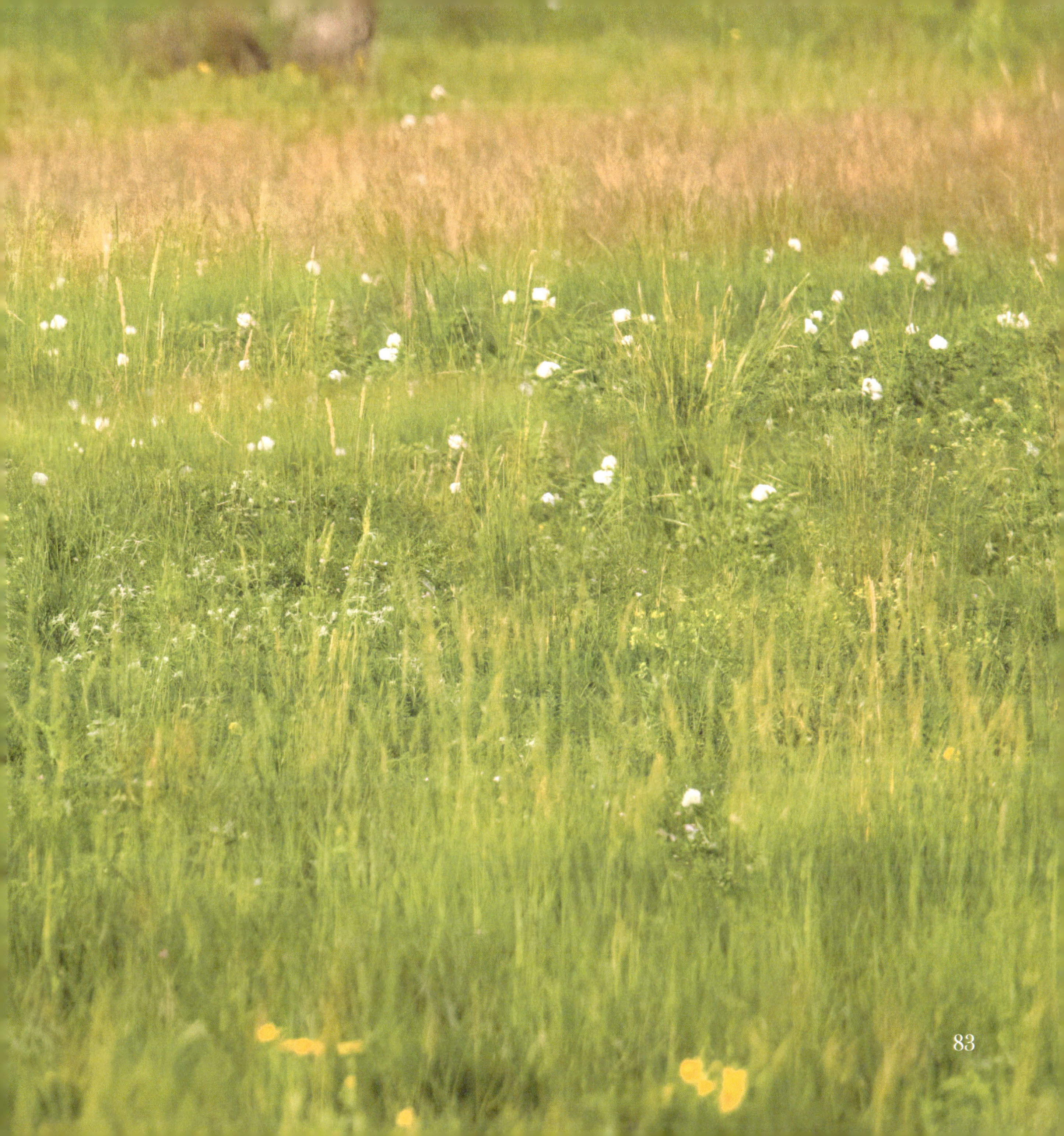

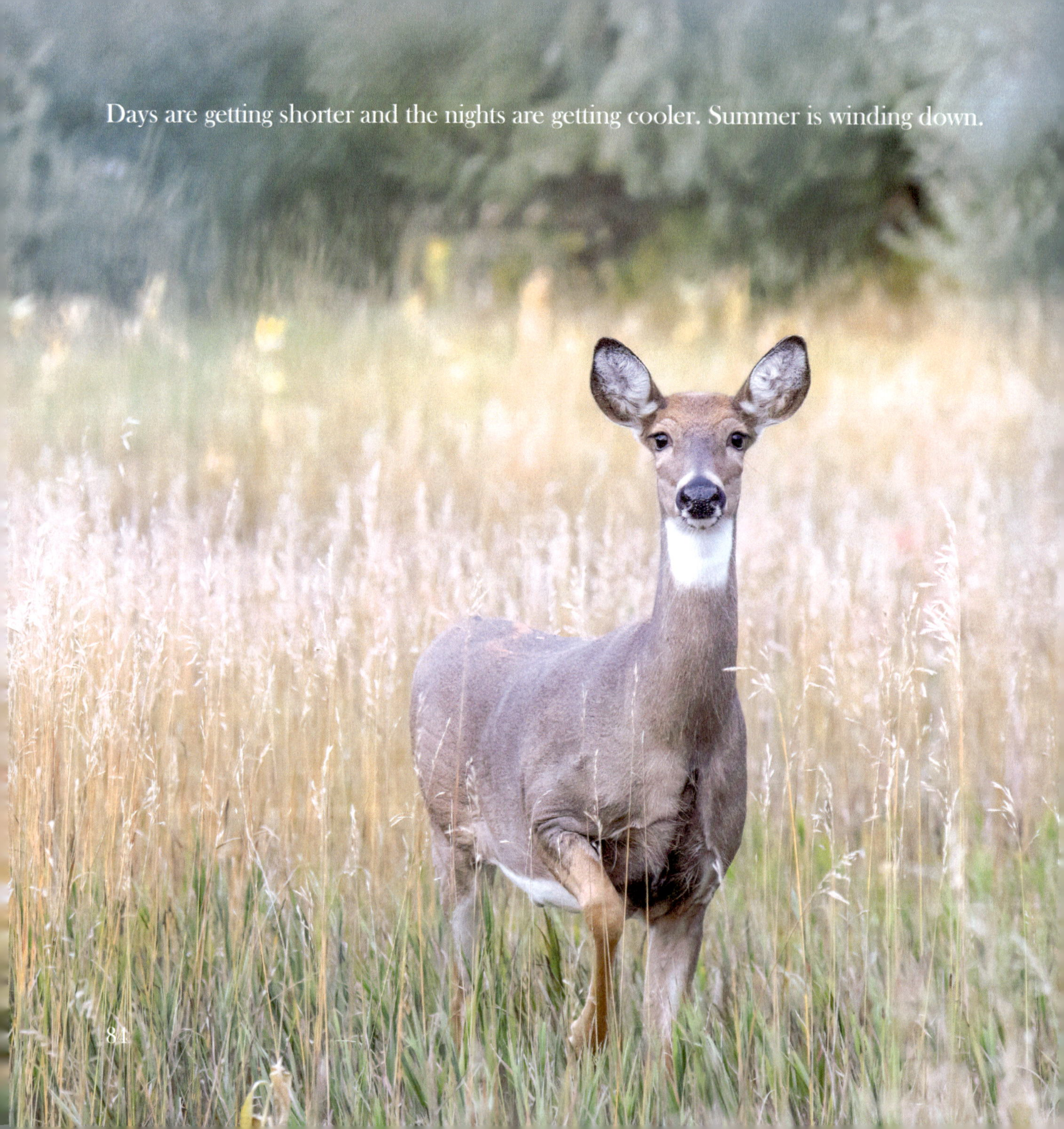

Days are getting shorter and the nights are getting cooler. Summer is winding down.

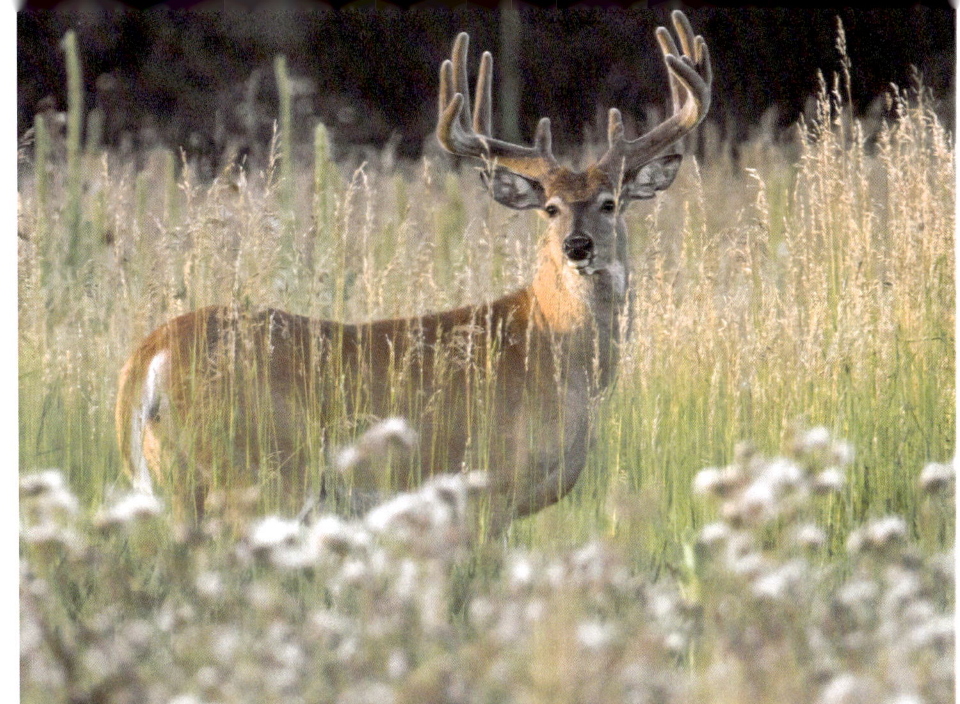

The deer are trying to get as much nutrition as they can to prepare for the upcoming months. Their thin and vibrant summer coats will soon be replaced with a duller colored coat that is thicker and much warmer.

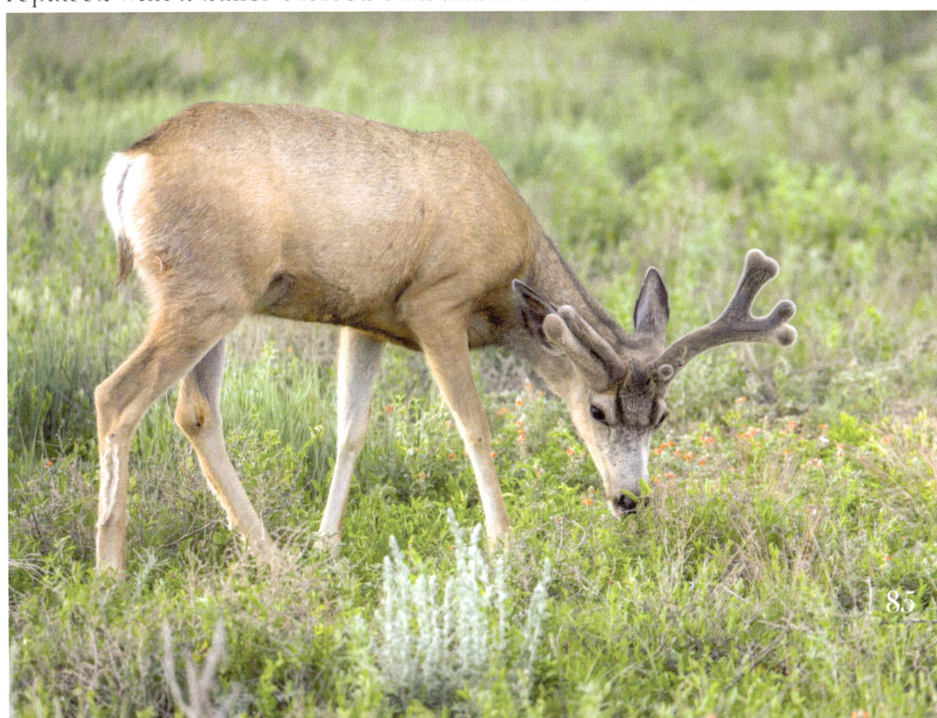

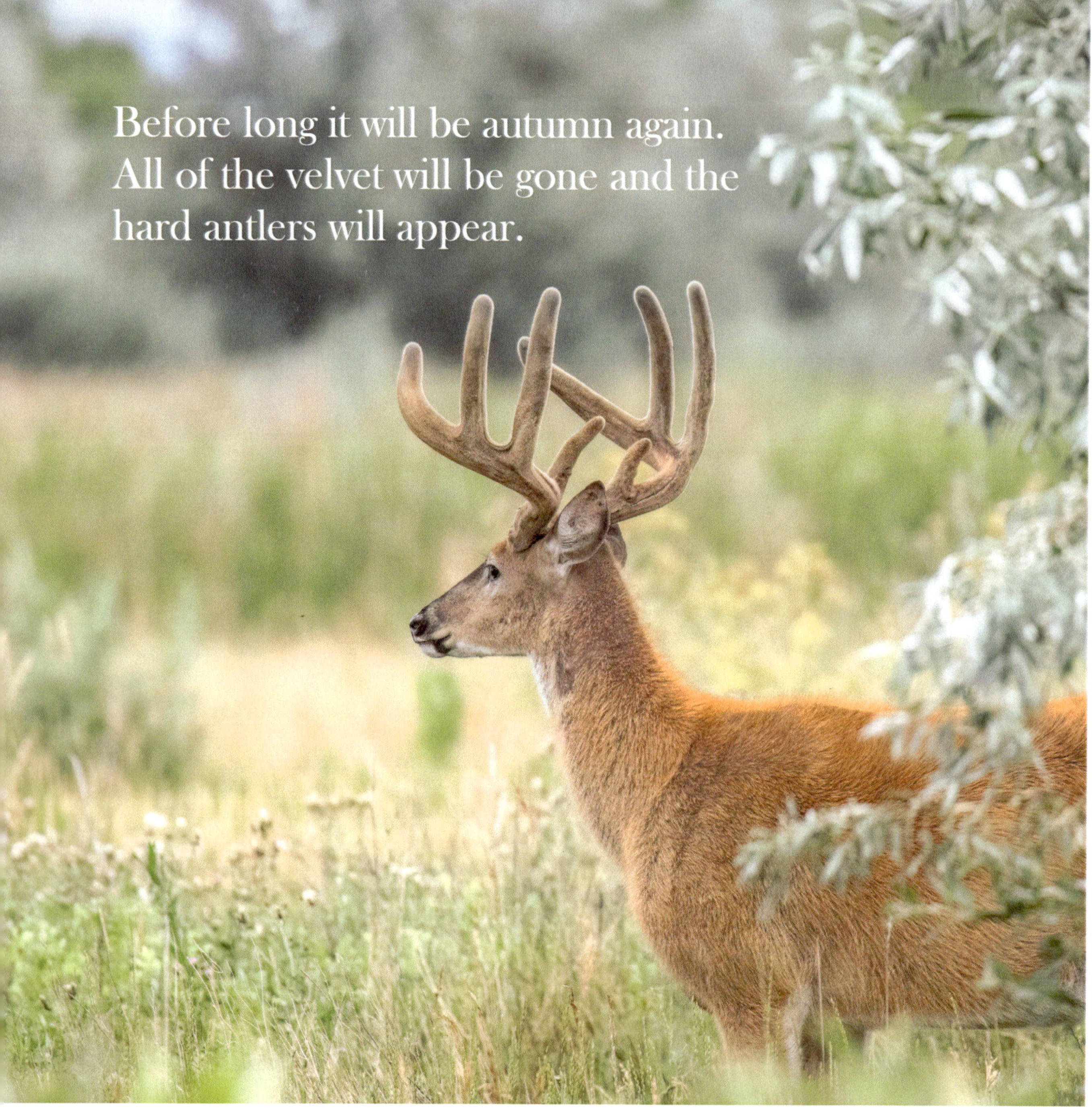
Before long it will be autumn again.
All of the velvet will be gone and the
hard antlers will appear.

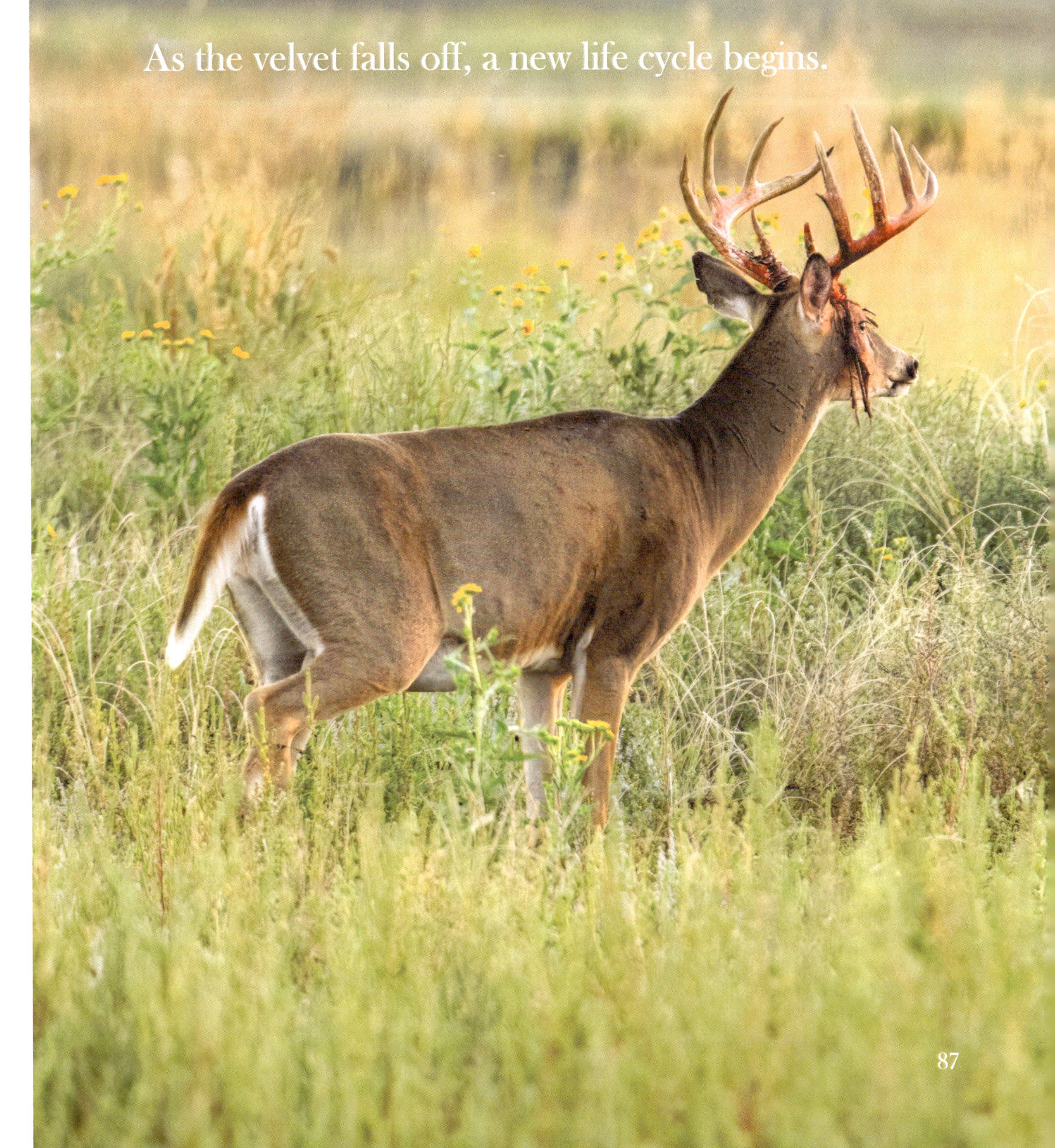
As the velvet falls off, a new life cycle begins.

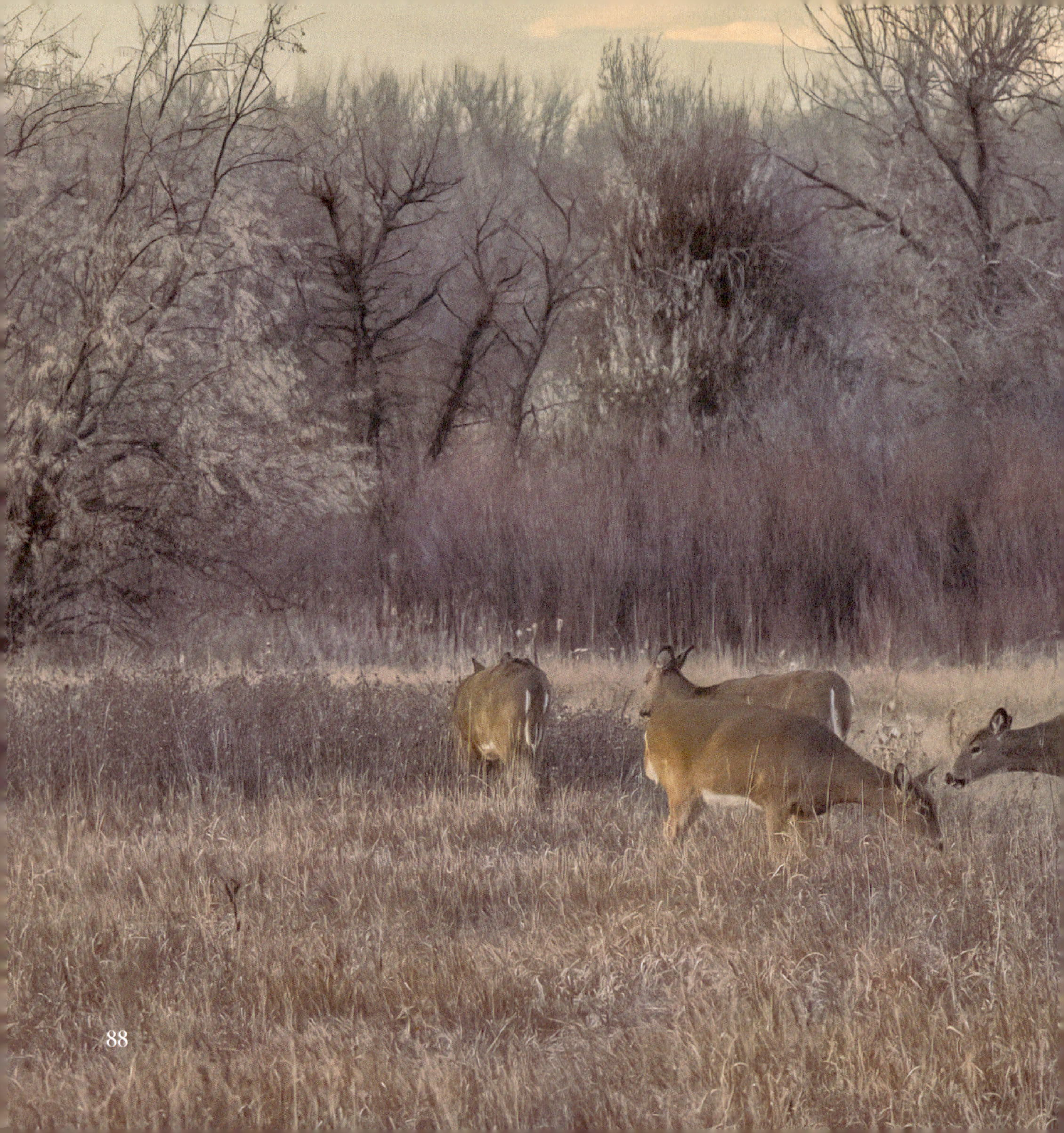

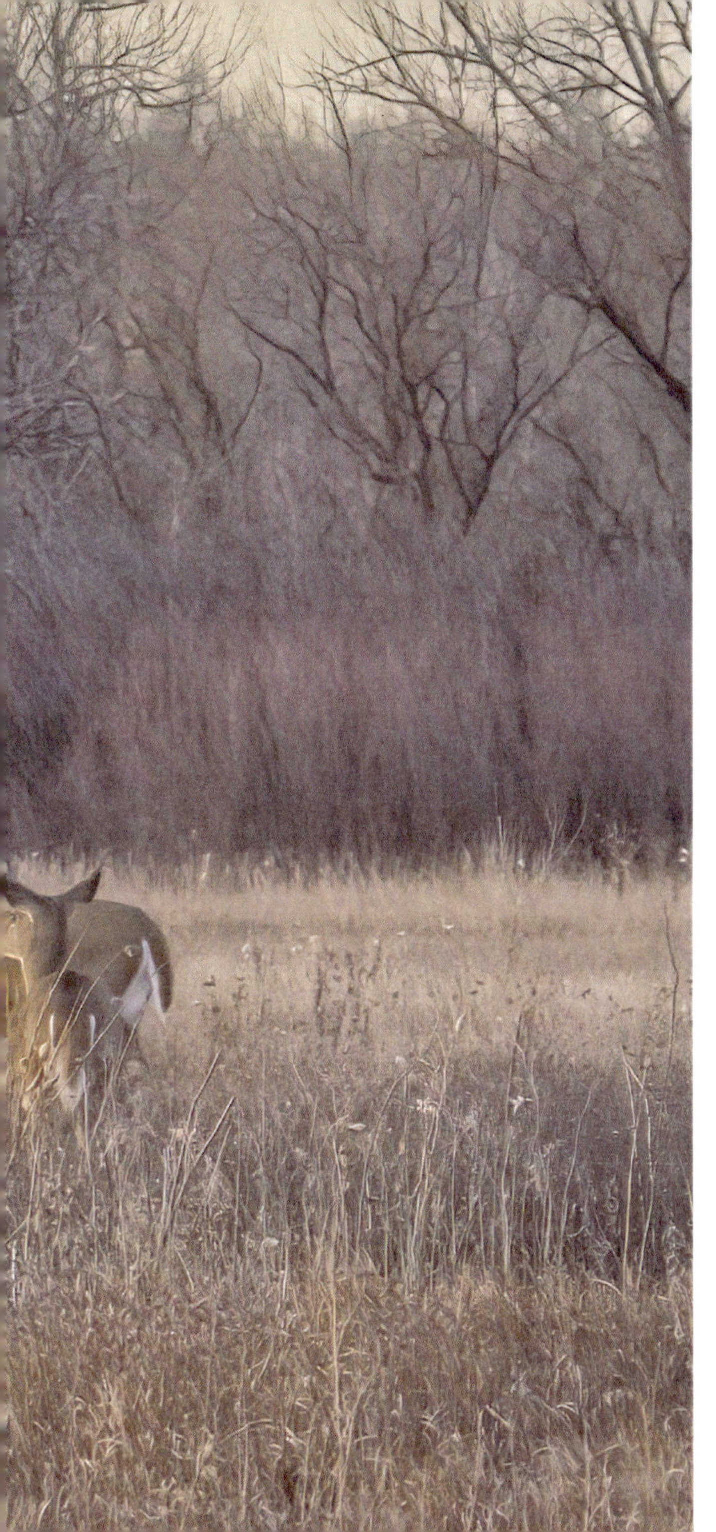

Field Notes

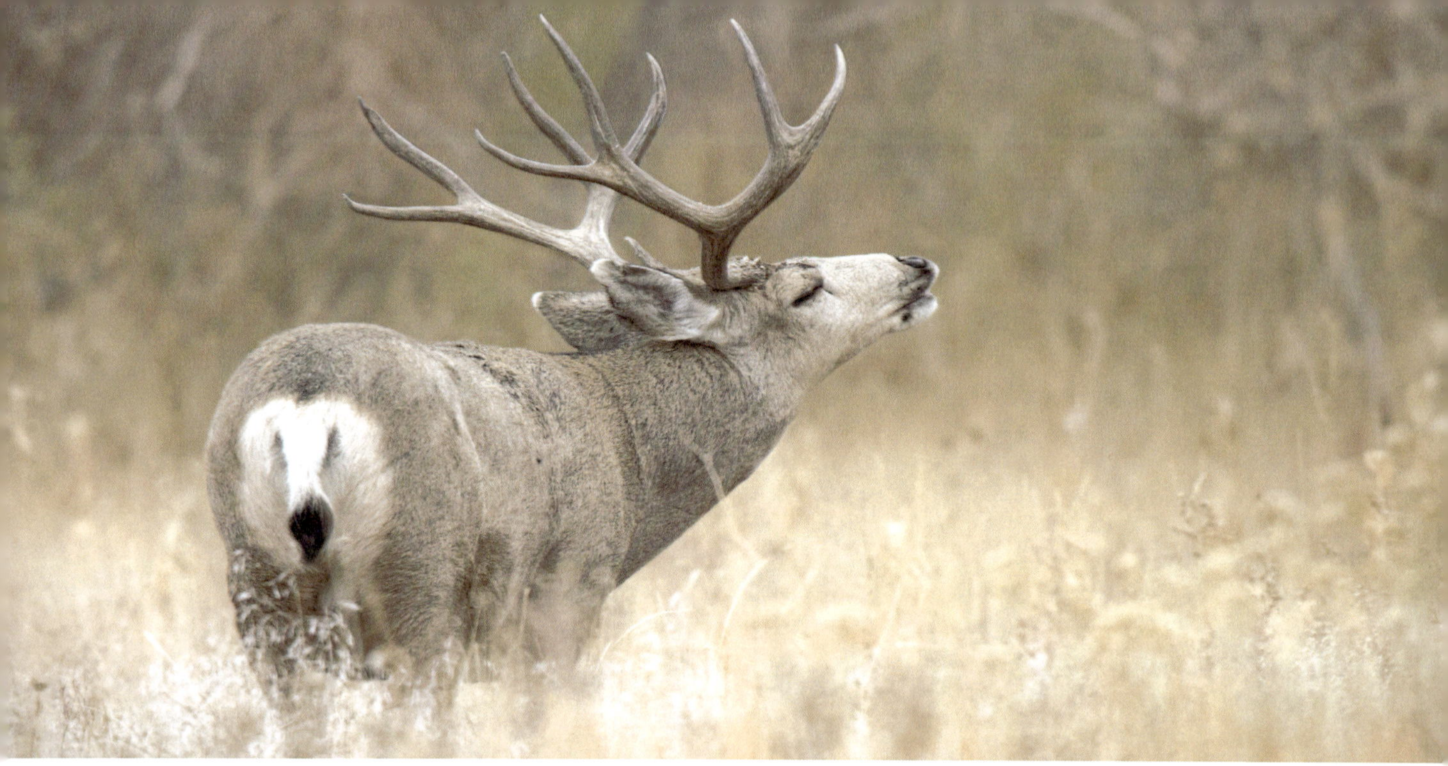

Two species of deer can be found in Colorado, Mule Deer and White-tailed Deer.

In general, Mule Deer are larger than White-tailed Deer.

Mule Deer live throughout Colorado. They were named after their large ears. Some thought their ears look like mule ears.

Both White-tailed Deer and Mule Deer have white on their tails, but Mule Deer tails look more like a white rope with black at the end.

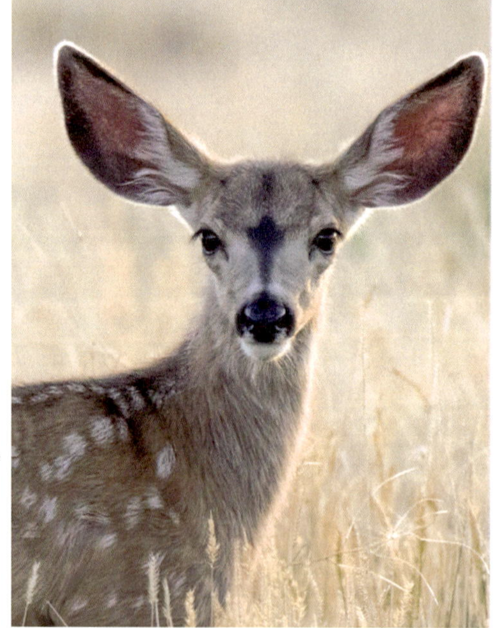

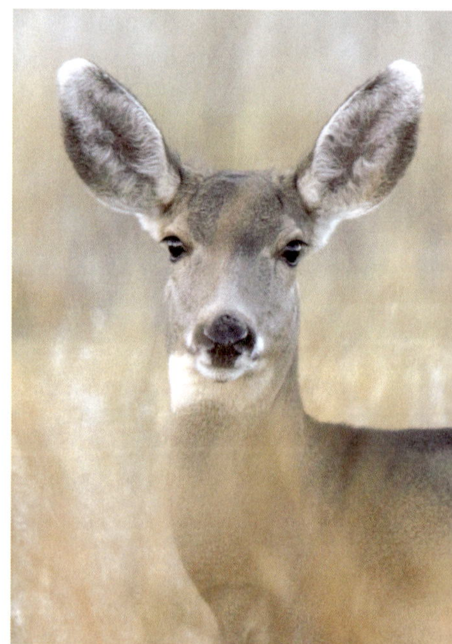

Mule Deer

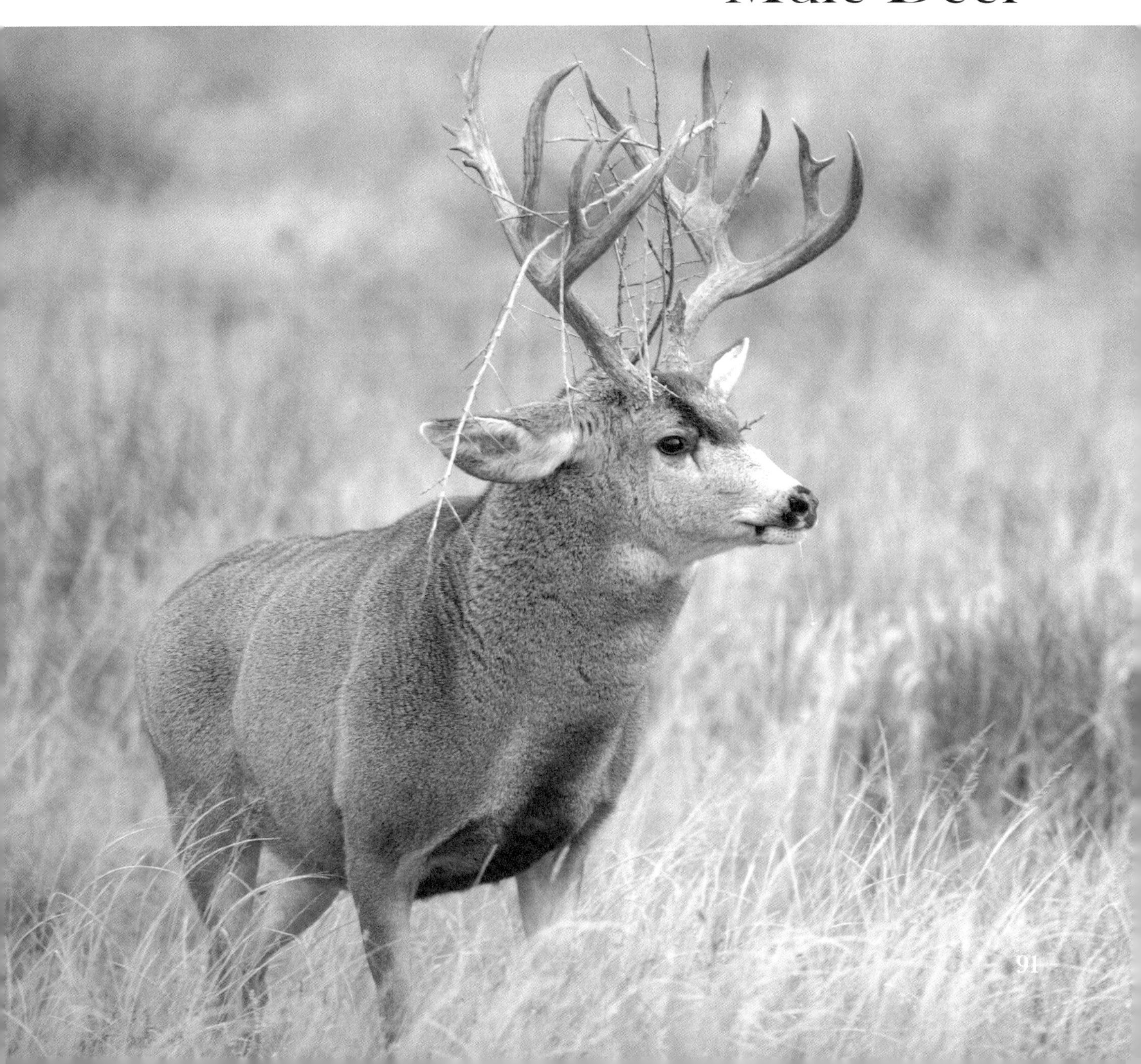

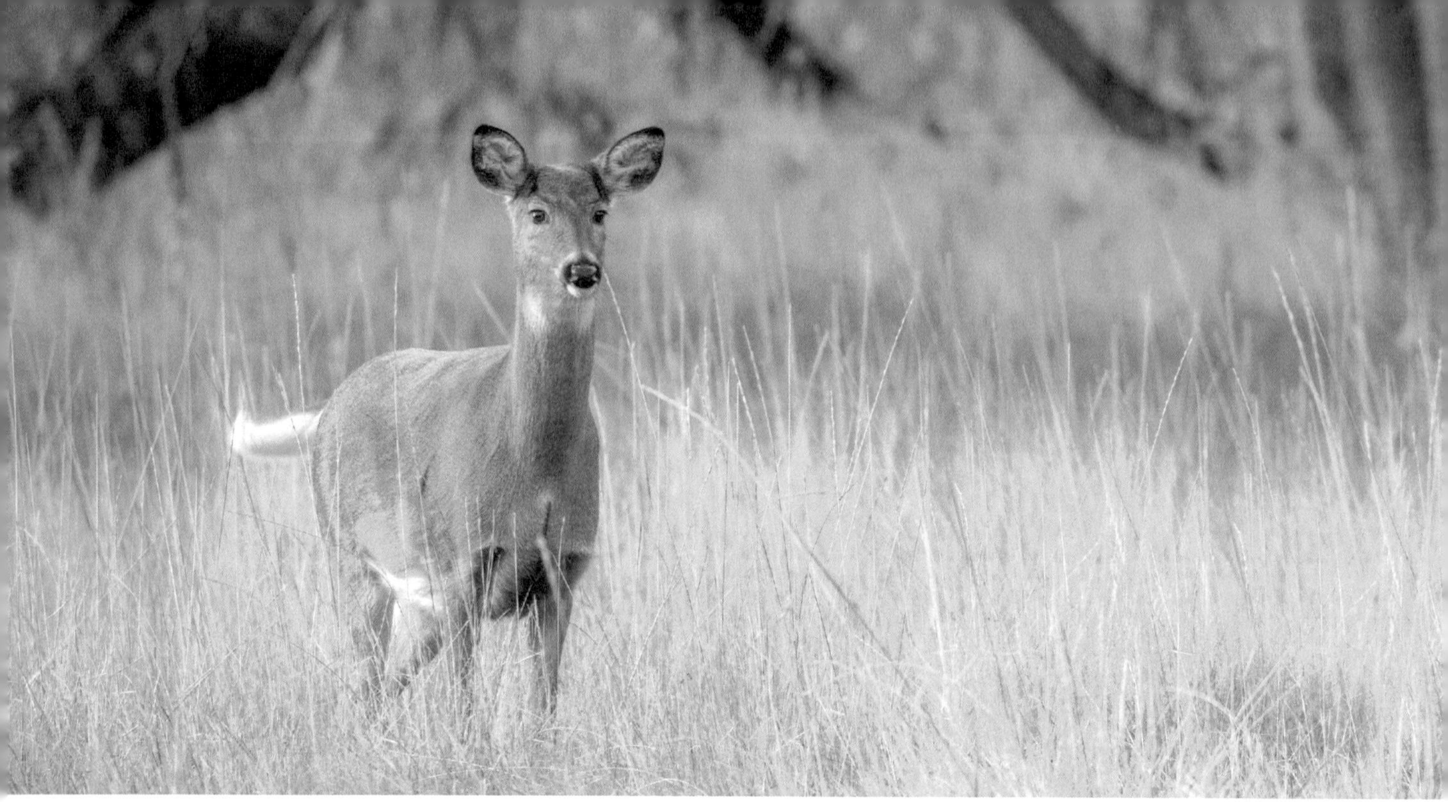

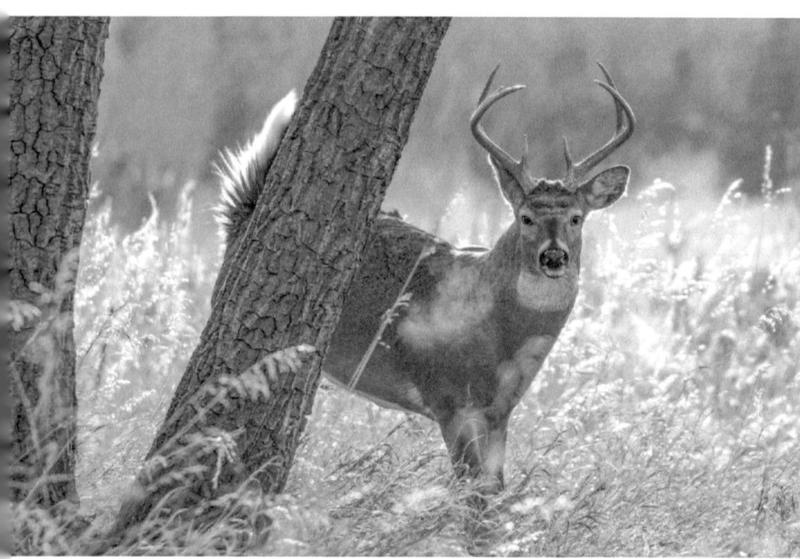

White-tailed Deer are named so because of their tails. The topside of their tails are mostly brown with white and maybe a little black.

However, it's the underside of the tail that is white. The tail can fan out when raised and the white underside will be seen.

If you see the tail raised, the deer is most likely on alert. White-tailed Deer also communicate with the position of their tails.

While Mule Deer can be found throughout Colorado, White-tailed Deer tend to stay on the Eastern Plains.

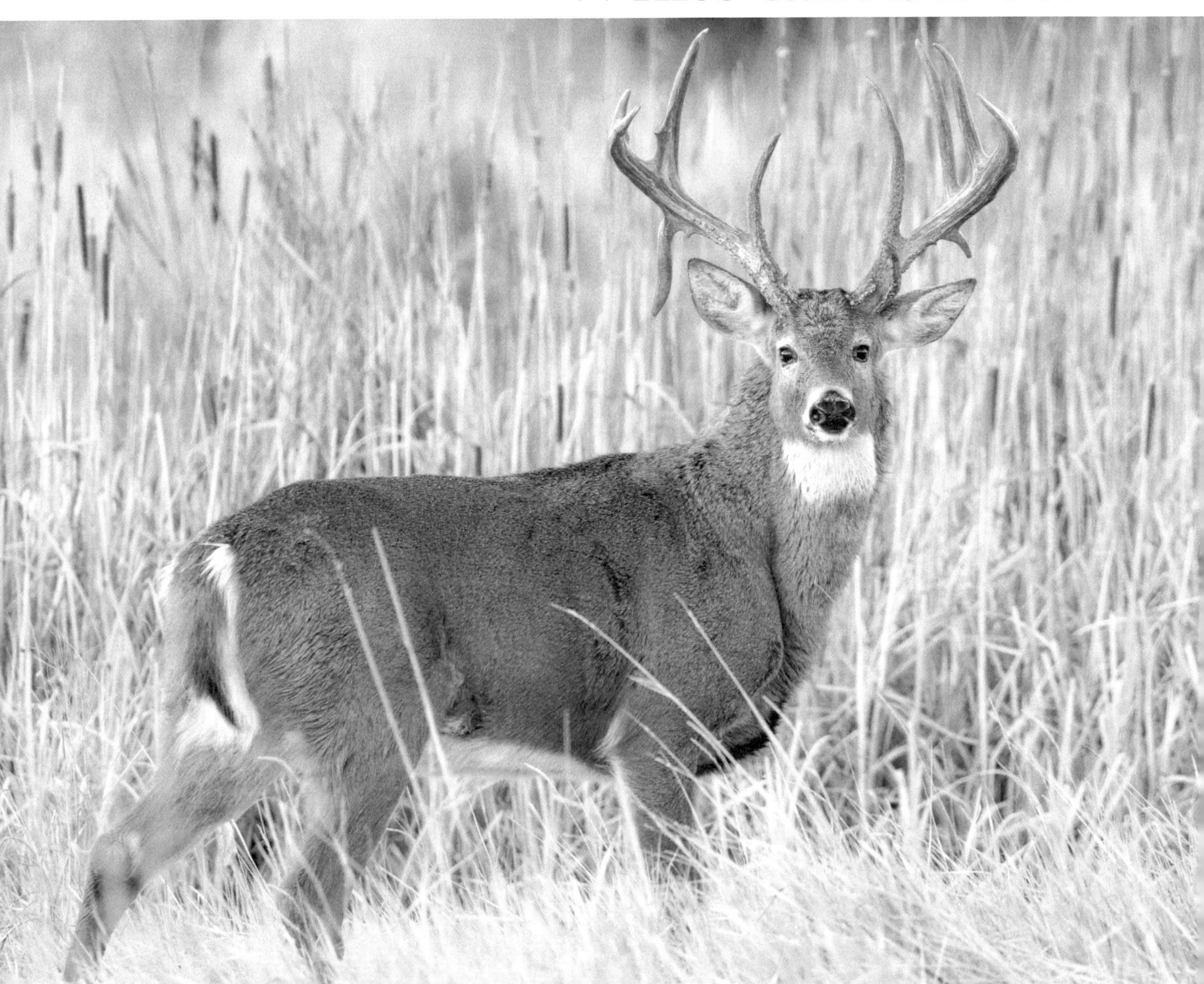

White-tailed Deer Antlers

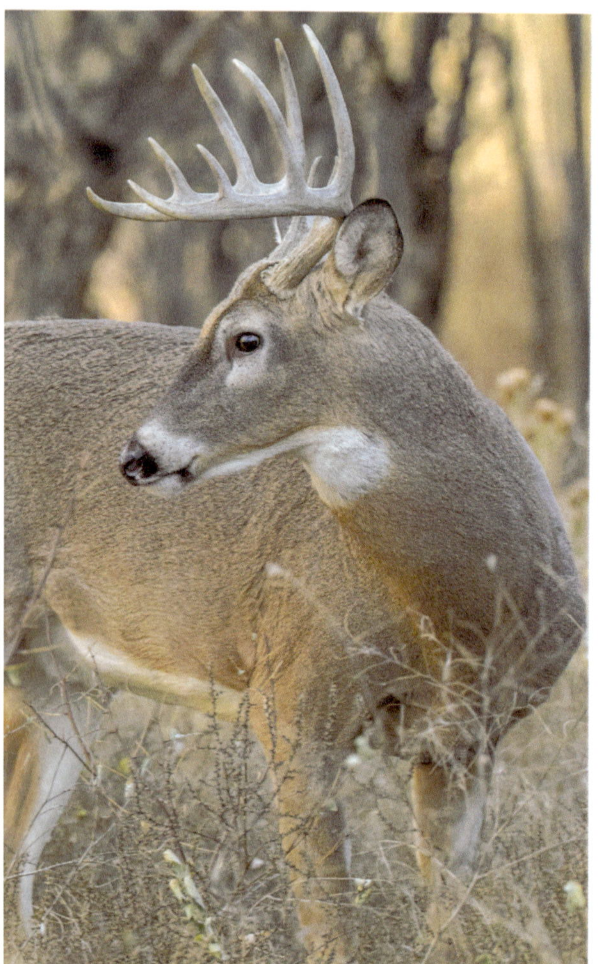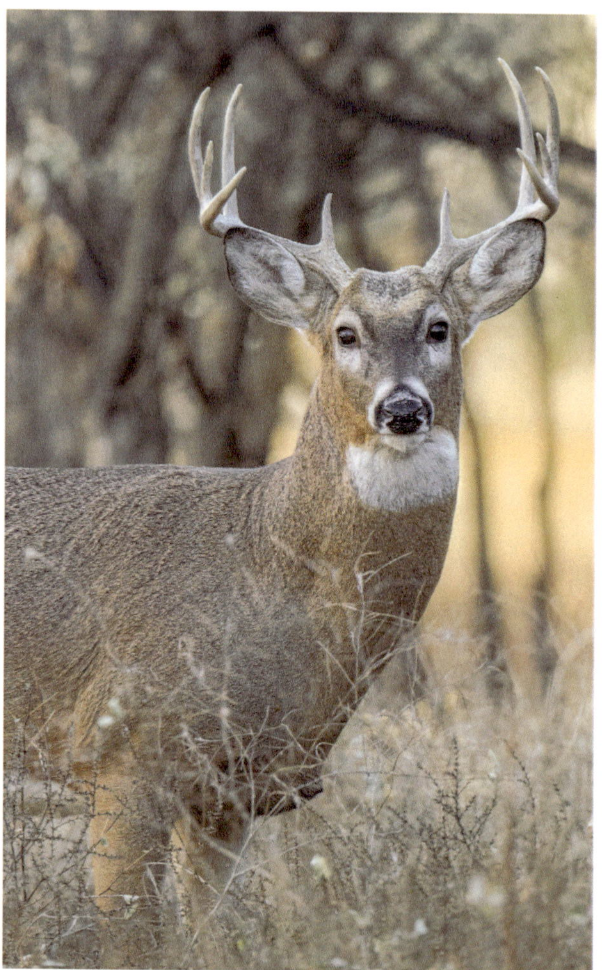

White-tailed buck antlers usually grow on a main beam or base. The points will grow from the beam. More points may be added every year. A buck's antlers are never the same twice. While they may be similar year to year, no set of antlers are the same.

Mule Deer Antlers

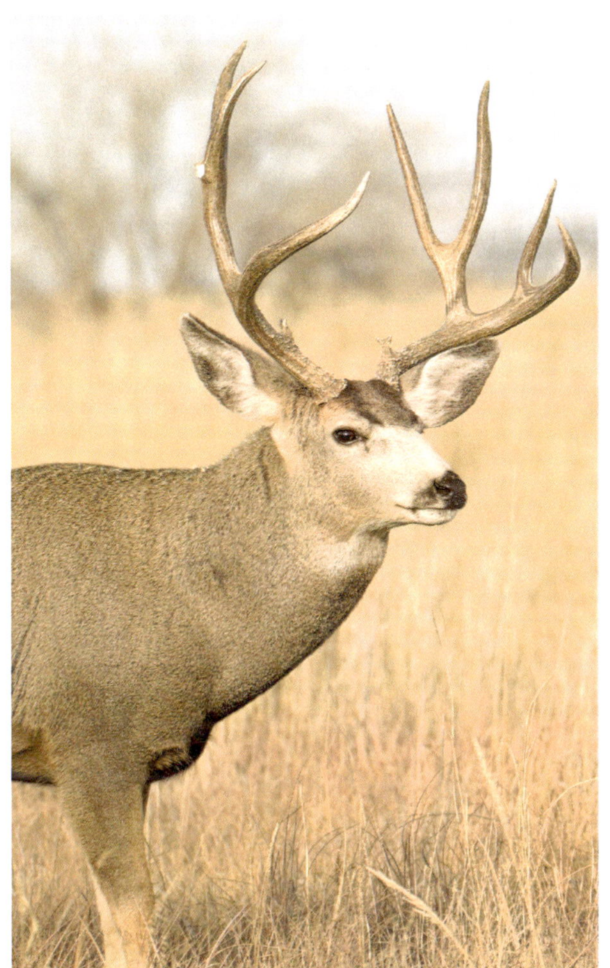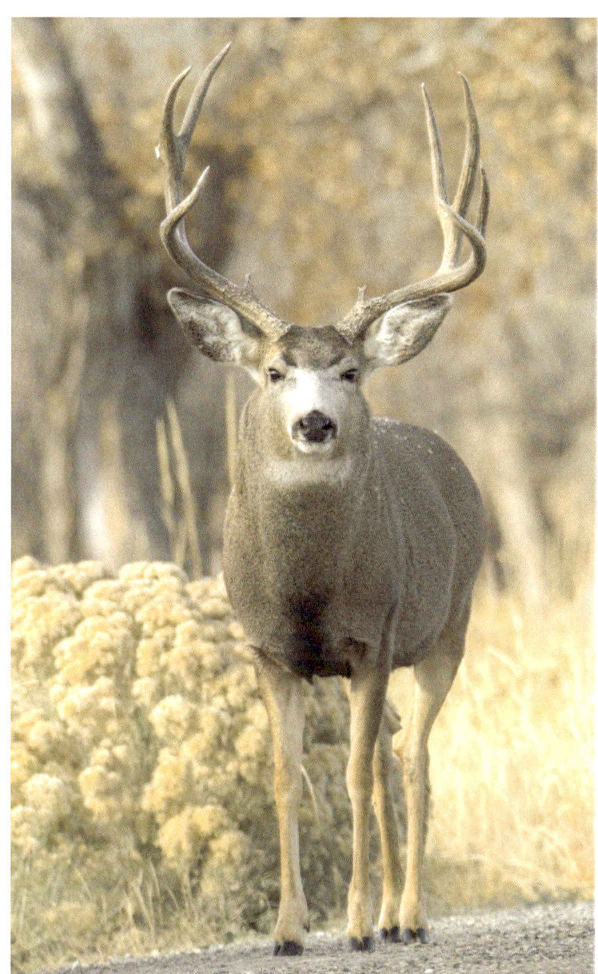

Not only do Mule Deer have bigger ears than White-tailed Deer, but they also have bigger antlers, generally speaking. A Mule Deer antler has a main beam like the whitetail, but the points will split or fork.

Velvet Antlers

White-tailed Buck

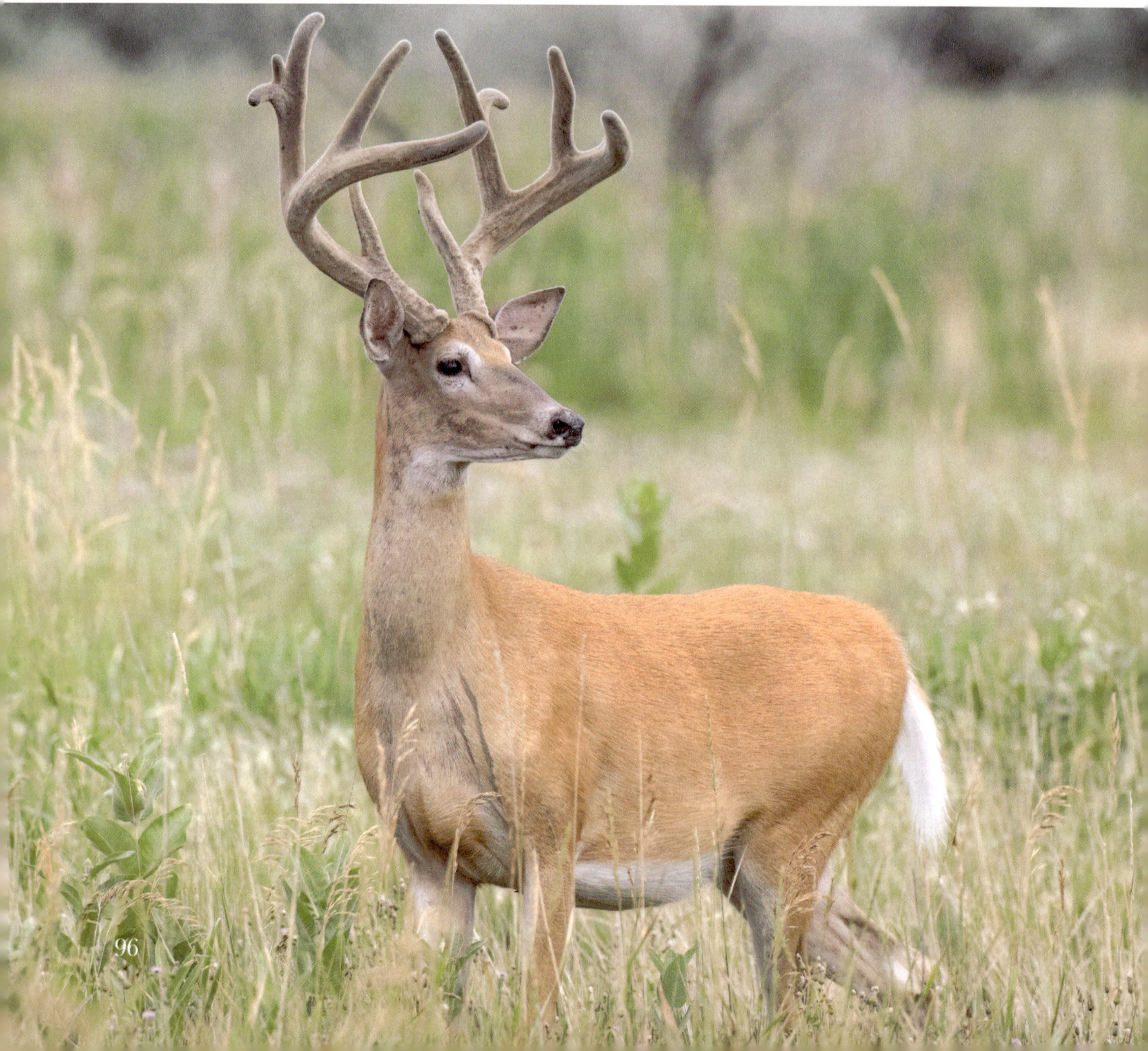

Velvet antlers start growing in the spring and continue to grow throughout the summer. Antlers are one of the fastest growing tissues in the natural world. White-tailed antlers may grow a quarter inch in a day. The velvet will fall off at the end of summer and the hard antler underneath will be exposed. The bucks will carry the antlers throughout the rut, and then they will fall off.

Mule Deer Buck

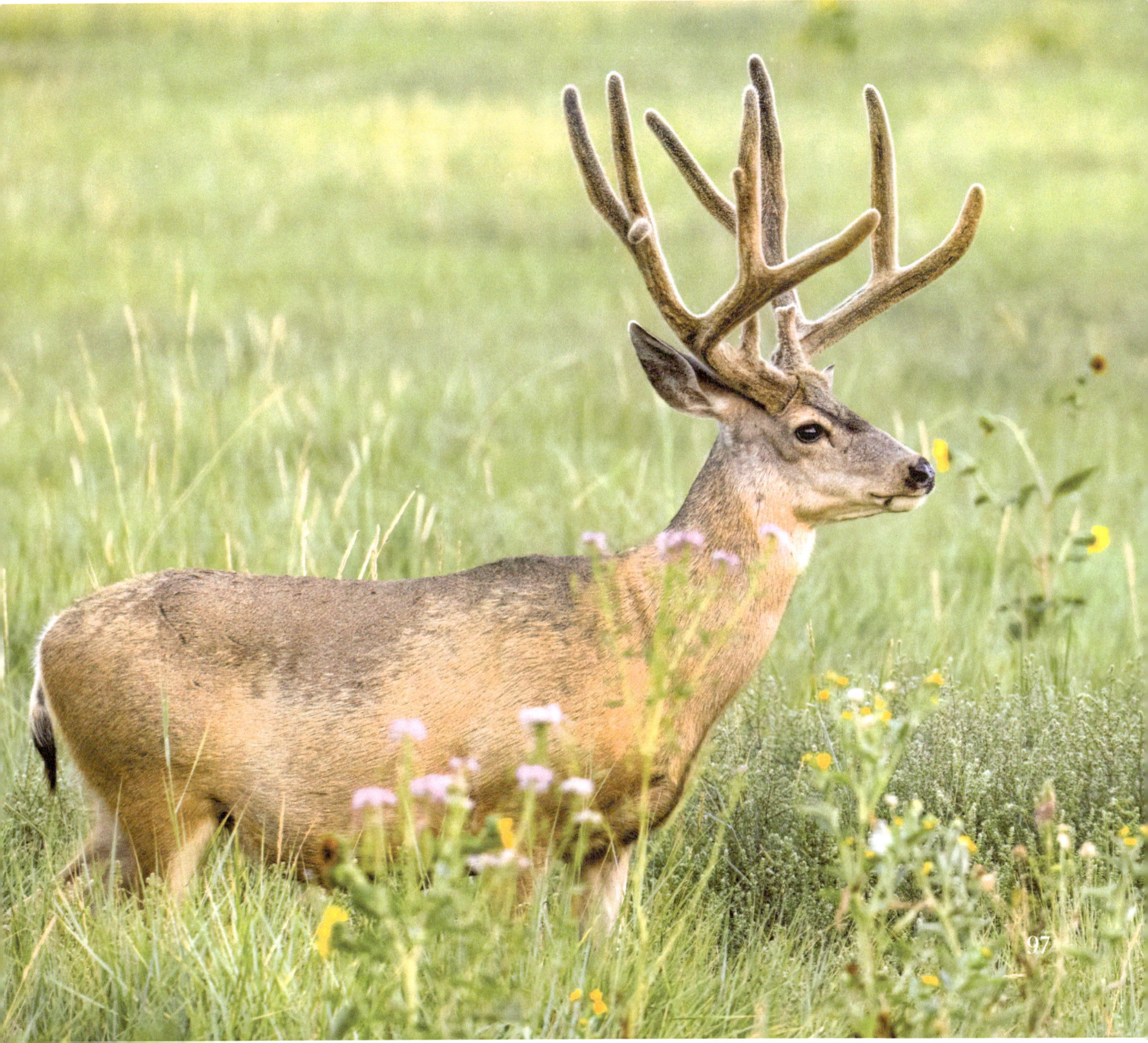

Antler Progression and Regression

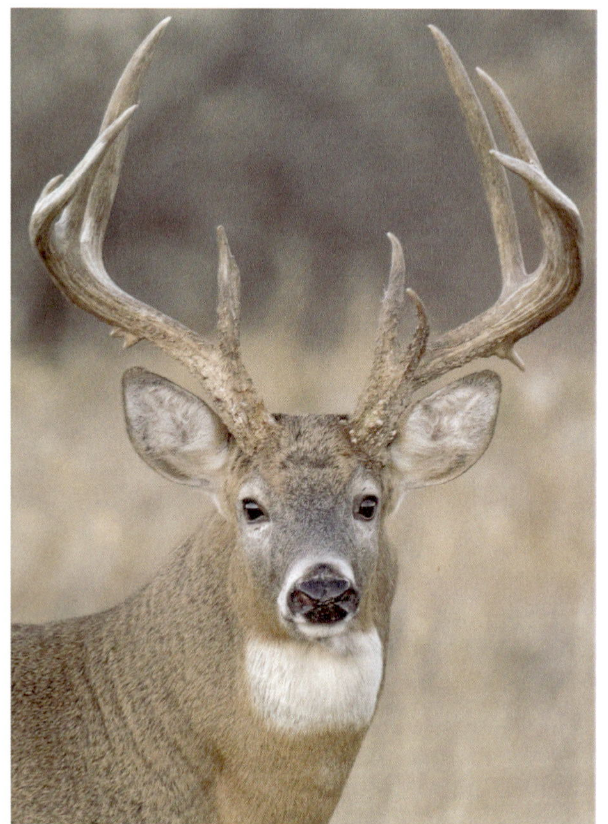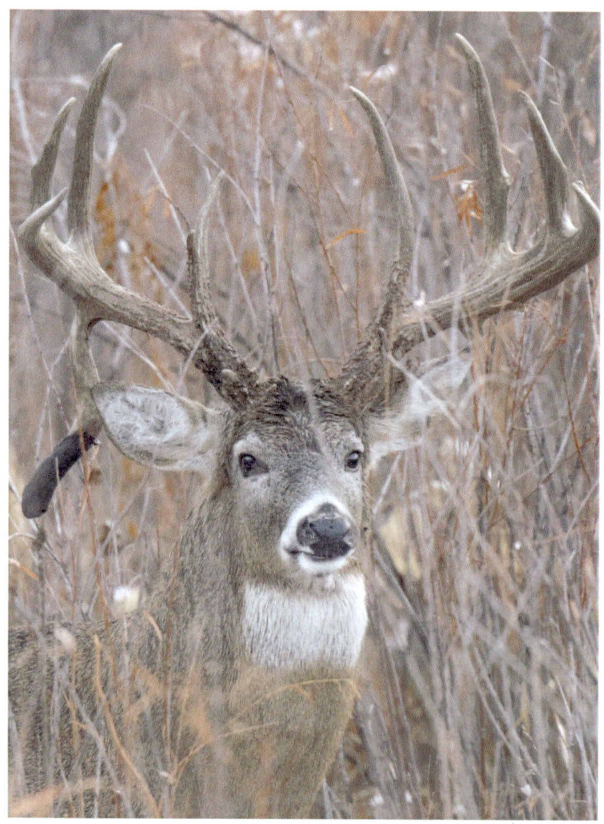

I took photographs of this mature White-tailed buck four different years all during the rut.

As you can see, his antlers grew even larger in the second year. He had a drop tine in both the second and third year.

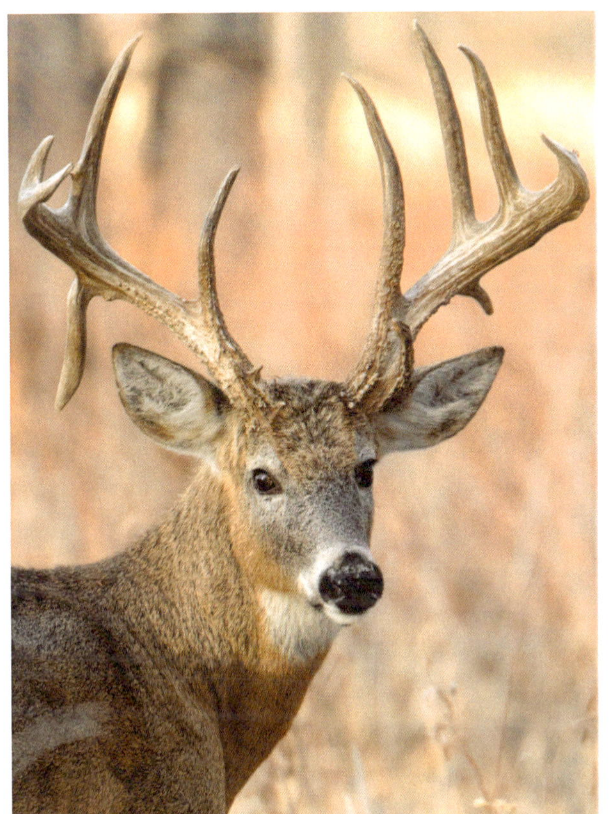 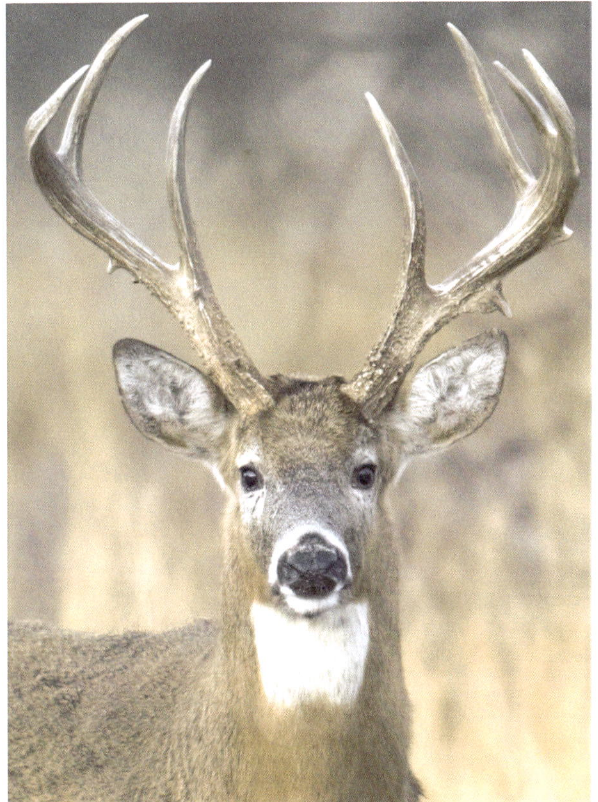

By the fourth year, his antlers are starting to regress. This is a natural occurrence as a buck ages.

Although antlers are different every year, you can see similar characteristics that are present year to year.

Home Range

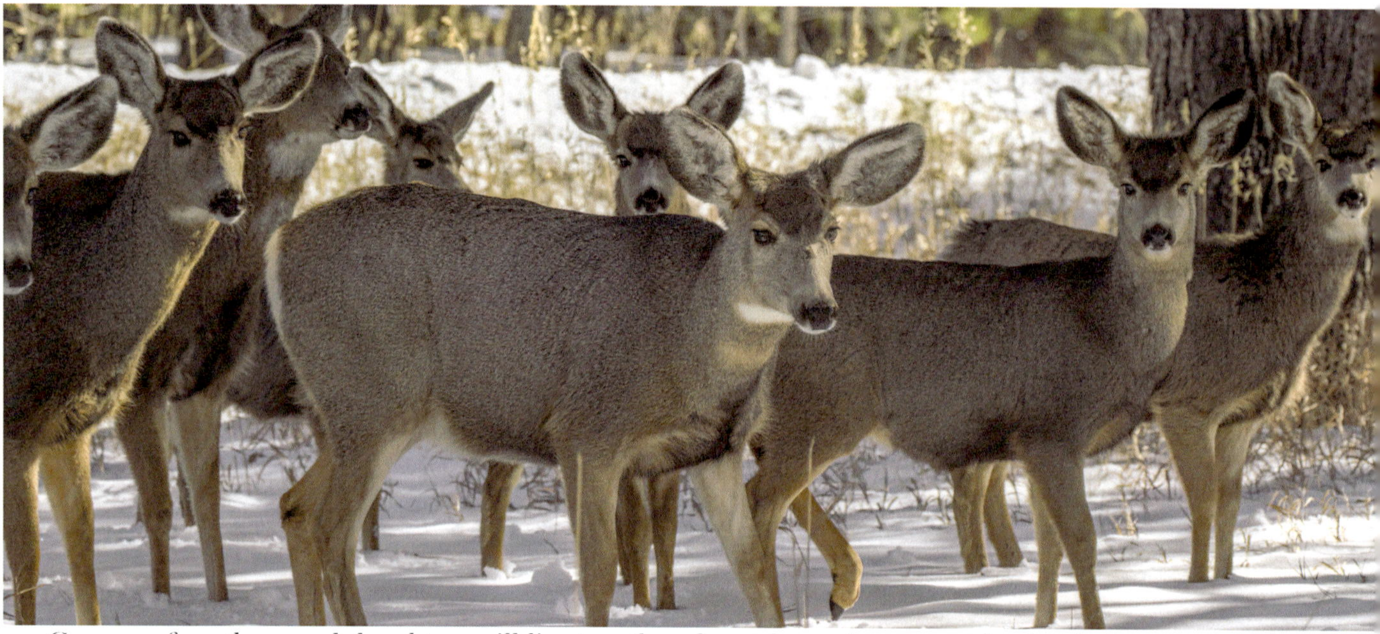

Groups of mothers and daughters will live together throughout the year and raise their young within their home range. You have heard it said before, there is safety in numbers. For deer, there are also predators around.

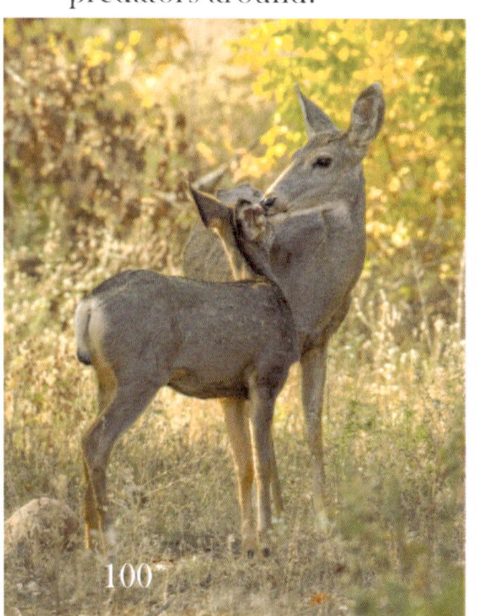

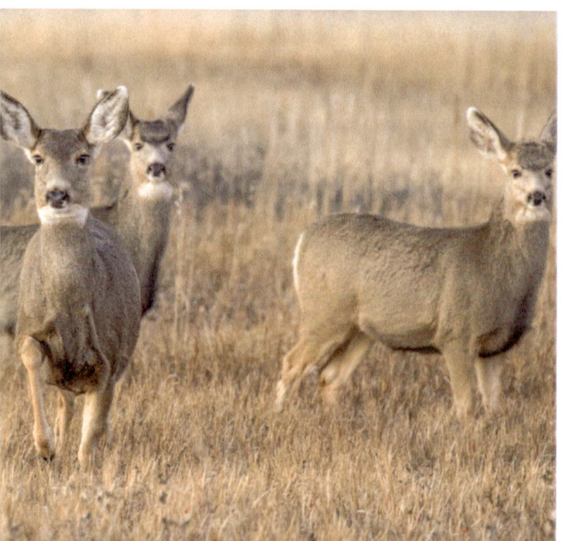

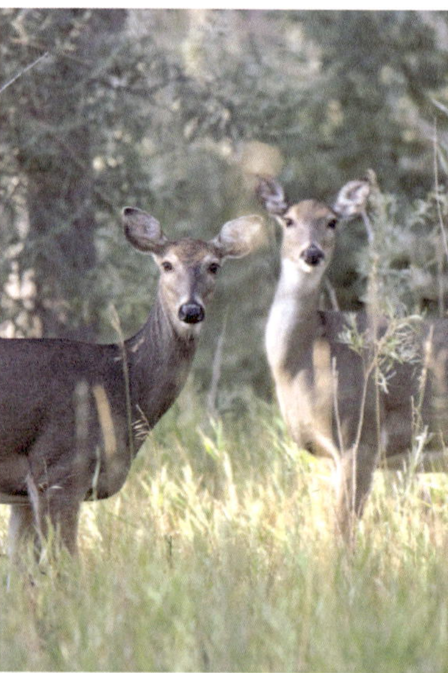

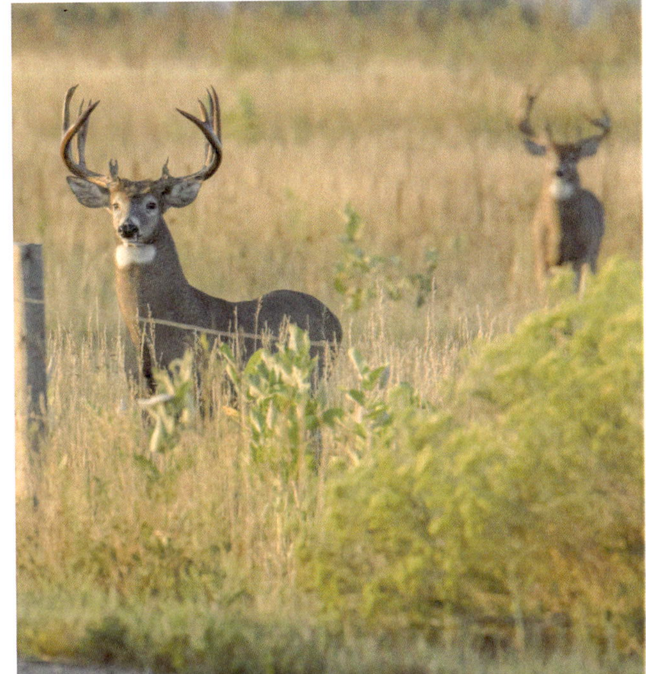

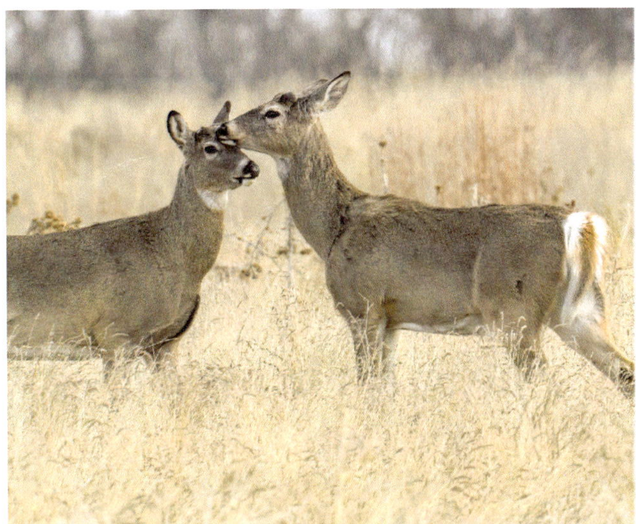

Throughout most of the year, except during the rut, bucks will join other bucks and live in groups called bachelor groups. They will eat, travel, and rest together. They will also protect each other.

Some bucks and bachelor groups will stay in the general vicinity with the does.

Other bucks will not. They will usually venture outside of the area, and sometimes travel miles away. This may help to ensure genetic diversity.

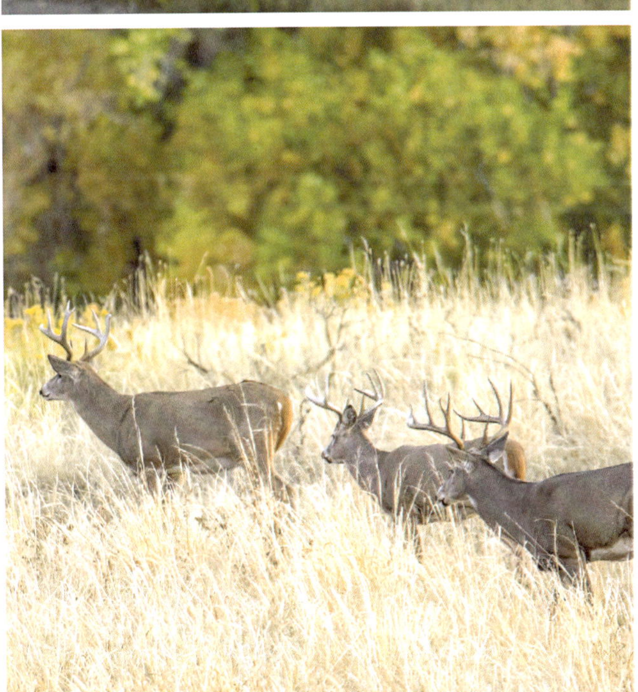

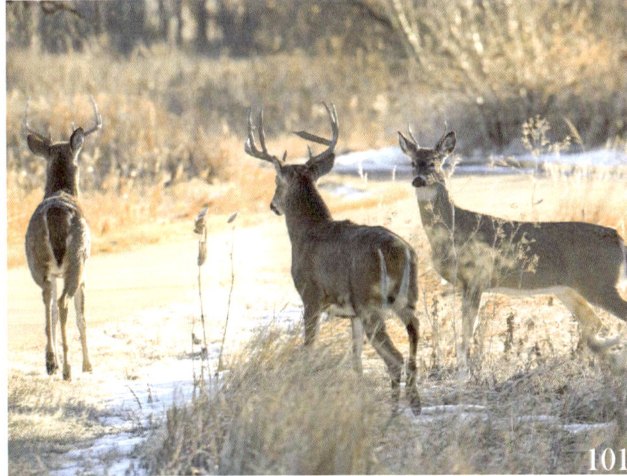

Guidance

Deer have very specific social structures within a herd.

Younger deer watch for guidance from the older deer.

The guidance may be with dominance and hooves, scent communication, or even a stern look.

Migration patterns are also learned from the older herd members.

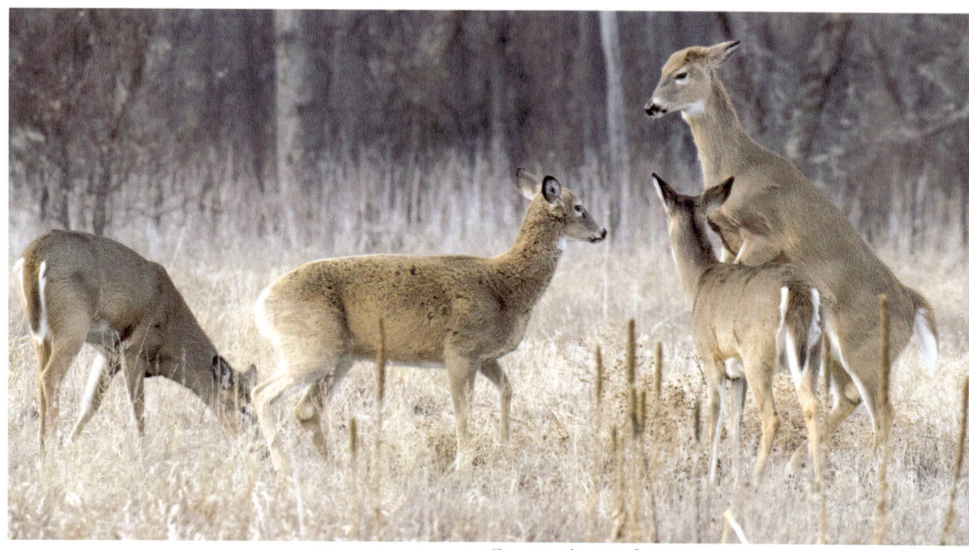

Sometimes hooves are involved.

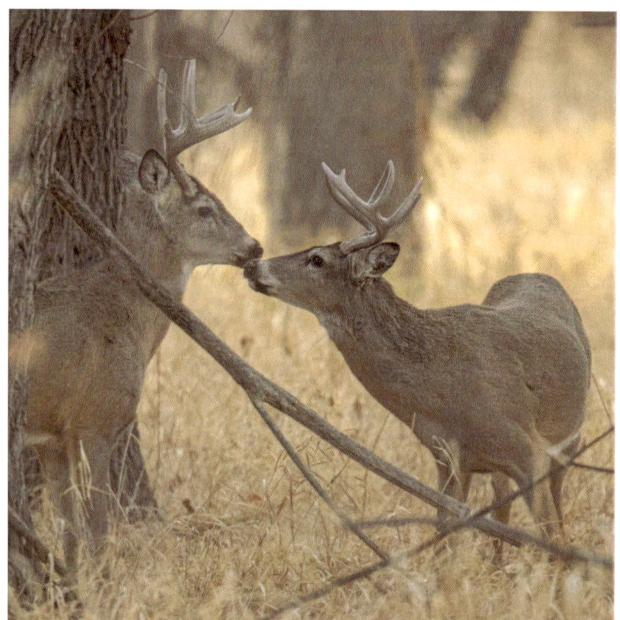

One of the ways deer communicate is through scent glands.

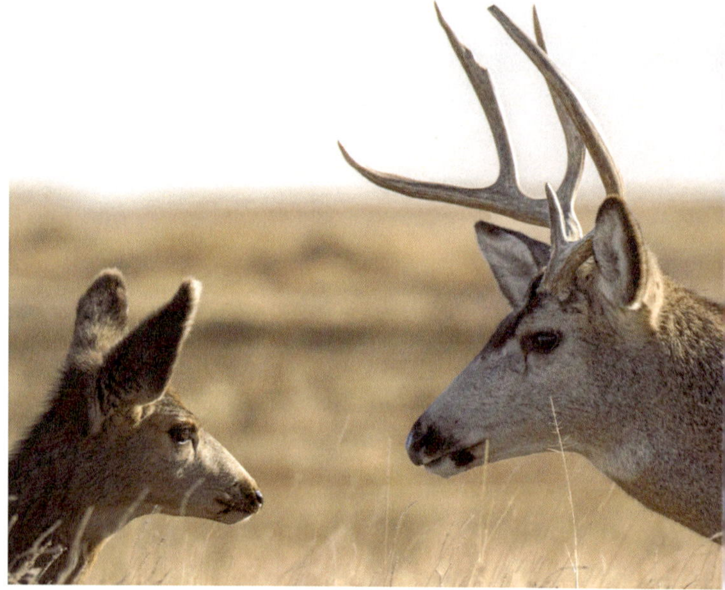

Sometimes a stern look is all that is needed.

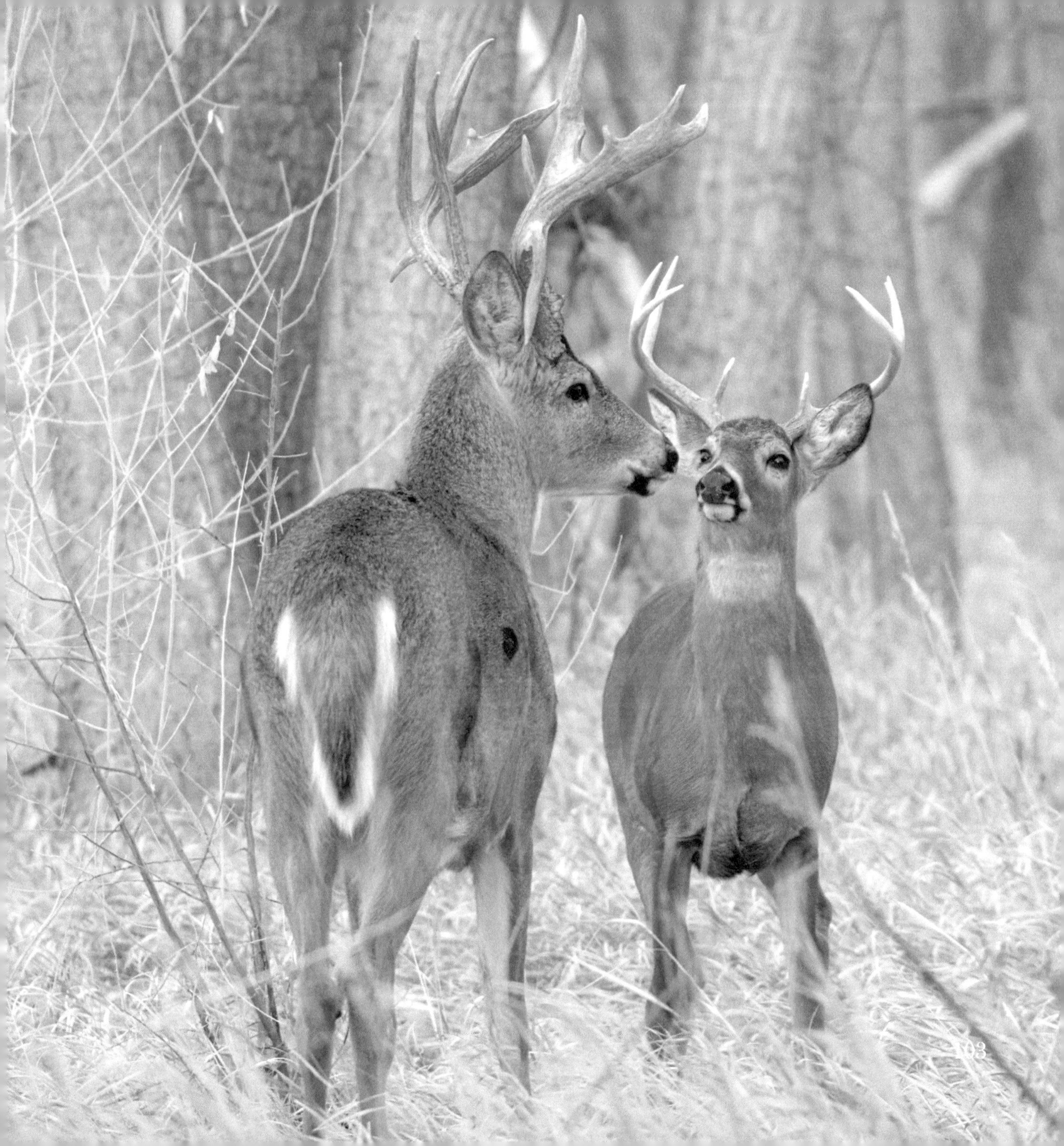

A Leucistic Mule Deer

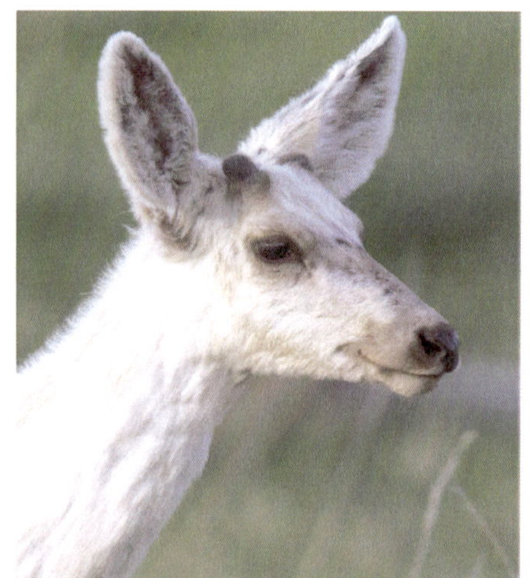

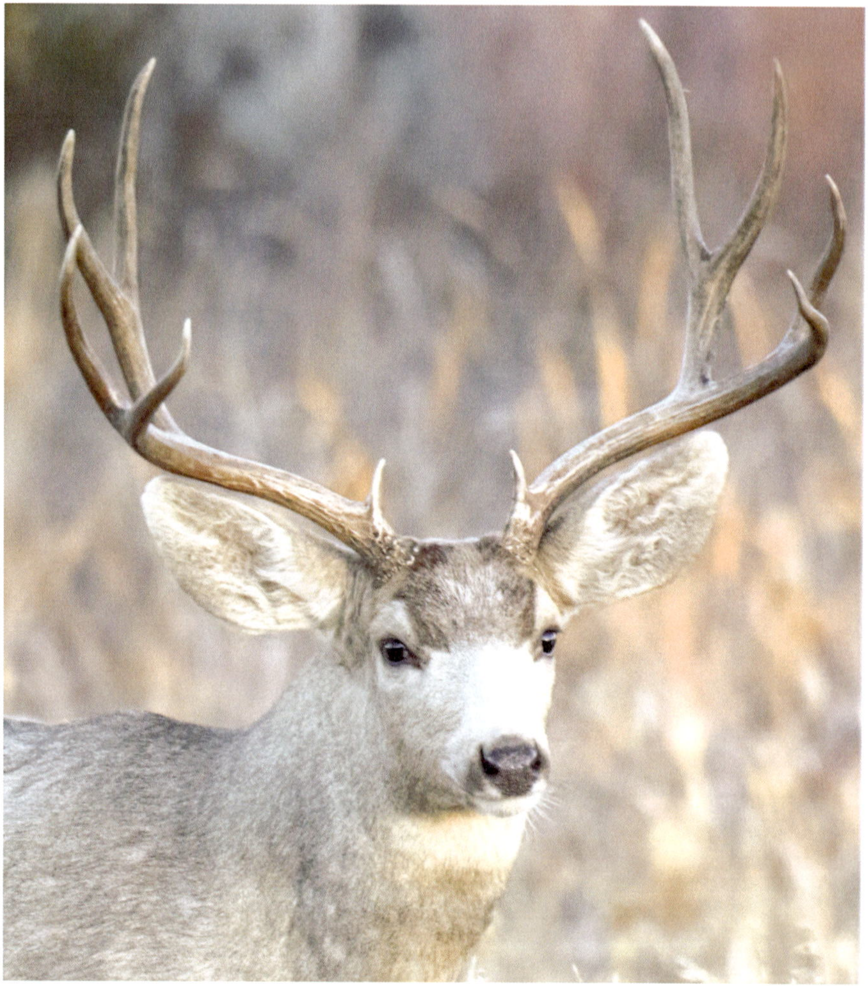

Leucism is a genetic condition. Animals with this condition have almost no color in their pigmentation, which is different from an albino which has no color at all.

This one-year-old Mule Deer buck is very light in color, almost all white.

At five years old, he is still lighter than the other Mule Deer, but not as light as he was when he was younger.

Junior, the White-tailed Buck

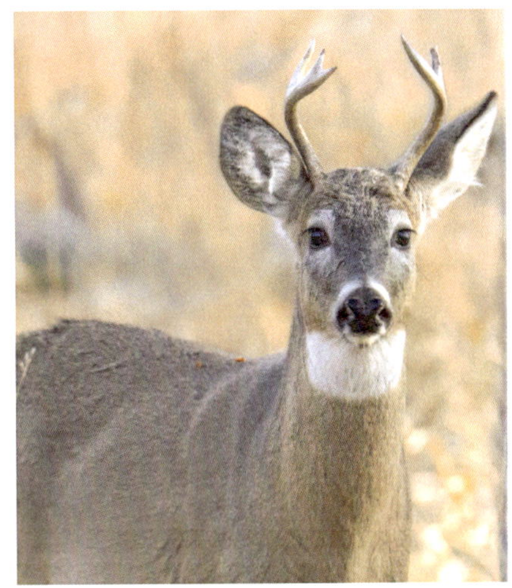

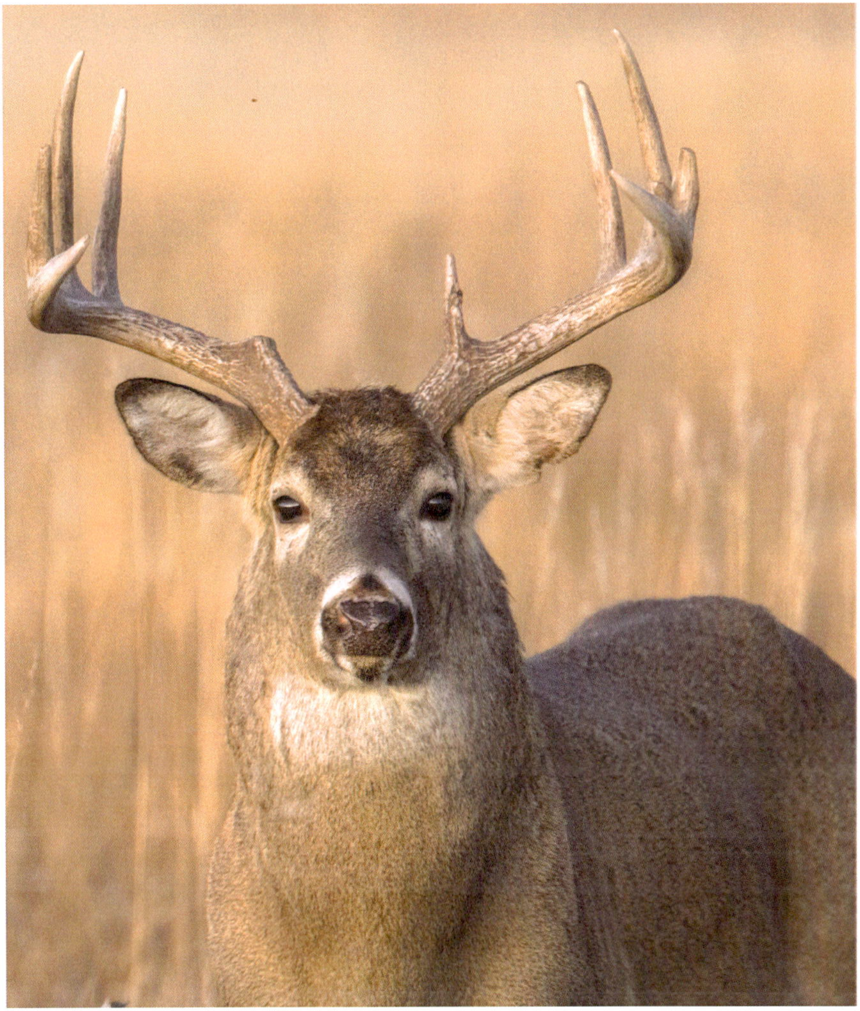

When Junior was two years old, his name seemed to fit him perfectly. He was smaller than many of the other White-tailed bucks in his age group.

However, as a mature six-year-old who is fighting the top bucks during the rut, maybe he should be renamed to J.R.

A Surprise Visitor

The first few years of my deer photography, I would walk the woods that I was very familiar with. One fall morning, I walked a regular trail where I usually saw White-tailed does and yearlings.

Suddenly, there was lot of noise in the bushes, much louder than the quiet steps of does.

Then a surprise visitor appeared. A huge Mule Deer buck!

He was looking at me, I was staring in amazement at him and was frozen in my tracks.

While I was used to photographing familiar White-tailed bucks, this unknown Mule Deer buck seemed very daunting to me. Although many of the deer I photograph are habituated to people, they are wild animals. One must always remember that and they need to be treated with respect.

This was a new opportunity for me, so I slowly raised my camera and started clicking the shutter. He posed for a few shots and then turned to his right and began eating leaves off a nearby bush.

I continued on the trail in awe of what had just happened.

This buck and I met up a few more times over the next two years. I loved taking photographs of him as he is such a beautiful animal.

Mule Deer migrate throughout the year, so hopefully he found other deer woods. Since this morning, I have photographed many Mule Deer bucks, but he will always be my favorite.

106

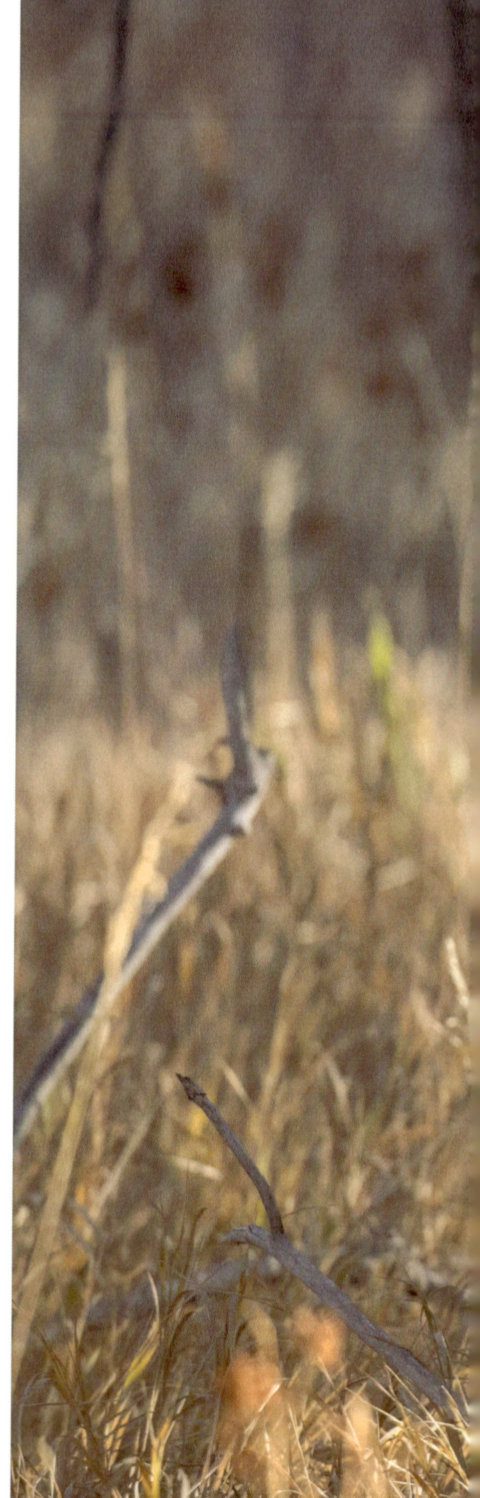

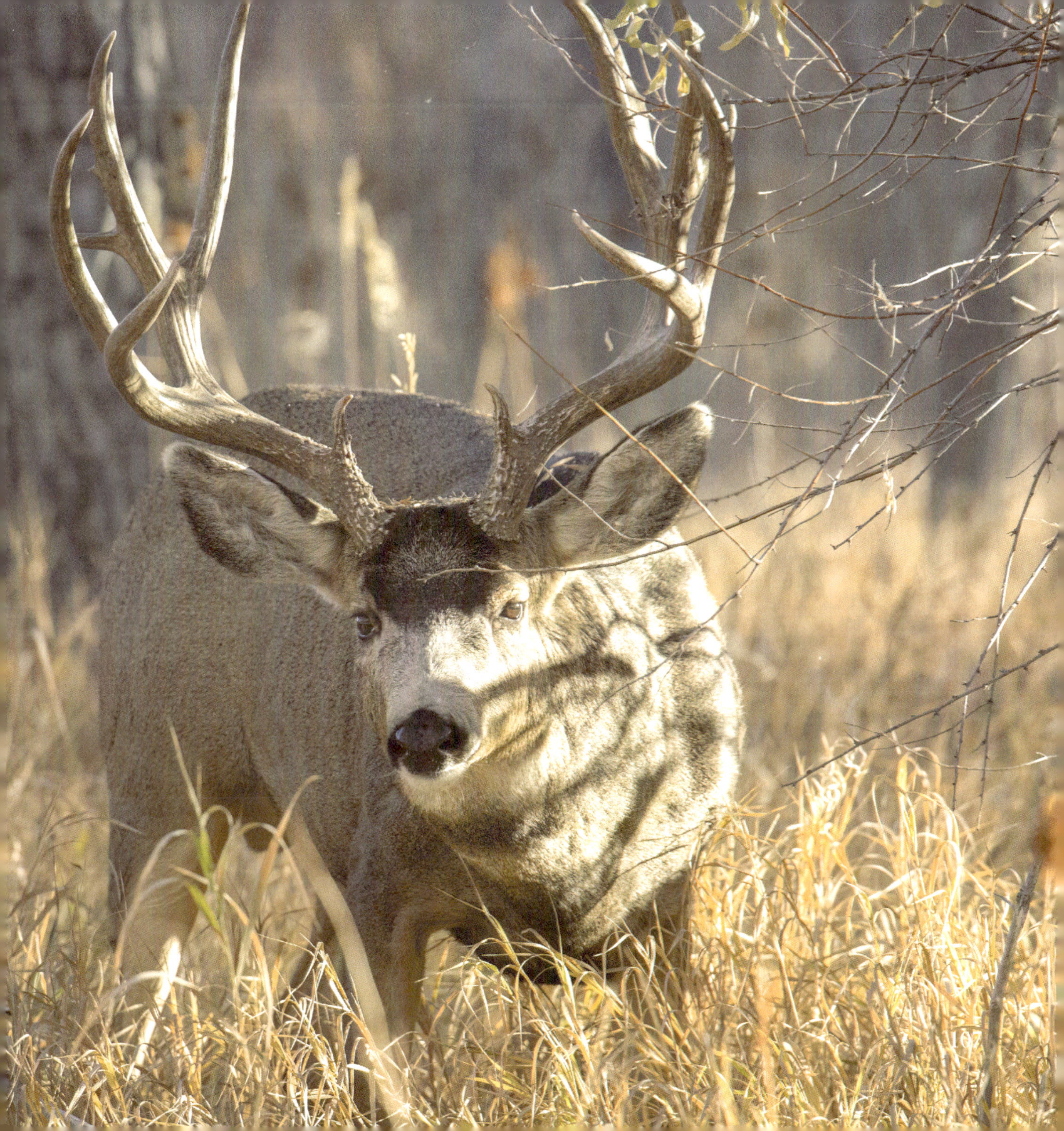

Big Red, The Fighter

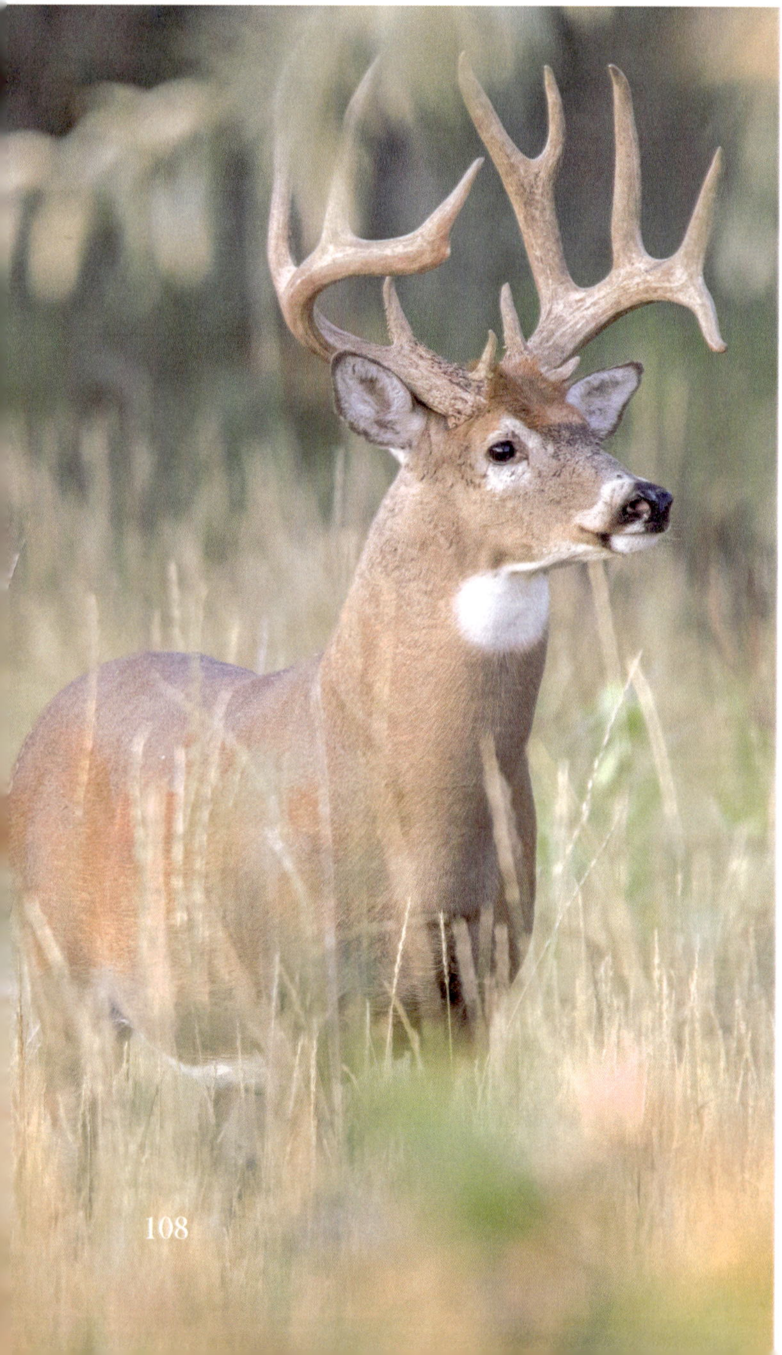

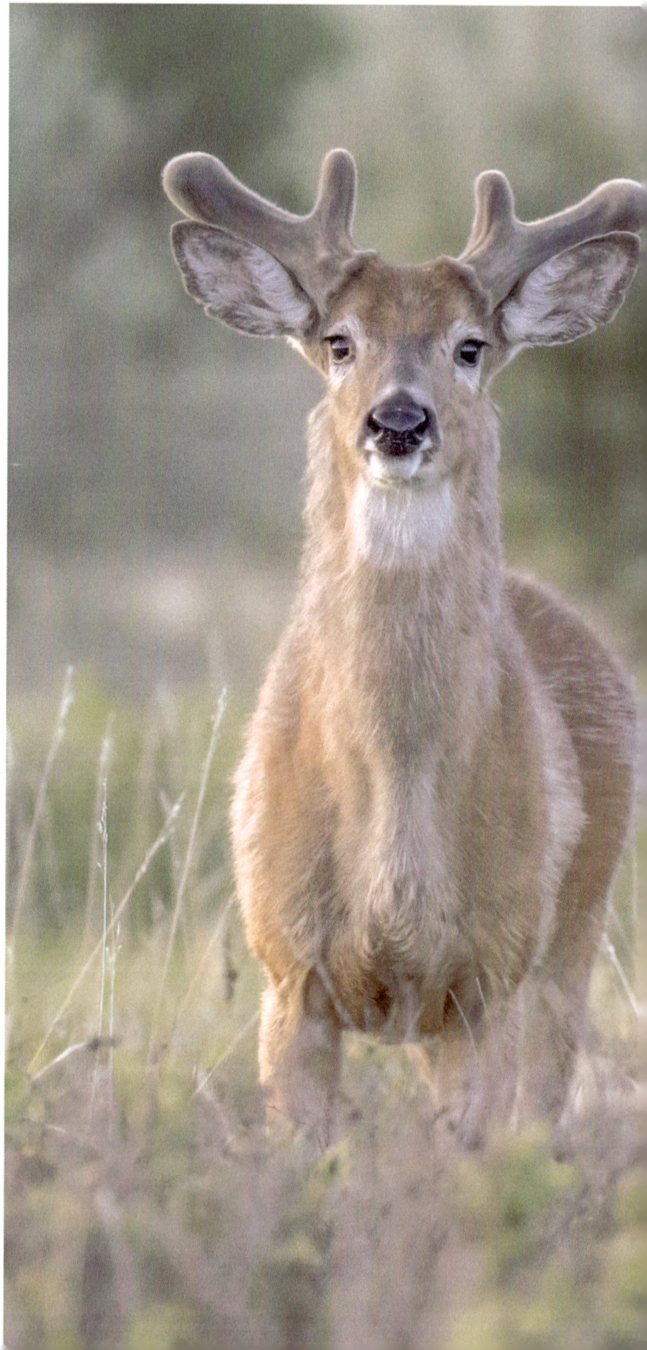

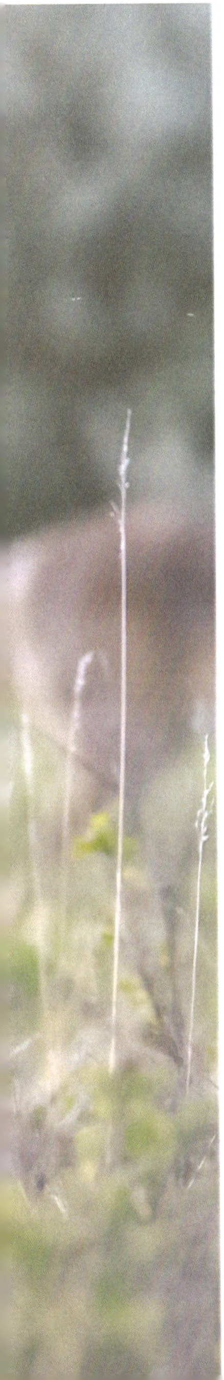

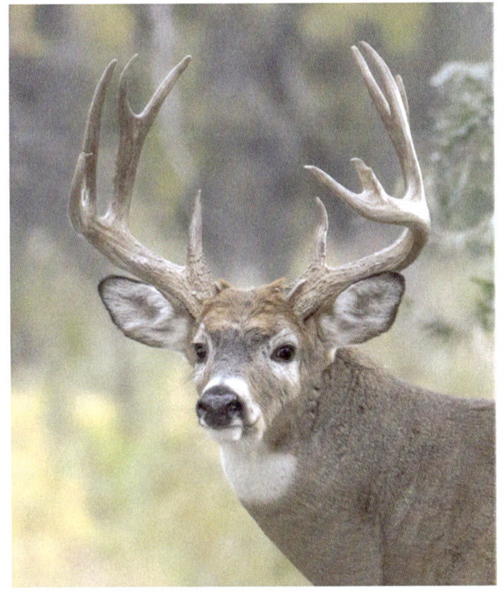

Big Red was a large, mature White-tailed buck with a reddish coat.

During the rut, he would run around and look at the other bucks to see if they wanted to fight. Usually, the other bucks ran away as quickly as possible.

However, some of the dominant bucks would fight him. One night he was involved in a fight that a few photographers witnessed.

It was an intense fight. Red was lying on the ground and breathing very heavily at the end. They weren't sure, if Red would make it through the night.

Red was not seen for several days, and we all feared the worst. Then one morning I saw him in a meadow. He had blood on his fur, but was chasing a doe like nothing had happened.

Ultimately, I heard that Red was killed in a fight.

Although, I was sad to hear the news, it seemed the only way for him to go.

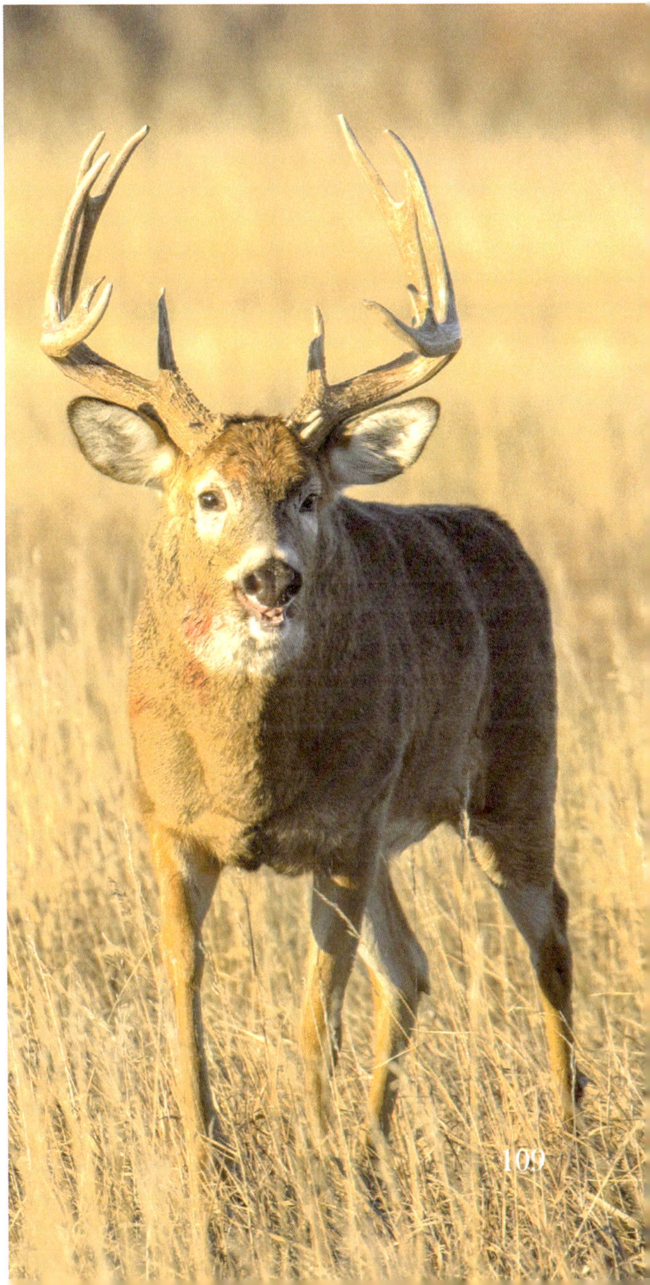

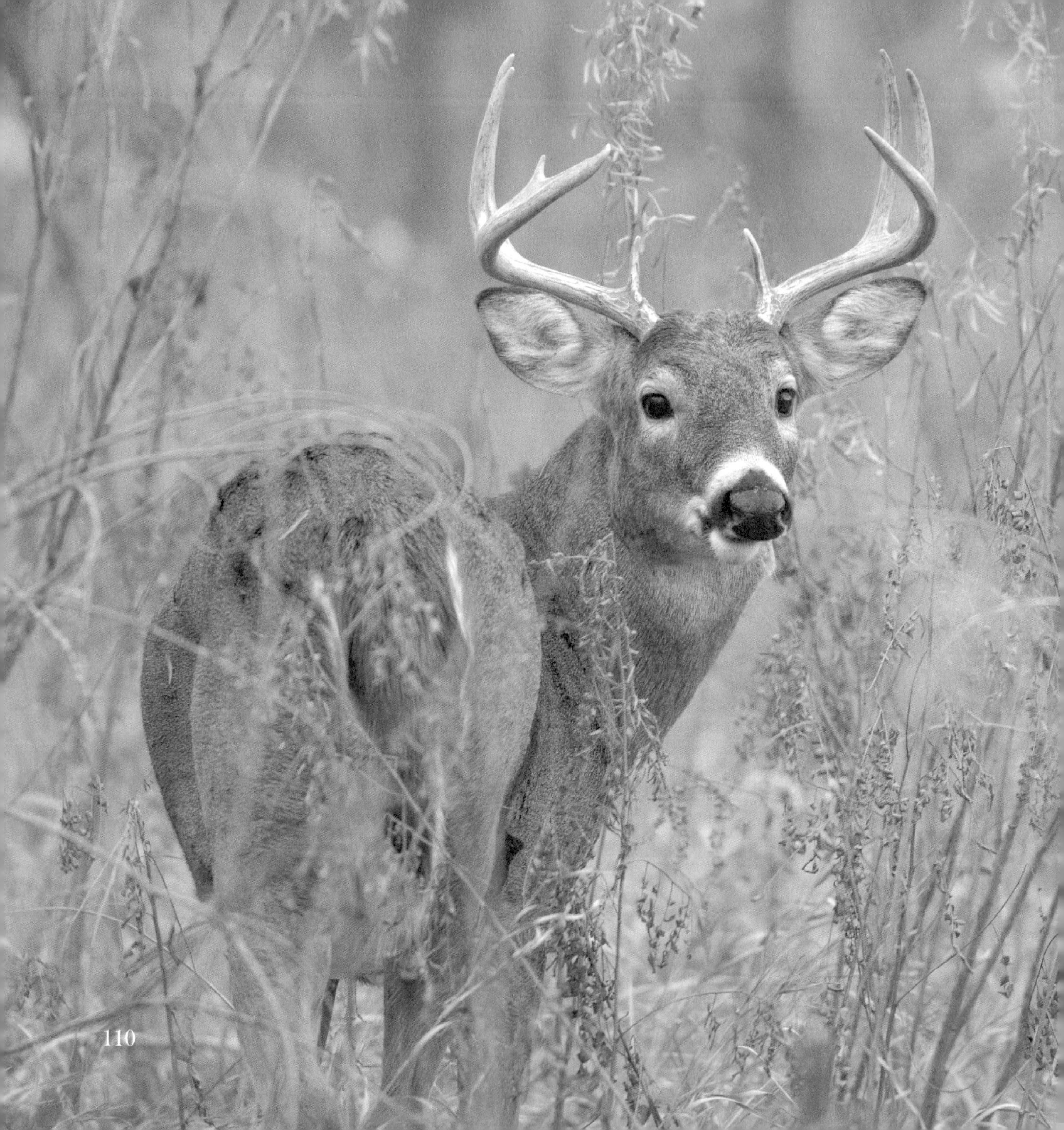

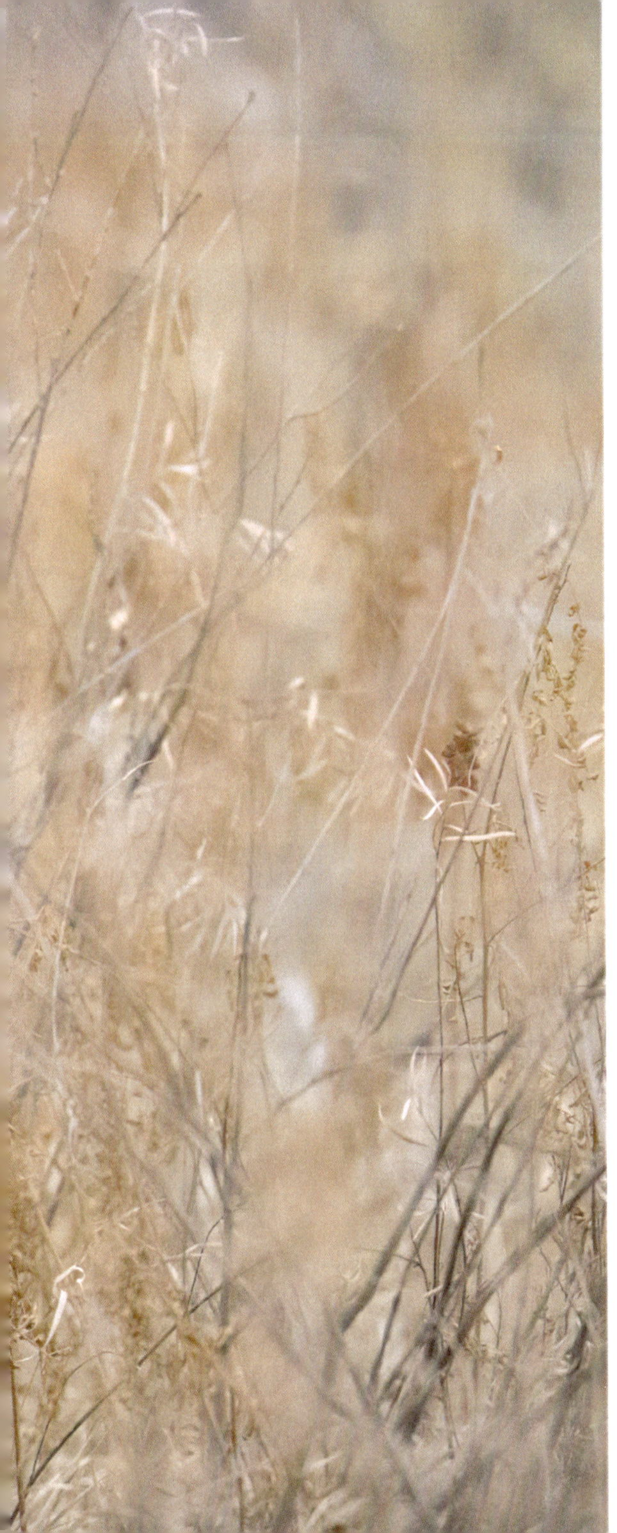

The Hand of the Lord

"But ask the animals,
and they will teach you,
or the birds in the sky,
and they will tell you;
or speak to the earth,
and it will teach you,
or let the fish in the sea
inform you. Which of
all these does not know
that the hand of the
Lord has done this?
In his hand is the life
of every creature and
the breath of all mankind."

—Job 12:7-10

About the Author

Robin Henderson-King resides in Colorado where she was born and raised. Her father, an avid outdoorsman, passed on his love of the outdoors and wildlife to her. The eldest of three girls, she accompanied her father on both fishing and hunting trips. While on family road trips he would encourage her to look at the side of the road for animals, especially deer. A skill that has come in handy with her photography.

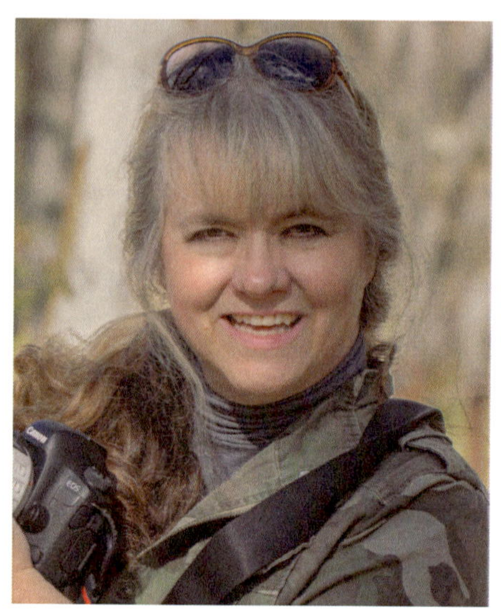

Robin graduated college with a liberal arts degree and worked in corporate communications. After the birth of her son and with the support of her husband, she decided to leave the corporate world. She started her own online home accents business, which she still runs today.

She connected back with nature after her son was diagnosed with stage-four cancer. When her son's treatment was completed, the side-effects of the chemotherapy left him with peripheral neuropathy in both of his calves and feet. A physical therapist recommended walking on uneven trails to help improve and reverse the condition. So that is what they did.

While walking on the trails, she took her camera and re-discovered her love of wildlife and the outdoors. But now, she had a camera to capture all the natural beauty of God's creation.

Any opportunity that she has, she is outside taking pictures. Robin's photographs have been published in *Colorado Outdoors Magazine* and she recently completed a naturalist training program to learn even more about the natural world that she loves to photograph.

www.ingramcontent.com/pod-product-compliance
Lightning Source LLC
Chambersburg PA
CBRC091240050726
47599CB00009B/955